THE PLAIN MAN'S GUIDE TO ETHICS

William Barclay has been Professor of Divinity
and Biblical Criticism in Glasgow University
since 1963, although he has been on the staff of
the University since 1947. His main job is to teach
the New Testament. Before that he was Minister
of Trinity Church of Scotland, Renfrew. Although
he has lived in the academic world for so long he
has always made it his aim to communicate the
Gospel to ordinary men and women with no
technical qualifications. His series of volumes on
the New Testament in the *Daily Study Bible*
have sold over a million copies; and his books
on prayer in the Fontana Series have sold by the
hundred thousand. For many years he has been
a regular contributor both to the *British Weekly*
and to the *Expository Times* and he has done
much work as a broadcaster both on radio and
television. He has made it his life work to try to
bridge the gap between the academic and the lay
world.

THE PLAIN MAN'S
GUIDE TO ETHICS

*Thoughts on
the Ten Commandments*

William Barclay

COLLINS
FONTANA BOOKS

First published in Fontana Books 1973

© William Barclay 1973

Printed in Great Britain
Collins Clear-Type Press
London and Glasgow

TO ALL MY STUDENTS, PAST AND
PRESENT

Scripture quotations are taken, unless otherwise stated, from the *Revised Standard Version* of the Bible, copyright 1946, 1952 and © 1971, by the Division of Christian Education, National Council of the Churches of Christ in the U.S.A. and are used by permission.

The author and publisher wish to thank Robert Hale and Company for permission to quote from Maurice Lindsay's *Portrait of Glasgow*.

CONTENTS

Foreword   *page* 9

1 The Ancient Foundation   11

2 The First Commandment   14

3 The Second Commandment   18

4 The Third Commandment   22

5 The Fourth Commandment   26

6 The Fifth Commandment   48

7 The Sixth Commandment   61

8 The Seventh Commandment   94

9 The Eighth Commandment   174

10 The Ninth Commandment   183

11 The Tenth Commandment   193

FOREWORD

The material in this book originally formed a series of articles on the Ten Commandments in the *British Weekly*. I am grateful both for the opportunity originally to write them and now to republish them in book form. The original material has been completely revised, and there is considerable additional material.

In the case of certain of the Commandments there has been extended treatment, and particularly in the case of three of them. The Commandment on the Sabbath has been used to discuss the history and the Christian obligation contained in the demand for Sabbath Observance, or Lord's Day Observance. The Commandment which forbids killing has been used to discuss such subjects as euthanasia, capital punishment and war. The Commandment which forbids adultery has been used to discuss the whole question of sexual relationships between men and women. Especially in these cases the scope of the discussion has been much widened.

There has been a very considerable amount of total rewriting. To take, for instance, the matter of the Seventh Commandment, when this series was originally written in the *British Weekly*, the oral contraceptive pill had not emerged; abortion had not yet had its legality extended; and homosexuality was still without exception a crime. The vast changes which have occurred in so short a time demanded in this case much rewriting.

I would be sadly lacking both in courtesy and in gratitude if I did not testify how much this book owes to Lady Collins. It was at her suggestion that its publication was first considered. To go over old material and to revise it is not a task in which an author finds much joy. And had it not been for Lady Collins' always gracious, yet always determined, encouragement, persuasion and sometimes coercion, this book would certainly have never been finished. I can only express my thanks for this, as for many other kindnesses, to so charming and so persuasive a taskmistress.

WILLIAM BARCLAY

The University of Glasgow
July 1972

CHAPTER ONE

THE ANCIENT FOUNDATION

Christianity did not come into this world without roots and foundations. There was in history a preparation for the coming of Jesus Christ. Jesus himself said that he did not come to destroy but to fulfil (Matthew 5:17). There was already something there out of which Christianity emerged and upon which it was built and could build. This was of course specially true of Judaism, for the history of the Jewish nation was the history of the preparation for the coming of God into the world in a unique way in Jesus Christ.

This is to say that the Christian Ethic had a foundation. Jesus did not come into a society which knew nothing of goodness and of morality and of ethics and of God. He came into a society which, as the New Testament itself would put it, already possessed the Law and the Prophets (Matthew 5:17). It is clearly a duty to look at that which Jesus himself said he had come to fulfil.

The Jewish ethic, which was the foundation of the Christian Ethic, was itself founded on the Ten Commandments. But these Commandments might well be called the universal foundation, not only of Jewish ethics, but of all ethics. They contain the basic laws of human conduct in society, laws which are not so much particularly and exclusively Jewish, but which are the starting-point of life for all men who have agreed to live together in any community. Let us then set down these Ten Commandments in their simplest form.

   i. You shall have no other gods before (or besides) me.

  ii. You shall not make for yourself a graven image.

 iii. You shall not take the name of the Lord your God in vain.

 iv. Remember the Sabbath day to keep it holy.

  v. Honour your father and your mother.

 vi. You shall not kill.

vii. You shall not commit adultery.

viii. You shall not steal.

ix. You shall not bear false witness against your neighbour.
x. You shall not covet.

Here then is the code which may be said to be the foundation of all social ethics, and certain facts stand out about it even at first sight.

(i) This code falls quite clearly into two sections. The first section deals with God, and the second section deals with man. The lonely supremacy of God is laid down. The impossibility of expressing God in any material form is stated. The reckless use of the name of God in promises and pledges is forbidden. The rights of God's day are safeguarded. The code then moves on to the human side. Father and mother are to be honoured and thus there is a rampart round the home. Human life is sacred. Sexual purity and fidelity are demanded. The rights of human property are conserved. False and slanderous speaking about others is condemned. The desire for that which is not ours and which is not for us is branded as wrong.

It may be said that this code inculcates two basic things – it demands *reverence for God* and *respect for man*. The majesty of God and the rights of human personality are alike conserved. This is intensely significant, for it is of the very essence of Judaism, and of the very essence of Christianity, that both have a two-directional look. They look both to God and to man. They recognize a duty to God and to man. They both know that a man must love God with every part and fibre of his being, and that he must also love his neighbour as himself. No man dare say that he loves God, unless he also loves his fellowmen; and no man can really and truly love his fellowmen, unless he sees that the true value of a man lies in the fact that he is a child of God. Without the manward look religion can become a remote and detached mysticism in which a man is concerned with his own soul and his own vision of God and nothing more. Without the Godward look a society can become a place in which, as in a totalitarian state, men are looked on as things and not as persons. Reverence for God and respect for man can never be separated from each other.

(ii) The second thing to note about the Ten Commandments is that they are a series of principles, and not a body of detailed rules and regulations. They do not attempt to give a man a series of rules ready-made to apply to any situation. What they do give a man is a certain attitude to God and to his fellowmen. Circumstances may change; the situation may alter; what remains constant is the attitude of reverence to God and respect for man. That reverence and that respect may be expressed in different ways at different times and in different situations; but the expression is always the expression of the same fundamental attitudes to God and to man. The Ten Commandments say: 'Here is how you ought to feel towards God and towards man. In each separate situation work out the expression in action of that feeling for yourself.' In other words, in this Jewish ethic, which is the foundation of the Christian Ethic, there is ideally an unchanging attitude with an infinite flexibility in the expression of it.

(iii) The third thing to note about the Ten Commandments is in fact the thing which is most often used as a criticism and even a condemnation of them. With the exception of the fourth and the fifth commandments they are all stated in negatives, and even in the case of the fourth commandment the injunction to keep the Sabbath day holy is largely expressed in negatives. By far the commonest criticism of the Ten Commandments is that they are a series of 'Thou shalt not's'.

But there is something to be said about this. Whether or not we are to regard the events of the book of Exodus as factual and actual history, it remains true that the structure of the story is dramatically and essentially correct. The people came to the wilderness of Sinai on the third new moon after their exodus, and it was then, according to the old story, that the Ten Commandments were given to them. They came from Egypt (Exodus 19:1). It was just three months after their escape from Egypt. They had been slaves for years in Egypt. It was inevitable that their spirit was gone, as indeed their conduct at the Red Sea when Pharaoh was in pursuit of them makes quite clear (Exodus 14:10–12). At this stage they were a people who had been slaves and who had escaped as little more than a disorganized rabble. In order that a mob of people may become a nation they must have a law which they will obey and which will weld them into a community. There can be no community without law. It was at this stage that the people received the Ten Commandments through Moses. *The Ten Commandments are the law without which nationhood is impossible.* They are the basis of community existence. It was the receiving and accepting of these laws which changed the people from being a rabble and a group of slaves into being a nation.

This is why the Ten Commandments are largely negative. They are negative because at this stage they could not possibly be anything else. They represent the voluntary and accepted principles of self-limitation and self-discipline without which no group of people can ever become a nation. They are not a finished ethic; they are a primary and foundational set of principles which are only a beginning, but nonetheless a beginning which was and is absolutely essential.

It may well be that we should stop criticizing the Ten Commandments because they are a series of 'Thou shalt not's' and begin recognizing that they are the necessary laws of nationhood, the charter of democracy. The beginning was the acceptance of self-limitations without which a community cannot come into being at all. True, they were very far from being the end, but it is never right to criticize a beginning for being a beginning, and that is what the Ten Commandments are, and we shall go on to look at each one of them.

CHAPTER TWO

THE FIRST COMMANDMENT

The Only God

The first words of the Bible are 'In the beginning God', and just as the Bible begins the story of history with God, so it begins the Law with God. 'You shall have no other gods before me' (Exodus 20:3).

Men's belief about God passed through three stages. The first stage was *polytheism*, which means the belief in many gods. At that stage men believed in a whole host of gods. They believed in a god of the sun, and a god of the moon, and a god of the sea, and a god of the sky, and a god of the fire, and a god of the wind, and a god of the river, and a god of the mountain, and a god of the wood. The world at this stage was crammed with gods and goddesses, competing, as it were, for the gifts and the worship of men.

The second stage was *henotheism*. At this stage a nation would accept one god as its god and would worship no other; but it was quite prepared to believe that the gods of the other nations were quite as real as its own god. At this stage a god was, as it were, supreme within his own territory, but other territories had other gods. We get this stage in the early part of the Old Testament. Chemosh was the god of the Amorites, and the Israelites sent a message to the Amorites; 'Will you not possess what Chemosh your god gives you to possess? And all that Jahweh our God has dispossessed before us, we will possess' (Judges 11:24). At this stage a conflict between nations was a conflict between their gods, because the territory of the nation and the territory of the god were co-extensive.

This stage of belief had one curious result. If a king or a prince of one land married a princess of another land, when the princess came to her new land and her new home she brought her own gods with her; and, therefore, a foreign marriage with the princess of another land was always liable to add another god to a nation's worship. One of the sins of Solomon was that he married many foreign princesses and each brought with her her own gods, and so the worship of Israel was defiled. Later, exactly the same happened when Ahab married the foreign Jezebel, for she, too, introduced her strange new gods into the worship of Israel (1 Kings 11:1–8; 16:19–23). At this stage there is, so to speak, a god for every nation; his power is limited to his own people, unless he is brought into another nation by a foreign marriage alliance. Such marriages marked the alliances of nations and the alliances of gods.

The last and final stage is *monotheism*, and this is the belief that there is not simply one god for each nation, but that there is only one God for all the earth. This is the belief of the Psalmist who thinks of the God whose presence fills the whole world and the uttermost parts of the earth and of the sea, and from whom even death could not separate him (Psalm 139:1–12). If religion was ever really to mean anything to a man in all the circumstances of his life, this stage had to come. If a man left his god behind him when he left his native land, his religion was but a broken reed; and especially in the bitter days of the exile the people of Israel had to learn to think of God as with them not just in Palestine but even in the distant and in the strange lands.

So then the Jews came in the end to believe in one God. In the Revised Standard Version this first commandment is given in two forms, 'You shall have no other gods *before* me,' and in the margin, 'You shall have no other gods *besides* me.' The first form is *henotheism*, the form in which Jahweh was the God for Israel, although there were other gods for other nations; the second form is *monotheism*, the belief that there is no other god besides Jahweh at all.

It might be thought that to begin like this is to begin with theology rather than with ethics, but theology and ethics cannot ever be separated. It is necessary to begin with God, for the very simple reason that, if men believe in gods at all, they will necessarily wish to be like the gods in whom they believe, and, therefore, the kind of gods they believe in will make all the difference to the kind of life which they live.

It is just here that we find the explanation of something that runs through the earlier parts of the Old Testament. In the Old Testament it is plain that the prophets regarded Baal worship as a very serious and dangerous threat to the purity of religion. Baal is not really a proper name; it means Lord; and among the peoples amidst whom Israel lived there were many Baals. The basic idea of Baal worship was this. The most mysterious force in life is growth. What makes the corn grow, and the grape swell, and the olive ripen? Where does this strange mysterious force come from, this force on which everything depends? That, said the other nations, is Baal or the Baals at work. Baal is the power of growth behind all living and growing things. As God said sadly to Hosea: 'And (Israel) did not know that it was I who gave her the grain, the wine, and the oil' (Hosea 2:8). It was God not Baal who was behind this wonderful growth, but there were many who worshipped the Baals and forgot God.

But Baal worship was more dangerous than that. There is one growth which is more wonderful than any other, one power which is more mysterious and unpredictable than any other. That is the power which begets a child, the sex force which gives life. The other nations believed that this was also the power of Baal. They saw in the power of sex the power of Baal. This turned the sexual act into a sacred act; and so the temples of Baal had crowds of priestesses who were sacred prostitutes.

Hosea rebukes those who sacrifice with cult prostitutes (Hosea 4:14). The very word to describe these cult prostitutes is a Hebrew word which means 'holy women'. To have sexual intercourse with one of them was to be united with the life force of Baal the god. This was the danger. The danger was that the people of Israel would drift into this Baal worship which surrounded them. Obviously it was a worship which had a fatal attraction for the lower side of human nature. It turned sexual immorality into an act of worship, and gluttony and drunkenness into an act of praising the Baals.

That is why the Ten Commandments begin by insisting that there is only one God, and all these other so-called gods are false imposters.

So then we come back to the point with which we started. It is of the first necessity to get the idea of God right, for a man will quite inevitably become like the god he worships. If he worships a licentious god like the Baals, he will become a licentious man. If he worships a hard stern god, then he will, as the world has so often tragically seen, become a hard stern man. If he worships a sentimentalized god, he will have a sentimentalized idea of religion.

It is from here that ethics takes its start. A man's god dictates a man's conduct, consciously or unconsciously.

The Christian believes in the God who is the God and Father of our Lord Jesus Christ, the God whose mind and heart and character is seen in the life and death of Jesus. And for that very reason the Christian Ethic might well be said to be the imitation of Christ.

CHAPTER THREE

THE SECOND COMMANDMENT

The Invisible God

The second commandment is the prohibition of the making or the worshipping of an idol. 'You shall not make for yourself a graven image' (Exodus 20:4).

An idol is a paradoxical thing. In one sense there is nothing more unnatural and even more ridiculous than an idol. Isaiah pours scorn on the man who makes an idol. He takes a piece of wood and with one bit of it he makes a fire to warm himself; with another bit of it he makes a fire to cook his dinner; and with the third bit of it he makes a god (Isaiah 44:14–20). He takes his tools and he designs and measures and cuts and carves and the resulting product of his own hands is his god (Isaiah 44:12, 13). The idol is there, incapable of movement, fixed to the one place as fast as a scarecrow in a cucumber field (Jeremiah 10:3–5). When in the day of war a town is invaded, the citizens flee from it staggering under the weight of the idols, the gods, that they are carrying on their shoulders (Isaiah 46: 1, 2, 7). There is no more savage and scathing indictment of the gods who are no gods than in the seventy-three verses of the little book of the Apocrypha called *The Letter of Jeremiah*. The craftsman makes crowns for the idols in the same way as ornaments are made for girls. The priests will steal the gold and the silver from the gods who are idols and may well spend it in a brothel. The gods who are idols have got to be dusted like furniture every morning. Their faces are blackened by the temple smoke, and the bats and the swallows and the birds and even the cats settle on them. Set them upright, and they cannot move; tip them over, and they cannot raise themselves. They are no more than that which a carpenter or a goldsmith made them. If there is a fire in a temple, the priests can flee, but the gods can only stay and be burned. The temple has to be locked up at nights, lest robbers steal the gods and their ornaments. Strong men strip them and go off with the booty, and they can do nothing to help themselves. They are no better than a scarecrow or a thorn-bush in a garden, on which every bird sits. They are no better than a dead body, cast out in the darkness.

From one point of view it is quite incredible that a man should regard as a god that which he himself cut and carved and manufactured, that which he has to carry about, like a piece of unwieldy baggage on a porter's back. It seems the most unnatural thing in the world to regard a thing like that as in any sense divine.

On the other hand it is also true that there is nothing easier to understand than the process by which an idol does come to be regarded as divine. God is unseen, a spirit and a power invisible to the eyes of men. It is very hard for simple people to remember and to think about, and to worship, an unseen god. Well, then, let us try to make it a little easier for people. So we make a little image which is meant in the first place to *remind* us of God when we look at it. We make a little image to represent God. We make a little image and the first intention is that by looking at the image we can better focus our thoughts on the God for whom it stands. But bit by bit the image ceases to represent God and begins to take the place of God.

You can see this process happening in the Old Testament itself in one particular story. In their wilderness days we find the old story of the way in which the people were attacked and tortured by fiery serpents. Then Moses on the instructions of God made a bronze serpent and set it up on a pole and those who had been bitten and who looked at the bronze serpent were healed (Numbers 21:6–9). And then centuries afterwards, we find that bronze serpent making another brief appearance. But this time we find Hezekiah breaking the serpent in pieces, because the people had been burning incense to it (2 Kings 18:4). This is exactly how a thing becomes an idol. Originally, the serpent had been meant to be a *reminder* of God; bit by bit, it *became* a god.

There is a parallel to this even in Christian action. We find something very like this happening in the case of the crucifix. A crucifix is meant to be a reminder of the love of the Cross; it is meant to help men and women, by looking at it, to fix and concentrate their minds and hearts on the one who bled and died there. It is meant to be a reminder and a picture which make meditation easier and prayer more real. But the danger is – it happens often – that the crucifix itself comes to be regarded with superstitious reverence; it itself becomes a holy thing. The symbol is identified and confused with the reality for which it stands.

Here then is the paradox of idolatry. It seems ridiculous that any man in his senses should ever worship as a god an immobile thing which his own hands have manufactured. But the fact is that there never was in the beginning any intention that he should. The idol was meant originally to be a representation of the divine which would make memory easier and worship more real. But bit by bit superstition turned the symbol into the reality, the representation into the thing it represented, the idol into God.

When we see what idolatry is, and when we see how it comes into being, then it is no longer possible comfortably to feel that in the twentieth century idolatry is no longer a possibility for sensible men. We are bound to see that idolatry is an ever present danger, and it is all the more dangerous in that that which was originally meant to be an aid to worship becomes the barrier to worship. Idolatry is not an antiquarian relic of the past; it is a present threat. In particular, in this twentieth century idolatry can mean two things.

(i) Idolatry means making *means into ends*. In the beginning an idol was, as we have seen, a means towards making memory and worship easier; in the end it became itself the object of worship. The means had become the end.

This is constantly happening in the Church. A liturgy is a means of worshipping God; but an elaborate liturgy can become an end in itself, so that the means and the method of worship end by becoming more important than the worship itself. Any system of Church government is a means towards the welfare of the Church; but a system of Church government can and does become an end in itself, so that people end by being more concerned with the way in which the Church is governed than with the Church itself. A Church building is a means whereby a group of people can worship God; but people can end by worshipping the building itself, so that they become more concerned with the place of worship than the worship itself.

Whenever means become ends, whenever we are in reality worshipping systems more than we are worshipping God, whenever we are more interested in liturgies than we are in prayer, whenever we are more concerned with forms of Church government than with the Church which is the body of Christ, whenever we are more concerned with worshipping in a certain building than with the good of the Church, then idolatry exists today as threateningly as it ever did.

(ii) The second danger of idolatry is even more obvious. *Idolatry substitutes the thing for the person.* The very essence of idolatry is that it is the worship of a thing instead of the worship of a person; the dead idol has taken the place of the living God.

A man's god is that which he thinks to be the most important thing in life. His god is that to which he is prepared to give his whole time, his whole thought, his whole strength. Whenever things become more important than persons to us, then idolatry has entered into life.

Whenever things become more important than people, trouble is sure to follow. In the days of the industrial revolution, the age when the machine was invented and discovered, the fatal mistake – from which industrial relationships have not even yet recovered – was that the machine was regarded as more important than the person, than the human being. Men, women and even little children were regarded as no more than machine-minders, to be used to keep the machines going and the profits rising. People were used as things, and it takes a long, long time to undo the damage that using persons as things can do to the relationships between master and man.

This worship of the thing can invade the home. It has been told that once a crossword puzzle had a clue in it, 'What makes a home?' And the required answer was 'furniture'. That is precisely what does not make a home, and yet that is precisely what so many people really worship. A better house in a better neighbourhood, a better television set, a bigger car, a continental holiday – these are things which people tend to think will make them happy. And they are all things, and a life based on the worship of things is a life based on idolatry. We do well to examine ourselves in order that we may see if it is possible that we have given things the first place in our lives.

Idolatry is by no means dead. Idolatry is not the ridiculous mistake of primitive people. Whenever means become ends, and whenever things become more important than people, and whenever anything usurps the place that God should have, idolatry is still there.

CHAPTER FOUR

THE THIRD COMMANDMENT

In the Name of God

In the Authorized Version the third commandment runs: 'Thou shalt not take the name of the Lord thy God in vain' (Exodus 20:7) and apart from altering the *thou* to *you* the Revised Standard Version keeps the same translation.

The main question obviously is: What is the meaning of the phrase *in vain*? In Hebrew the phrase literally means *for unreality*. The word is the word which the A.V. often translates *vanity*. It is used of the man who has lifted up his soul to vanity (Psalm 24:4). It is used in Exodus 23:1 for a false report. The word describes that which is empty, idle, insincere, frivolous. This commandment, then, lays it down that the name of God must never be used in an empty, frivolous or insincere way. There are two main ways in which that may be done, and it would be the first of them which was mainly intended when the commandment was first laid down.

(i) The commandment is a prohibition of taking the name of God in vain in a promise or a pledge, that is, of making such a promise or pledge in the name of God, with no intention of keeping it, or of making a promise in the name of God and then afterwards breaking it, because it was inconvenient or uncomfortable to keep it. This is a condemnation of the man who takes a pledge in God's name to do something, and who then breaks his pledge.

The breaking of such a pledge is something which the Bible looks at with the utmost seriousness. Again and again swearing falsely is regarded as a grave and serious sin. 'And you shall not swear by my name falsely, and so profane the name of your God' (Leviticus 19:12). Jeremiah condemns those who say, 'As the Lord lives' yet swear falsely (Jeremiah 5:2). To swear falsely is ranked with stealing, murdering, committing adultery, and going after strange gods (Jeremiah 7:9). Zechariah promises destruction to the thief and to the man who swears falsely by the name of

God (Zechariah 5:4). Malachi classes the man who swears falsely with the sorcerer, the adulterer, those who oppress the hireling, the widow and the orphan, those who thrust aside the sojourner, and those who do not fear God (Malachi 3:5). There is no doubt of the heinousness of this offence in the eyes of the prophets and the law-givers of Israel.

There is an obvious connection between this commandment and the passage in Matthew 5:33–37 in which Jesus forbids oaths altogether, and insists that an unadorned Yes or No is all that is needed. But there is a background to that passage. In the time of Jesus there were Jews who were masters of evasion. If they did take an oath in the name of God, they would keep it, but they did everything possible to avoid doing so. They would swear by heaven, or by earth, or by Jerusalem, or by their own heads, and they would feel themselves quite free to break such an oath, because it did not actually include the name of God. God, so to speak, had not actually been made a partner to the transaction by name, and therefore the transaction was quite breakable.

Jesus declares that heaven is God's throne and earth is God's footstool and Jerusalem is God's city. The point that Jesus is making is that you cannot possibly keep God out of any transaction, for God is everywhere present, and, whether his name is mentioned or not, he is there present when any promise is given or taken. All promises and pledges are made in the presence of God, just as all places are in the presence of God, and therefore an oath in the name of God is unnecessary, for God is there anyway.

There have been people, like the Quakers, who took this as an absolute prohibition and who would never take an oath in a law-court. But it is clear from the New Testament itself that the prohibition is not as absolute as all that, and that it must be read against its background of evasion. Jesus himself did not refuse to be put upon oath when he was before the High Priest. He was asked a question under oath and he answered it without comment (Matthew 26:63). Paul himself gives his sworn pledge to the Galatians (Galatians 1:20) that he is telling the whole truth.

It is true that an oath should never be necessary, but there are clearly times when it has to be taken. Nevertheless, we do well to read this commandment in the memory that anything we say and anything we promise is said and promised in the name and presence of God, whether we use the name of God or not. This lays down the sanctity of all promises. Let us then look at all the promises we make, and must keep.

(a) There are the ordinary promises and undertakings of life; and in this matter a little self-examination will show that life is littered with broken promises. We promise to do this, to see to that, to be here, to go there – and again and again the promise is broken, and normally we think nothing of it. We promise ourselves and others not to do, or to stop doing, something – and there is no difference. We would do well to give our promises with more thought and to keep them with more resolution. Life can easily get to a stage when a promise is lightly given and broken without a qualm, and sometimes even without a memory that it was ever given.

(b) There is the promise which is implicit in every contract of work. When we enter on any contract of work, our employer undertakes to give us so much money, and we undertake to give him our work. It is one of the modern tragedies that efficiency and conscientiousness are increasingly becoming lost virtues, because the promise implicit in any kind of work and wages agreement is not realized, or is disregarded or forgotten.

(c) More technically, there is the promise in the law-courts, the promise, before God by name in this case, to tell the truth, the whole truth and nothing but the truth. Nothing is clearer than that daily that oath is broken. Either to save himself or someone else from penalty, or to gain something for himself or for someone else, a man twists or suppresses or denies or falsifies the truth. We may well hope that we will never arrive in a position when we have to take this oath, but if we do, the truth is not something to evade, but something to face, whatever the consequences may be.

(d) There are at least three specifically religious pledges. There is the marriage vow which is taken as we shall answer for it to God. The state of modern society makes it clear that the marriage vow is lightly taken and lightly broken. To this we shall later be returning, but it is the basic truth to say that the marriage pledge is taken for better or for worse, and is not to be broken by caprice, or when for a time it may become difficult to keep it. There is no pledge in which it is more necessary to know what we are doing and to reckon up the consequences of doing it, and if we are not prepared to face the consequences, we should not take it.

(e) There is the pledge of baptism in which parents pledge themselves to bring up a child in the knowledge and the love and the fear of God. It is all too true that there are many parents who delegate that task to the Sunday School and the day school and the youth club. It is very often the case that parents have nothing to say to their children, and children nothing to say to their parents. There is no real contact, let alone any real intimacy. There are things which only the parents can teach the child, if the vow is to be kept. As has been so often said before, there would be fewer delinquent children and young people, if there were fewer delinquent parents.

(f) Lastly, there is the pledge of the sacrament. The word *sacrament* has many meanings. Its simplest is that the word *sacramentum* is the standard Latin word for a soldier's oath of loyalty to his general and to his emperor. When a man comes to the sacrament of the Lord's supper, he comes for many things, but one of them – and it must never be forgotten – is to take or renew his *sacramentum*, his oath of loyalty to Christ as his Saviour and King.

(ii) The other way in which the name of the Lord may be taken in vain is in swearing in the sense of bad language. A man may use bad language in many a different way and with many a language expression, but surely nothing causes such a shudder as the name of God and of Jesus Christ as an oath. If a man does so carelessly, he will do well to remember that he will give account for every chance word that he speaks. If he does it in anger, he will do well to learn to bridle his tongue. If he does so, thinking that he is lending stress and emphasis to what he says, he will do well to learn that there is nothing so impressive as utter simplicity of language. Let a man think, and think long before he takes the name of God, or the son of God irreverently upon his lips.

This is one of the commandments which will never go out of date, for it asserts the sacredness of every promise and it rebukes the blasphemy of irreverence.

CHAPTER FIVE

THE FOURTH COMMANDMENT

God's Day and how to use it

Set out in full the fourth commandment runs: 'Remember the sabbath day, to keep it holy. Six days you shall labour, and do all your work; but the seventh day is a sabbath to the Lord your God; in it you shall not do any work, you, or your son, or your daughter, your manservant, or your maidservant, or your cattle, or the sojourner who is within your gates; for in six days the Lord made heaven and earth, the sea, and all that is in them, and rested the seventh day; therefore the Lord blessed the sabbath day and hallowed it' (Exodus 20:8–11). We shall have to spend more time in the study of this commandment, for it has been, and is, and no doubt will continue to be, the centre of much dispute and controversy.

The division of time into the week of seven days was not a Jewish invention. It very probably originated in Babylon, and the seven days were probably in the first place the days sacred to the seven gods or spirits of the seven planets. Thus even the Romans much later assigned a day to each one of the gods, to Saturn, Apollo, Diana, Mars, Mercury, Jupiter and Venus. Even the names that we still use in the English-speaking countries come from the names of the corresponding Scandinavian gods and goddesses. Woden and Thor and all the rest of them still have their names in the days of the week.

But although the Jews found the seven-day week there already when they came into Canaan, they alone were responsible for the exaltation of the Sabbath into the most sacred of all days. For the Jew the Sabbath was inextricably connected with the creation story. In six days God made the world, and on the seventh day he rested after the toil of creation. 'So God blessed the seventh day and hallowed it, because on it God rested from all his work which he had done in creation' (Genesis 2:–3). So then for the Jew the Sabbath was the last day of the seven-day week, the day on which God rested after the work of creation, and the essential way of keeping the Sabbath was for man to rest as God had rested.

As it stands in the Ten Commandments, the fourth commandment is primarily a great piece of social and humanitarian legislation. It is not primarily a religious regulation at all. There is nothing at all said about worship or about religious services. What is laid down is a day of rest on which even the serving men and women lay aside their tasks and on which even the toiling beasts are not forgotten, and when even the stranger and foreigner share in this rest. In its original form the fourth commandment is supremely one of the great merciful laws of the Old Testament. It is social legislation based on religious belief.

If the Jewish approach to the Sabbath had remained like this, all might have been well, but it did not. Principles became regulations, and law became legalism. There was a reason for this. Centuries of subjection to greater nations robbed the Jews of all possibilities of outward expansion, and, as it were, drove the nation in upon itself. Their scholars and experts and theologians began to study their own laws under the microscope. And worse, they began to be dissatisfied with principles and to insist upon rules and regulations to cover every conceivable event that might happen to a man. There came a passion for definition, and for the fragmentation of principles into rules and regulations.

Nowhere was this so evident as in the Sabbath law. The law forbade work. But what is work? There were laid down thirty-nine different classifications called 'fathers of work', each classification capable of infinite sub-division. One class of work which was forbidden was the carrying of a burden. But what is a burden? So it comes to be argued whether or not a man may lift his child on the Sunday. Yes, he may, but not if the child has a stone in his hand, for the stone is a burden even if the child is not. Then there comes the inevitable question. What is a stone? And so the matter went on and on.

It was forbidden to tie a knot, to light a fire, to move a lamp, to go on a journey, to prepare a meal on the Sabbath. It was forbidden to heal on the Sabbath. In the case of illness or injury steps could be taken to keep a man from getting worse, but not to cure him or to make him better. It was the Scribes who carefully worked out these rules and regulations and the Pharisees who as carefully kept them. Inevitably the whole character of the

Sabbath changed. Instead of being a day designed to protect the rights and the health and the welfare of the working man, it became a day of prohibitions, with the list of things which might not be done stretching out into an almost endless series of rules and regulations.

This process went on between the Old and the New Testaments, and in New Testament times this is what the Sabbath had become like for the strict orthodox Jew, although it must always be remembered that, besides being the day of endless prohibitions, it was also the day of worship in the Synagogue, and for many a devout and simple soul it would be the worship and not the legalism which gave the Sabbath its character.

The length to which the Jewish devotion to the Sabbath law would go can best be seen from the fact that at the beginning of the Maccabean struggles the Jews would stand and be killed in cold blood without defending themselves rather than take up arms on the Sabbath day (1 Maccabees 2:29–38); and in the later struggles against Pompey they would stand and watch their enemies building a vast mound from which to attack the city, and deliberately doing the work on the Sabbath, and not lift a hand to stop them lest they should break the Sabbath law (Josephus, *Antiquities of the Jews* 14.4.2). The Sabbath law was literally dearer than life itself.

With the coming of Christianity two things would happen. All the early Christians were Jews and in the beginning they would quite certainly worship as their fathers had done, even if they put a new meaning into the worship. It certainly would not occur to the early Jewish Christians that the Sabbath was anything else but binding on them too. But there was another fact to lay beside that. There was another day of the week which to the Christians was bound to be a supremely sacred day – the first day of the week, because it was on that day that their Lord Jesus had risen from the dead (Mark 16:2; Luke 24:1; John 20:1; Matthew 28:1). They might still observe their ancestral Sabbath, but for them the first day of the week was the day on which there had happened what for them was the supreme event of history – the Resurrection.

There are signs that in the New Testament itself, even as early as that, the first day of the week, the day of the Resurrection, is becoming the Christian day. The Sabbath is not listed as one of the basic things which Gentile Christians must accept and observe (Acts 15:20, 29). It was on the first day of the week that the congregation met to break bread at Troas (Acts 20:7). It was on the first day of the week that the Corinthians were to put something aside for the collection for the Jerusalem Church (1 Corinthians 16:2). It is clear that the first day of the week is acquiring a very special place in the life of the Church.

And then in one of the latest books of the New Testament, in the Revelation which dates to between A.D. 80 and 90, we find the expression the Lord's Day for the first time (Revelation 1:10). 'I was in the Spirit on the Lord's day,' writes the John of the Revelation. It is quite true that there are some scholars who think that that phrase means not *the Lord's Day*, but *the Day of the Lord*, and who believe that what it means is that John by the Spirit was projected forward in history to the Day of the Lord, the end of time, and saw in advance what was going to happen then. That is very unlikely. The Lord's Day and the Day of the Lord are two quite different phrases in Greek, and they are not ever interchangeable. We may safely take it that here we have the first instance in literature of the expression the Lord's Day to describe the first day of the week, the day of the Resurrection, the great day of the Christian Church.

So then we have now got this length in our study. The Sabbath was a uniquely Jewish institution, although the Jews got the seven-day week from Babylon; it commemorated God's rest after the work of creation; it began by being a great humanitarian institution, a piece of social legislation based on religious conviction; as time went on it became more and more a day of legalistic rules and restrictions and prohibitions, although it never ceased to be the day of worship. At first the early Christians, being Jews, naturally accepted it; but there are signs even within the New Testament that the first day of the week, the day of the Resurrection, the Lord's Day, was to be the great day of the Christian Church.

So the Jewish Sabbath had tended to become increasingly a day of restrictions and prohibitions observed in a legalistic spirit. Now it is clear that to one man at least any such day would be the reverse of the whole Christian gospel, and that man was Paul. And we do in fact find Paul condemning those who observe days and months and seasons and years (Galatians 4:10), and insisting that the Christians must not get involved in questions about festivals and new moons and Sabbaths (Colossians 2:16), and holding that the man who is really strong in the faith will require no special holy days at all, but will regard all days as holy (Romans 14:5, 6). We may take it as certain that in Paul's churches there would be a strong move away from the legalistic Sabbath towards the Resurrection joy of the Lord's Day.

There was one theoretical possibility which was at the same time an obvious practical impossibility – to observe both the Sabbath and the Lord's Day festival, because the former is the memorial of creation, and the latter of the Resurrection (*Apostolic Constitutions* 7:23). But it clearly never could have been a practical possibility to have two holy days in one week, the disruption of everyday work would have been too severe.

By the beginning of the second century, it is quite clear that the Lord's Day had conquered. The steps of the process we know nothing about, the result is quite clear. The Didache, the teaching of the Twelve Apostles, the first service book of the Church, dating to shortly after A.D. 100, instructs: 'On the Lord's Day come together, break bread, and hold Eucharist' (The Didache 14.1). Ignatius (about A.D. 110) is quite definite. They who walked in ancient customs have come to a new hope 'no longer living for the Sabbath, but for the Lord's Day' (*To the Magnesians* 9.1). For him the Sabbath is a dead letter. From then on there is absolute and unbroken unanimity that the Christian day is the Lord's Day, often with the corollary that the Sabbath is no longer binding on the Christian and that it is a culpable error to seek to go on observing it. Justin Martyr (A.D. 170) writes: 'On the day called the day of the Sun all who live in cities or in the country gather together to one place' (*First Apology* 67). In his discussion with Trypho the Jew he says: 'We do not live after the law, we are not circumcised in the flesh, we do not keep the Sabbath' (*Dialogue with Trypho* 10); and he says to the Jew, 'Because you are idle for one day, you think you are pious (*Dialogue with Trypho* 12). Dionysius of Corinth writes to Soter of Rome 'Today we have passed the Lord's holy day' (Eusebius, *Ecclesiastical History* 4.23). Barnabas speaks of the Lord's Day as the eighth day, and he thinks of it as the day on which the new creation was begun. 'We cultivate with gladness,' he says, 'the eighth day on which Jesus rose from the dead' (*Letter of Barnabas* 15). Tertullian (about A.D. 200) says that sometimes the heathen think that the Christians worship the sun because they meet on the Sun's day (*Apology* 16). Athanasius (about A.D. 360) writes, 'We keep no Sabbath day: we keep the Lord's Day, as a memorial of the beginning of the second new creation' (*Concerning the Sabbath and Circumcision*). Canon 29 of the Council of Laodicea (A.D. 363) lays it down: 'Christians must not judaize by resting on the Sabbath, but must work on that day, and, if they can, observe the Lord's Day, resting then as Christians.' Augustine (A.D. 420) insists on the festal character of the Lord's Day, for on it Jesus rose from the dead. The fourth commandment, he says, is not in any literal sense binding on a Christian; its obligations have not been transferred to the Lord's Day, for on it Jesus rose from the dead. The first book on the Lord's Day was written by Melito of Sardis about A.D. 170. Origen (A.D. 240) apologizes for the special observance of any day at all. The Sunday is observed as a concession to the weaker brothers because they are either unable or unwilling to keep every day in this way, and so require some visible reminders to prevent spiritual things from passing altogether out of their minds (*Against Celsus* 8.22.23).

There is no doubt at all that from the early second century onwards – and perhaps even earlier – the Lord's Day has completely displaced the Sabbath, and that the two are never confused, and are even contrasted with each other. It is even said, as in the decisions of the Council of Laodicea, that it is an error for a Christian to keep the Sabbath. At first sight the curious thing about this is that there is nothing at all about the cessation of work. There is no indication that the Lord's Day was a day when all work was suspended. Simply on general grounds it could not have been. In the very earliest days it was to the humbler members of society that the Christian faith most appealed. It was obviously impossible for a servant, and still more for a slave, to take a whole day off work in a pagan society. True, if he was a Jew he might do so, partly because the Jews were a self-contained community, and partly because the ancient world had become used to the stubborn idiosyncrasies of the Jews. It is, for instance, true that the Jews alone of all people in the Empire were exempt from compulsory military service, because their strict

adherence to their food laws and their refusal to bear arms on the
Sabbath made it impossible to integrate them into any army. But
it had taken centuries for the ancient world to realize that a Jew
inflexibly kept his law, and to accept that fact. A like latitude
would never be granted to slaves and servants who had adopted
a new and upstart religion. Complete cessation of work on the
Lord's Day was not within the realms of possibility for the early
Church.

. But what is more significant is that even in cases in which such
a cessation was possible in many cases it was not observed.
Jerome (*Letters* 108.20) tells of the Lord's Day practice of the
nuns of the famous religious community at Bethlehem. 'On the
Lord's Day only they proceeded to the Church beside which
they lived, each company following its own mother superior.
Returning home in the same order, they devoted themselves to
their allotted tasks, and made garments either for themselves or
for others.' In other words, after the worship of the Lord's Day
the normal work of the community went on. And it must be
remembered that this refers to a time early in the fifth century,
when a cessation of work would have been perfectly possible, if
it had been considered obligatory and desirable.

This then is one side of the matter, but there is another. There
are indeed signs that the Christian community was on its way
to a Lord's Day when ordinary activities were suspended. There
are two references in Tertullian early in the third century which
show the trend. He speaks of Christians deferring even their
business on the Lord's Day, lest they give any place to the devil
(*On prayer* 22). He compares the position of the Christian with
the position of the heathen in regard to festal days. If any indulgence to the weakness of human nature is necessary, the
Christians have the advantage. For the heathen each festive day
occurs only once a year. 'You have a festive day every eighth
day' (*On Idolatry* 14).

A series of factors influenced the movement to a Lord's Day in
which work was prohibited. There were the heathen festivals;
there was the undoubted influence of the Jewish Sabbath; there
was the fact that Christianity was penetrating the higher ranks of
society in which people could, if they so chose, observe a work-
less Lord's Day. Above all, there was the increasing stress laid
on the obligatory nature of the services of the Church. The more

the Church was organized, the more the Lord's Day became specifically a 'religious' day.

This tendency was soon to find official support. The day came when the struggles of the Church were almost at an end, although trouble was to flare again in the days of Julian the Apostate, for the time came when Constantine, the first of the Christian Emperors, accepted the Christian faith. In A.D. 321 Constantine passed an act which is an epoch in the observance of the Lord's Day. The act laid it down that work in the cities must stop on the Lord's Day, although the agricultural work of the country was allowed to go on, lest crops be ruined and lost by inactivity (*The Code of Justinian*, book 3, title 12.12.3).

It will always remain something of a problem why Constantine passed this piece of legislation. Perhaps by this time so many religions were having so many festal days that the real reason was social and economic and not religious at all, and that Constantine was seeking mainly to standardize a national weekly holy day. It may be that his interest was genuinely religious. Eusebius says that he ordained that one day should be a day of prayer, because his earnest desire was 'gradually to lead all mankind to the worship of God' (*Life of Constantine* 4.18).

One of the odd by-products of Constantine's action, if Eusebius is to be believed, was the institution of the first military Church parades! Constantine laid it down that all Christian soldiers were to be given the opportunity to worship. Non-Christian soldiers were to be paraded, and they were all together to recite a prayer which they had been taught and learned by heart: 'We acknowledge thee the only God; we own thee as our King, and implore thy succour. By thy favour we have gotten the victory; through thee we are mightier than our enemies. We render thanks for thy past benefits, and trust thee for future blessings. Together we pray thee and beseech thee long to preserve to us, safe and triumphant, our Emperor Constantine and his pious sons' (*Life of Constantine* 4.20).

Clearly, we now have a new situation, and it was a situation which tended to follow a course of progressive hardening. The continuous edicts and pronouncements of councils show that it is one thing to lay down an edict and another to enforce it. Theodosius in A.D. 386 forbade on the Lord's Day all litigation, and all spectacles in the theatre or in the circus. In A.D. 538 the

Council of Orleans forbade even the field work that the previous edicts had allowed, and in A.D. 585 the Council of Macon ordained a complete cessation of business, and declared that the Lord's Day was a day of perpetual rest. But it is still to be noted that there was nothing ascetically grim about this, for the Council of Grangra forbade fasting on the Lord's Day. Canon 18 runs: 'If anyone under pretence of asceticism, shall fast on Sunday, let him be anathema.'

And now we come to the influence of two famous men, influence which altered the whole emphasis and influence which lasts to this day. Alcuin (A.D. 735–804) was the first to identify the Sabbath and the Lord's Day. All work on the Lord's Day became a breach of the fourth commandment. This was a complete reversal of the position of the early Church. The early Church had again and again distinguished between the Sabbath and the Lord's Day, and now Alcuin – and it is perhaps not too much to say fatally – identified them. The matter was taken beyond recovery when Thomas Aquinas (A.D. 1225–74) did exactly and explicitly the same. 'The Sabbath is changed into the Lord's Day' (*Summa* 2.1, question 103, article 3). It was not long before the Church was drawing up as detailed Lord's Day prohibitions as ever the Pharisees did. The Sabbath came to be more and more glorified. In medieval times there circulated a so-called 'Letter from Heaven' which associated the Sunday with all kinds of things, with the creation of the angels, with the grounding of the ark on Ararat, with the Exodus, with the baptism of Jesus, with his greatest miracles, with his Ascension, with Pentecost. The entanglement of the Lord's Day with the Sabbath had begun, and it has never been fully unravelled.

But over against this there is one astonishing thing to be said. It is true that work was forbidden, but the odd and curious thing is that amusement was not forbidden. The only things forbidden up to the fifteenth century were dancing, the singing of ribald songs, theatrical performances and races in the circus, and in the sixteenth century there were complaints about the markets, the open shops, the hawking, the dicing, the sports, the conjuring, the theatrical performances, the dancing, the singing, the revelry which marked the Sunday. It was then that the law was laid down – so very recently repealed in Scotland – that only bona fide travellers might be served in inns on Sunday.

So as the Reformation approached, we have a situation when, from the point of view of work, Sunday and Sabbath are identified, but from the point of view of pleasure the greatest laxity prevailed.

With the Reformers we reach a new stage, and the interesting and significant thing is that the position of the Reformers was almost the same as the position of the early Church. The Reformers were unanimous that the Lord's Day and the Sabbath were not the same day, and they were equally unanimous that the fourth commandment, like the rest of the Jewish law, was for the Christian abrogated.

Luther's position was quite clear. In the *Larger Catechism* he insists that serving men and maids must have a day of rest and refreshment, a day when they can gather to hear God's word, and to praise and pray. But in principle it is of no importance what day it is. It is not necessarily a fixed day as it was for the Jews, for in itself one day is no better than another. Calvin is equally clear (*Institutes* 2.8.32, 34). The Sabbath is abrogated. 'It being expedient to overthrow superstition, the Jewish holy day was abolished, and as a thing necessary to retain decency, order and peace in the Church, another day was appointed for that purpose.' 'The observance of days among us is a free service and void of all superstition.'

The Helvetic Confession (chapter 24) summarizes the position of the Reformers: 'The Lord's Day itself ever since the apostles' time was consecrated to religious exercise and to a holy rest. . . . Yet herein we give no place to the Jewish observance of the day or to any superstitions. For we do not count one day to be holier than another, nor think that mere rest itself is acceptable to God. Besides, we do celebrate and keep the Lord's Day, and not the Jewish Sabbath, and that with a free observance.' 'There can be no doubt,' said Calvin, 'that, on the advent of Our Lord Jesus Christ, the ceremonial part of the commandment was abolished.'

Here, then, is the position of the Reformers. They utterly refused to identify the Lord's Day and the Sabbath. The necessity was, as they saw it, that men and women should have one day to rest their bodies and to refresh their souls, but the day in itself did not matter. And the observance was a 'free observance', a matter of personal responsibility and not of legal coercion.

This was a really and truly Christian view, but it ran into difficulties. Personal responsibility, free observance, leave much to the individual, and one of the Homilies, written in 1563, has it: 'The Lord was more dishonoured and the devil better served on Sunday than upon all the days of the week besides.'

Further, it was desperately difficult to get away from the identification of the Lord's Day and the Sabbath once that identification had been made. And in 1595 that identification was made again in a book with the English title of *True Doctrine of the Sabbath* by Nicholas Bound, a Suffolk clergyman. He claimed literally and absolutely that all the authority and observances of the Jewish Sabbath had been transferred to the Lord's Day, and he insisted that they should be enforced by the state and by the law of the land. Few books have had more influence and few aroused a longer continued controversy, for in the next hundred years it produced at least one hundred and twenty books for or against. But it did open the way to the legalized enforcement of the sabbatizing of the Lord's Day.

There followed a time of sway and conflict the legacy of which is not yet fully past. This may be seen in the vicissitudes of a little book written by James I. It was entitled *The King's Majesty's Proclamation to his Subjects concerning Lawful Sports to be used*, and is commonly called *The Book of Sports*. It was an insistence on the right of the people to enjoy all traditional pastimes on the Sunday except bull and bear baiting. It first saw the light of day in 1618. It was republished by Charles I in 1633, with instructions to Justices that all disorders should be duly punished, but that 'all neighbourhood and freedom with manlike and lawful exercises be used'. And then in 1643 that same book, the voice of two kings, was publicly burned by the public hangman.

It was then that the Puritans came to power. They ordered every maypole in England to be cut down, and they turned Christmas into a penitential fast and between 1644 and 1656 a series of ever more severe Sunday Observance laws was passed, including the notorious law which forbade 'all vain and profane walking' on the Sabbath. Sabbatarianism was for a time supreme and the Lord's Day had become the Jewish Sabbath.

The important thing is that it was just at this time, in 1648, that the Westminster Confession emerged. It emerged at the time of the most acute Sabbatarianism in the history of this country. Its section on the Sabbath, for so it calls the Lord's Day (21.7, 8), repeated in the Larger and Shorter Confessions, runs as follows: 'As it is the law of nature, that, in general, a due proportion of time be set apart for the worship of God; so, in his word, by a positive, moral and perpetual commandment, binding all men in all ages, he hath particularly appointed one day in seven for a sabbath, to be kept holy unto him; which, from the beginning of the world to the resurrection of Christ, was the last day of the week; and, from the resurrection of Christ, was changed into the first day of the week, which in Scripture is called the Lord's Day, and is to be continued to the end of the world, as the Christian Sabbath. This Sabbath is then kept holy unto the Lord, when men, after due preparing of their hearts, and ordering of their common affairs beforehand, do not only observe an holy rest all the day from their own works, words and thoughts about their worldly employment and recreations: but also are taken up the whole time in the public and private exercises of his worship, and in the duties of necessity and mercy.'

That is the doctrine by which my own Church, the Church of Scotland, was officially bound. Almost from beginning to end it is a departure from Reformed doctrine, particularly in its identification of the Sabbath and the Lord's Day, an identification which can be supported neither from the Scriptures nor from the doctrines of the Reformation.

Nowhere did the identification of the Sabbath and the Lord's Day have more effect than in Scotland. Maurice Lindsay in his book *Portrait of Glasgow* cites certain examples of this. On the so-called Sabbath day, 'some people "did not sweep or dust the house, nor make the beds, nor allow any food to be cooked or dressed", while others "opened only as much of the shutters of their windows as would serve to enable the inmates to move up and down, or an individual to sit at the opening to read".' He tells how the first Sunday train from Glasgow to Edinburgh ran on 13 March 1842. A contemporary journalist wrote that it was 'filled with peaceful and respectable persons, gliding quietly away on its mission'. The Presbytery of Glasgow had already denounced the running of Sunday trains as 'a flagrant violation of the law of God as expressed in the Fourth Commandment, a grievous outrage on the religious feelings of the people of Scotland, a powerful temptation to the careless and indifferent to abandon the public ordinances of Grace, and most disastrous to the quiet of the rural parishes along the line of the railways, by the introduction into them every Sabbath, of many of the profligate and dissipated who inhabit the cities of Glasgow and Edinburgh'. Maurice Lindsay goes on: 'In Edinburgh a threatening battery of ministers, presumably unaware of the inclusion of their city in their Glasgow brethren's condemnation, lined the platforms and informed the detraining passengers that they had bought tickets to hell, a claim which does not seem to have deterred many of them from making their way towards Princes Street.'

But there was worse, much worse than that. Peter Mackenzie, one of the leaders of the reform movement in the city of Glasgow, described 'the plight of an Irish family destitute on the street on a snowy January night in 1847, one child out of seven dead, the mother herself dying of consumption, victims of a Church ruling that soup kitchens for the destitute were not to be opened on the Sabbath for fear of offending the Lord'.

To return to history, with the Restoration, there came a natural swing of the pendulum far too far in the opposite direction. And in 1677 a Sunday Observance Act was passed regarding trade, labour and travelling with very reasonable provision for what necessity demanded. We may note one last Act. In 1781 Bishop Porteus drew up a Sunday Observance Act in which it was laid down that 'any place of public entertainment or debate where a charge is made for admission may be deemed a disorderly house.' This Act was directly aimed at bear baiting and infidel propaganda, and this is the Act which has been used in a way that its sponsor never intended.

We must here leave the history of the matter, for in principle there is nothing to add. We shall go on to try and deal with the matter constructively, but at the moment we may simply note once again that neither the early Church nor the Reformers ever at the time identified the Lord's Day with the Sabbath. That identification did not emerge until the eighth century. It was roundly denied at the Reformation, but it emerged again stronger than ever in the sixteenth and seventeenth centuries. It is that identification which has bedevilled the whole question of the use of the Sunday, and the question has been acutely complicated by the fact that it was at a time when that identification was supreme that the Westminster Confession was drawn up. It can hardly be denied that a rethinking of the whole position has been long overdue.

It has been necessary to spend a good deal of time looking at this matter historically, because it is often necessary to see how a situation arose before anything can be done to mend and to reform it. We have to understand a situation before we can do anything about it.

One thing has become completely and inescapably clear. The Sabbath day and the Lord's Day are different days and commemorate different events. The Sabbath is the last day of the week and commemorates God's rest after the toil of the week of creation; the Lord's Day is the first day of the week and commemorates the Resurrection of our Lord. Here we must be very plain and very definite. For the Christian the Sabbath has ceased to exist. The Sabbath is simply a day which he does not observe, and to speak, for example, of a Sabbath School is quite wrong, because for the Christian there is no such thing.

Again to put it very plainly and very definitely, this fourth commandment is not binding on the Christian at all, for there is no evidence in Scripture that the rules and regulations which govern the Sabbath were ever transferred by divine authority to the Lord's Day. The Sabbath is not a Christian institution, the Lord's Day is. To this day the Jews observe the Sabbath, on our Saturday, and, from the point of view of Jewish religion, correctly so. But the Christian has his own day, commemorating the greatest event in his faith, that is, the Resurrection. This means we are not asking: How ought I to keep the Sabbath? We are asking, How ought I to keep the Lord's Day? The Lord's Day is not primarily and essentially a day when this, that, or the next kind of work and action is prohibited, which is what the Jewish Sabbath is. The Lord's Day is primarily and essentially a day when we remember that Jesus Christ is risen from the dead and is alive for ever more, and therefore with us here and now. Every time we become involved in arguments about what may or may not be done on the Lord's Day we are, in fact, being Jewish instead of Christian, and we are, in fact, turning the Lord's Day into the Sabbath again. So then our real question is not: How shall we keep the Sabbath? But: How shall we keep the Lord's Day?

(i) The prior question is: Ought we to observe and keep any special day at all? It was clearly Paul's point of view that the really strong Christian would observe all days alike (Romans 14:1–6). But he also knew human nature well enough to know that to observe all days alike would in all probability simply mean to observe none at all. In theory we can argue that no special day is necessary and all days are God's days, but in practice we need a special day on which to focus our thoughts on God and on our risen Lord.

(ii) What then shall be the purpose of this day? In the first instance, a day of rest is still a necessity. As the old Greek proverb had it, the bow that is always bent (that is, always stretched taut) will soon cease to shoot straight. In the days of the French Revolution the revolutionaries abolished everything that had to do with religion, and they abolished Sunday, only to find that they had to bring it back again, because the health of the nation was suffering because there was no day of rest. It is a known fact, confirmed by those who study the technique of work, that, if a worker is working really hard, his efficiency diminishes towards the end of the week; and his efficiency is restored by the day of rest. It is proved that a day of rest is a social and industrial necessity without which health and work inevitably suffer.

It is just exactly here that we run into trouble. There is no difficulty at all in getting almost, if not quite, everyone to agree with this general principle; the difficulty lies in the practical application of it. We have the principle that the Lord's Day should be a day of rest. But it is entirely necessary to define what rest is.

When the commandment itself was laid down, it was laid down in a society where almost all work was physical work. A man tilled the soil, or reaped the harvest, or fished in the lake, or watched the flock. He would come to the end of the week with aching muscles and a body exhausted, physically weary and tired, and for such a man rest was undoubtedly a time in which he did nothing, in which he lay back and eased the tired limbs. But the modern situation is quite different. There is much less work which is purely physical work, and there is much more work which is done with more or less no physical effort at all.

One of the great problems of the modern health situation is

that too many people take too little exercise, and many of the modern occupational diseases are the direct result of too little active use of the body. For the man engaged in a sedentary office job, or in a profession at which all his work is done in a chair at a desk, real rest will not be immobile inactivity; it will be some kind of action. For such a man a day of rest will be a day when he actively uses his body, and by so doing preserves his health.

And for that very reason no man need have a guilty conscience if on the Lord's Day he plays some healthy game, or swims in the sea, or climbs the hills, or walks in the country. It is to be carefully noted that this is not an argument for watching sport, and for organized sport on the Lord's Day. This is not what this kind of rest involves at all. But it is to say that the golf course and the tennis court and the cricket pitch and the sea and the hills are not forbidden to a Christian who is observing a day of rest.

In a situation in which a man can, so to speak, sit and eat himself into a thrombosis, a day of rest will be a day when he exercises his body as well as his soul. For the modern man, in the civilization and the way of life in which he lives, inactivity is not rest; it is the very thing which is ruining his body. Let a man interpret the word rest as his needs demand. If the end of the week finds him with a body which needs activity more than anything else, let him not fear to take it.

(iii) For a third thing, the Lord's Day will surely be a family day. No faith sets a higher value on the family than Christianity does. In the ancient times the family did live together on the farm and in the fishing boat and in the village. Day and daily they lived, worked, ate and slept together. Even when the children grew up and married, they still remained within the clan. But in modern conditions it can happen that the members of the family rarely see each other through the week. They have their own work during the day; they have their own studies or activities in the evening; in many families not even the midday meal is eaten together.

When the children grow up and marry, they do not stay in the old home; they leave it and go their own ways. In such circumstances the Lord's Day can be, and ought to be, the family meeting day, the day when members of the family meet as a family, the day when the sons and daughters who have gone out come back home again, the day when the grandchildren meet their grandparents, the day when the family circle, so interrupted and broken by modern life, comes together again. Even to this day there is a certain symbolism in the Sunday midday meal. It can become a kind of sacrament of the home.

We have thought of the Lord's Day as the day of rest, not necessarily in the sense of inactivity, but in the real sense of the term. We have thought of the Lord's Day as the day of the meeting of the family. But the Lord's Day goes much deeper than that, and we must go on to see its still greater meanings and its still more precious values. We, therefore, now turn to look at the things which belong more to what may be called the divine side of the day.

(iv) The Lord's Day was always the day when God's people met and assembled together, and if we can work out the reasons why they did meet together, then we will go far towards finding the most important uses of the Lord's Day.

The way in which we can best do this is by going back to the early Church, and setting down that Church's own description of the meeting together of the Christians.

We begin with a description, which is not given by a Christian at all. It is the description sent by Pliny the governor of Bithynia to Trajan the Roman Emperor in A.D. 111. Trajan had sent Pliny to be governor of Bithynia. Pliny enjoyed the friendship of Trajan, and it was his custom to seek directly Trajan's advice on any problems which arose. One of the problems was what to do with the Christians, whether or not to treat them as criminals, law-breakers and evil-doers. So Pliny examined the Christians and then sent a letter to Trajan telling him what they had said (Pliny, *Letters* 10.96), and it is clear that Pliny's sympathies were with the Christians: 'They were in the habit of meeting on a certain fixed day before it was light, when they sang in alternate verses a hymn to Christ as to a god, and bound themselves by a solemn oath not to commit any wicked deeds, but never to commit any fraud, theft or adultery, nor deny a trust, when they should be called upon to deliver it up, after which it was their custom to separate, and then to reassemble to partake of food – but food of an ordinary and innocent kind.'

Here is the first description of a Christian service, and, since it comes from a Roman governor, it must be quite unprejudiced.

The second description is from the defence of Christianity

written to the Roman government by Justin Martyr about A.D. 150 (Justin, *First Apology* 67): 'On the day called Sunday all who live in cities or in the country gather together to one place, and the memoirs of the apostles or the writings of the prophets are read as long as time permits. Then, when the reader has ceased, the president verbally instructs and exhorts to the imitation of these good things. Then we all rise together and pray, and, as we said before, when our prayer is ended, bread and wine are brought, and the president in like manner offers prayers and thanksgivings according to his ability, and the people assent, saying Amen. There is a distribution to each, and a participation in that over which thanks has been given, and to those who are absent a portion is sent by the deacons. And they who are well-to-do and willing to do so give what each thinks fit. What is collected is deposited with the president, who gives help to the orphans and widows, and to those who through illness or any other cause are in want, and to those who are in bonds, and to the strangers among us, and to all who are in need.'

The third description comes from the defence of Christianity by Tertullian (*c.* A.D. 155–222). It is long but it is so important that it must be quoted in full (Tertullian, *Apology* 39): 'We meet together as an assembly and congregation, in order that, offering up prayers to God as with united force, we may wrestle with him in our supplications. This violence God delights in. We pray too for the Emperors, for their ministers, and for all in authority, for the welfare of the world, for the prevalence of peace, for the delay of the final consummation.

'We assemble to read our sacred writings, if any peculiarity of the times makes either forewarning or reminiscence needful. However it be in that respect, with the sacred words we nourish our faith, we animate our hope, we make our confidence more steadfast; and, no less, by inculcation of God's precepts we confirm good habits. In the same place also exhortations are made, rebukes and sacred censures are administered. For with a great gravity is the work of judging carried on among us, as befits those who feel assured that they are in the sight of God; and you have the most notable example of judgment to come, when anyone has sinned so grievously as to require his severance from us in prayer, and the meeting and all sacred intercourse.

'The tried men of our elders preside over us, obtaining that honour not by purchase, but by established character. . . .

'On the monthly collection day, if he likes, each puts in a small donation, but only if it be his pleasure, and only if he is able; for there is no compulsion; all is voluntary. These gifts are, as it were, piety's deposit fund. For they are not taken thence and spent on feasts and drinking bouts, and eating-houses, but to support and bury poor people, to supply the wants of boys and girls destitute of means and parents, and of old persons confined now to the house; such too as have suffered shipwreck; and if there happen to be any condemned to the mines, or banished to the islands, or shut up in prisons for their fidelity to the cause of God's Church, they become the nurslings of their confession.'

He then goes on to speak of the *Agapē*, the Love Feast. Every early Christian congregation had on the Lord's Day a communal meal, to which those who had plenty brought much, and to which those who had little brought what they could, and to which the slave must often have brought nothing but his hunger, and in which all shared in joyous fellowship: 'Our feast explains itself by its name. The Greek word means love. . . . As it is an act of religious service, it permits no vileness or immodesty. The participants before reclining taste first of prayer to God. As much is eaten as satisfies the craving of hunger; as much is drunk as befits the chaste. They say it is enough, as those who remember that even during the night they have to worship God. They talk as those who know that the Lord is one of their hearers. After they have washed, and after the lights have been brought in, each is asked to stand forth and sing, as he can, a hymn to God, either one from the Holy Scriptures, or one of his own composing. . . . As the feast began with prayer, so with prayer it is closed. We go from it, not like troops of mischiefdoers, nor bands of roamers, nor to break out into licentious acts, but to have as much care of our modesty and chastity, as if we had been at a school of virtue rather than a banquet.'

When we read these descriptions of the early Christian Lord's Day services, certain things emerge, and these things make a pattern.

(a) They used the Lord's Day for *study*. In both Justin and Tertullian the reading of Scripture is stressed. In fact, it is so stressed that it seems to be the main part of the service. The Christian should always use the Lord's Day to find out a little more about the faith he professes. It may be by listening to a sermon; it may be by taking part in a Bible school or Bible class; it may be by being one of a group who meet to talk and to discuss; it may be by the listening to what radio and television can give; it may be by the deliberate reading of a teaching book. One way or another, the Lord's Day should be a teaching or a learning day.

(b) They used the Lord's Day for *prayer*. This is to say, they used it to get to know God better. On the Lord's Day they took life and laid it before God. Prayer too was an unvarying part of the pattern of the early Christian Lord's Day. If the Lord's Day is nothing else, it must be the day when we stop – and remember God. It must be a day when we take our own needs, when we take all kinds of people, and lay all before God.

(c) They used the Lord's Day for *fellowship*. It was on that day, week by week, that they had their Love Feast, to which they came together in a togetherness which overcame all social barriers and made them one united band of brothers in Christ. The Church has lost and gained many things in the course of the years; it is one of the tragedies that it lost the Love Feast, and never really gained anything to put in its place. In a curious way, to have eaten together is the way to unity.

(d) They used the Lord's Day *to make that fellowship practically effective*. Part of the unvarying pattern is the voluntary offering for those in trouble and in need. This goes right back to the New Testament. When Paul was writing to the Corinthians and reminding them of the collection he was taking for the poor of the Church at Jerusalem, he said: 'On the first day of every week, each of you is to put something aside and store it up, as he may prosper' (1 Corinthians 16:2). The Lord's Day must surely always be used to help those less fortunate than we are. It may be that in the days of the week we do not have time to think of others; the Lord's Day is the day on which we remember. And today in the modern world that remembering may well be best done by not dropping a coin or even a note in a collection plate but by paying a visit or extending an invitation to someone who is old or lonely or a stranger in a strange place.

(e) They used the Lord's Day for *praise*. Both the heathen Pliny and the Christian Tertullian note how the Christian congregations sang. That too goes right back to the New Testament, for again in the Letter to the Corinthians Paul speaks about the man who comes to the Church's worship with a hymn (1 Corinthians 14:26). 'Let us sing to God's praise and glory', is a fit opening to any Christian assembly.

(f) They used the Lord's Day *to strengthen the moral fibre of life.* Even the heathen Pliny tells of the pledge the Christians took to live the good life. Both Justin and Tertullian tell of the exhortation delivered; and Tertullian tells of the Christian discipline exercised on those who lived unchristian lives. Their aim was to use the Lord's Day to emerge on the beginning of the new week morally strengthened and spiritually uplifted.

To know more about the faith we hold, to come nearer to God and nearer to our fellowmen, to remember others and to help them, to declare our praise to God, to walk with firmer steps the way to life – these were the aims of the early Christians in their use of the Lord's Day – and they are aims just as valid as ever they were.

(v) For the Christian the Lord's Day should be used for worship. The word worship is a very wide word. Worship is worth-ship, and to worship is to confess and to experience the supreme worth of God. It is through some means or other to find the presence of God, and through that discovery to find the inspiration and the strength to live a life which is fit for the presence of God. William Temple's definition of worship places worship in the wider context which it ought to have. 'To worship,' Temple wrote, 'is to quicken the conscience by the holiness of God, to feed the mind with the truth of God, to purge the imagination by the beauty of God, to open the heart to the love of God, to devote the will to the purpose of God.'

We must clearly and willingly admit that there are many ways to worship. However difficult it is for the conventional religious mind to recognize it or to admit it, the Church is not the only place in which worship in the real sense of the word is possible.

There are those for whom nature itself is the cathedral of God. Wordsworth writes of this experience of nature in 'Lines composed a few miles above Tintern Abbey':

> I have felt
> A presence that disturbs me with the joy
> Of elevated thoughts; a sense sublime
> Of something far more deeply interfused,

Whose dwelling is the light of setting suns,
And the round ocean and the living air,
And the blue sky, and in the mind of man.

There is no doubt that this is a description of worship, and un-questionably a man can worship in nature; it would be strange if we could not meet God in the world that God has made.

A man can worship in music. When Handel was asked how he had succeeded in writing the music of his *Messiah*, he answered: 'I saw the Heavens open, and God sitting on his great white throne,' and it is just that same experience that music can bring to some.

A man can worship in beauty. F. R. Barry in his life of that great bishop, Mervyn Haigh, repeats a story about Haigh that Dean Hedley Burrows told him. Burrows said that, when he was Dean of Hereford, Mervyn Haigh came to see him on one occasion. Burrows goes on: 'He (Haigh) took me into the cath-edral and led me to a certain point in the north nave aisle from which he could see the fifteenth-century vaulting in the south transept, and he said, "It was that light which decided me to be ordained".' It was through beauty that God spoke to Mervyn Haigh.

It may well be that in this modern world a man may find his worship in the services that come to him on the air on radio and television. One of the strangest experiences in broadcasting is that, if one is taking part in a well-established programme which has been running perhaps for many years, a programme such, for instance, as the People's Service, one is acutely aware of an un-seen fellowship; there is the clear consciousness that one is in the midst of a worshipping community which one cannot see but which one can vividly and intensely feel.

It may well be true that for the large majority of people wor-ship must be a corporate act within a church; it may well be that at least some of us hesitate, or refuse, to recognize anything else as worship; but, if worship be the realization and the aware-ness of the presence of God, and of God's greatness, and the dedication of life to him, then there are many kinds of worship, and a man must find his own way to God. He must somehow use the Lord's Day to rediscover, to realize and to remember that God is very near.

In the Lord's Day the Christian has a great possession. The

Lord's Day is not the Jewish Sabbath and must not be con-
founded with it. The Lord's Day is a day of rest, but rest must be
interpreted according to the needs of the individual; the Lord's
Day is the day of the meeting of families and friends; the Lord's
Day is the day when we seek to enter more deeply, in learning, in
reading, in study, in discussion into the meaning of the faith; the
Lord's Day is the day when we remember those who are lonely
and in need and who are less fortunate than we are; the Lord's
Day is the day when in worship we realize the presence of God in
order to go out and to walk in it through all the days of the week.

CHAPTER SIX

THE FIFTH COMMANDMENT

Father and Mother

The fifth commandment is: 'Honour your father and your
mother.' This commandment is built into the very structure of
human society. It occurs again in a slightly different form in
Leviticus 19:3: 'Every one of you shall revere his mother and his
father.' The Jewish rabbis with their passion for detailed exegesis
of Scripture were not slow to note that in the Exodus version the
father comes first, and in the Leviticus version the mother comes
first, and they used this to prove that the honour to father and to
mother must be the same. They expanded it thus: 'It is known
that a son naturally honours his mother more than his father,
because she pets him. Therefore God put the honour of father
before that of mother. It is known to God that a son reverences
his father more than his mother, because his father teaches him
the Law. Therefore God put the reverence of mother before that
of father.' The double form of the commandment, so the rabbis
argued, existed to make sure that the same honour was given to
father and to mother.

The sternest penalties were threatened against the person who
broke this commandment. Everyone who curses his father or his

mother shall be put to death (Leviticus 20:9; Exodus 21:17).
Two most significant things are to be noted. The commandment
to honour father and mother comes directly after the commandments which lay down our duty to God, and the penalty for
breaking the commandment is the same as the penalty for blasphemy against God (Leviticus 24:15).

There are various developments of this commandment in other
parts of the Old Testament. There are two references to it in
Proverbs. 'If one curses his father or his mother, his lamp will
be put out in utter darkness' (Proverbs 20:20). 'The eye that
mocks a father and scorns to obey a mother will be picked out
by the ravens of the valley, and eaten by the vultures' (Proverbs
30:17). No one is left in any doubt about the seriousness of breaking this commandment. The longest expansion of it, and the
most impressive, is in the apocryphal book Ecclesiasticus 3:1-16:
Listen to me your father, O children;
    and act accordingly, that you may be kept in safety.
For the Lord honoured the father above the children,
    and he confirmed the right of the mother over her sons.
Whoever honours his father atones for sins,
    and whoever glorifies his mother is like one who lays up
        treasure.
Whoever honours his father will be gladdened by his own
        children,
    and when he prays he will be heard.
Whoever glorifies his father will have long life,
    and whoever obeys the Lord will refresh his mother;
    he will serve his parents as his masters.
Honour your father by word and deed,
    that a blessing from him may come upon you.
For a father's blessing strengthens the houses of the children,
    but a mother's curse uproots their foundations.
Do not glorify yourself by dishonouring your father,
    for your father's dishonour is no glory to you.
For a man's glory comes from honouring his father,
    and it is a disgrace for children not to respect their mother.
O son, help your father in his old age,
    and do not grieve him as long as he lives;
even if he is lacking in understanding, show forbearance;
    in all your strength do not despise him.

For kindness to a father will not be forgotten,
  and against your sins it will be credited to you;
in the day of your affliction it will be remembered in your favour;
  as frost in fair weather, your sins will melt away.
Whoever forsakes his father is like a blasphemer,
  and whoever angers his mother is cursed by the Lord.

From the beginning to the end, the Old Testament reiterates
this commandment.

There are wonderful tales of how the rabbis specially carried
out this commandment. The most wonderful of these tales attach
themselves to a certain Rabbi Tarfon. In one of them it is told
that when Rabbi Tarfon's mother wished to get up on to her
bed, he would stoop down and make his bent back a step for her
on which to step up. It is told that on another occasion his
mother's sandals split and broke in such a way that she could
not mend them. So she had to walk across the courtyard bare-
foot. So Rabbi Tarfon put his hands under her feet at each step
she took, so that she might walk over his hands and not over the
cobblestones all the way. The rabbis felt that the glory of honouring a parent was even greater than any other glory that might
come to them; their only complaint was: 'You have not fulfilled
half of the commandment to honour.' This is a commandment
that Jesus twice quoted as binding. He does so in Mark 7:9–13
(cf. Matthew 15:4–6). In that passage he condemns those who
subtly evade this commandment. To avoid having to help their
parents, there were those who said that all their goods were
Korban, that is, formally dedicated to God. Then when an aged
parent asked for help, they would reply, 'We cannot help you.
All our goods are dedicated to God.' But it was in fact all a
clever trick to avoid giving the help. So also Jesus quoted this
commandment to the rich young ruler as one of the basic commandments which every man who sought goodness and life must
obey (Matthew 19:19; Mark 10:19; Luke 18:20).

There is still something more to be said about Jesus and this
commandment. It may well be said that he himself meticulously
obeyed it. Jesus died at the age of thirty-three and of these
thirty-three years he spent no fewer than thirty in the village home
at Nazareth. He who was the Saviour of the world spent ten-
elevenths of his life in a village home. Why should this be so? It
would seem that Joseph, the father of the family, died young. We

do not for instance find Joseph mentioned at all in the story of the wedding at Cana of Galilee (John 2:1–11). So since Joseph died, Jesus the eldest son, his mother's first-born, took upon himself the burden of the support of Mary his mother, and of his younger brothers and sisters. He faithfully and dutifully discharged his duties to his home and to his mother, and in John's story we find him still thinking of her on his cross (John 19:26, 27). The fifth commandment is a commandment which Jesus told others to keep, and which he kept himself.

The Greeks and the Romans were just as certain as the Jews that honour must be paid to parents. Plato in the *Laws* (717 C, D, E) writes of the honour that must be paid to parents. It comes second only to the honour that must be paid to the gods. Every honest man, he says, pays his debts, and there is no debt so primary, so essential and so universal as the debt which every child owes to every parent for the love and the care which gave him life, and which preserved his life. Plato goes on: 'And throughout all his life a man must diligently observe reverence of speech towards his parents above all things.... Wherefore the son must yield to his parents when they are wroth, and, when they give rein to their wrath either by word or by deed, he must pardon them, seeing that it is most natural for a father to be specially wroth when he deems that he is wronged by his own son.' The son should see that his parents are fittingly buried when they die and he should for ever cherish the memory of them. Plato, like the Jewish teachers, sets honour to parents in the highest place, and, also like the Jewish teachers, he lays it down that to honour parents brings blessings from the gods.

Aristotle lays down the same duty of honour. 'It would be felt,' he says, 'that our parents have the first claim on us for maintenance, since we owe it to them as a debt, and to support the authors of our being stands before self-preservation in moral nobility. Honour is also due to the parents as it is to the gods' (*Nicomachean Ethics* 9.2.8). It is remarkable how often the great ethical teachers both of Judaism and of Hellenism connect the honour of God and the honour of parents.

It could truthfully be said that no nation ever insisted on honour for parents as the Romans did. The Romans had the *patria potestas*, the law of the father's power, which, as Gaius the great Roman jurist said (1.55), has no parallel in the laws of any other nation. Throughout his whole lifetime a Roman father had absolute power over his son. So long as his father lived, a Roman son never came of age, and could not legally own one pennyworth of property. Legally and at least theoretically the father's power over the son was absolute. He could imprison him, scourge him, put him in chains, send him to work in the fields and even put him to death. The father could do this even if the son was famous and held the highest office of state. There was no legal power which could rescue a son from the father's power (Dionysius of Halicarnassus, *Roman Antiquities* 2.26.4).

Roman history is scattered with tales – many of them legendary – of how father after father used this unlimited power. There was Livy's famous story (8.7.1) of the fate of the son of Titus Manlius Torquatus in the wars with the Tusculans. Titus had given a precise and definite order that no Roman should engage in single combat with a Tusculan. Manlius' own son had gone out on a reconnaissance. Taunted by a Tusculan, he had engaged him in single combat and had won a glorious victory. He returned home amidst the acclamations of his comrades, carrying his spoils, and rejoicing that he was his father's son. But he had disobeyed the law which forbade single combat, and even in that moment of victory his father executed him. That story may well be legendary, but there is a story of the time of the Catiline conspiracy which is historical.

During the conspiracy, Aulus Fulvius, the son of a Roman senator, attached himself to the rebel Catiline. When Catiline had been defeated, Aulus Fulvius was arrested on his own father's orders and executed. The Roman father possessed this absolute power over his child, and right down to historical times there were occasions when he did not shrink from using it.

So, then, wherever we turn in the ancient world, to Judaism, to Greece or to Rome, we find the insistence that parents must be honoured and obeyed. When we turn to Christianity we find the same demand. Twice we find the injunction deliberately laid down. 'Children, obey your parents in the Lord, for this is right. "Honour your father and mother" (this is the first commandment with a promise), "that it may be well with you and that you may live long on the earth" ' (Ephesians 6:1–3). 'Children, obey your parents in everything, for this pleases the Lord' (Colossians 3:20).

We have then to ask just what it means to honour one's father and mother, and, when we do begin to work this out, we will find how delicately balanced a relationship the parent-child relationship is.

There is a Jewish rabbinic passage – one of many – on this subject. 'In what does reverence for a father consist? In not sitting in his presence, and in not speaking in his presence, and in not contradicting him. Of what does honour for parents consist? In providing food and drink for them, in clothing them, in giving them shoes for their feet, in helping them to enter or leave the house.' Rabbi Eliezer said: 'Even if a father ordered him to throw a purse of gold into the sea, he should obey him.'

(i) Gratitude will be a necessary part of honour for parents. It is literally true that the child owes the parent his life in a double sense of the term. He owes him his life through birth, but he also owes him his life in that the parent cared for him and provided for him in the days and years when he could not care and provide for himself, and when, if he had been left to himself, he would certainly have perished; and a human being's period of helplessness lasts for longer than that of any animal.

This is quite certainly true, but it is also true that no parent should ever blackmailingly hold over his child's head all that he has done for him. The simple truth is that it is both a legal and a moral duty for a parent to provide for and to care for and to support and nourish a child. When a parent has done that, he has done no more than his duty. Of course, it is true that often a parent has surrounded his child with love and has made very great sacrifices to give the child some special chance. Of course, the duty of gratitude is there, but, nonetheless it is an ugly thing for a parent to hold over a child's head what he has done for him.

(ii) Obedience will be a necessary part of honour for parents. It is but natural that the child should obey the parent. The child must believe that the parent's love will never ask him to do anything but what is for his good. The child must see that the parent's store of the experience of life gives the parent a right to offer guidance and advice. But there are certain things to be said.

First, a parent must earn the right to be obeyed. He can never resort to the method of the dictator and the tyrant and say: 'Do it because I say it.' A parent cannot in simple justice demand from the child any standard of conduct which he does not himself fulfil. We cannot order others to do what we ourselves are not prepared to do.

Second, in the last analysis a parent must always be trying to build up in his child that proper independence which will enable the child to stand on his own two feet and to face life on his own. The parent cannot therefore demand an obedience which takes from the child all power of decision. He must in the end respect the child as a person as well as seek to control him as a child. The great and difficult task of parenthood is to exercise control in such a way that in the end the child will not need it any more.

(iii) Support will be a necessary part of honour for parents. The child will wish to see that the parent in his old age or weakness does not lack for the necessities of life and is never left either in need or in loneliness.

This is an obvious duty, and yet there is this to be said, and it is to be said, not in any hardness of spirit, but simply as a fact. There have been cases when the support of a parent was too big a burden. Worse, there have been cases when a parent, brought into a child's home, has caused intolerable problems. There is seldom room for anyone outside the family in any home. It takes an enormous amount of grace for a situation in which an aged parent has come to be a permanent resident in the home of a married child, for it is very difficult for a parent ever to look on a son or daughter as anything other than a child, however old the child may be. No two people were ever closer to each other than my father and I, and yet, when my father was left alone, he would never come to stay with me permanently; he was much too wise a man for that.

No one can lay down general rules; of course, parents and married children have made a success of a situation in which they lived together, but if a parent cannot have a home of his or her own, then it is almost always much better to go into one of the homes for the aged which the Church and the community provide. It should be the right of all aged people that they should be entitled to some place of their own.

There is more still to be said. Gratitude, obedience, support will all be part of the honour given to a parent, but, as the years go on, there is a delicacy of adjustment in the parent-child relationship which both will need all the grace they can find to achieve and to maintain.

The study of this commandment is not completed by the statement of the duty of the child to the parent. Let us again set down the New Testament advice to the child, but this time let us continue the quotation a little further. 'Children, obey your parents in the Lord, for this is right. "Honour your father and mother" (this is the first commandment with a promise), "that it may be well with you and that you may live long on the earth." Fathers, do not provoke your children to anger, but bring them up in the discipline and instruction of the Lord' (Ephesians 6:1–4). 'Children, obey your parents in everything, for this pleases the Lord. Fathers, do not provoke your children, lest they become discouraged.' (Colossians 3:20–21).

These two quotations make very clear one of the characteristics of New Testament ethics, a characteristic that we shall meet again and again. The New Testament ethic is always a reciprocal ethic. It never lays all the duty on one side. If there is a duty on one side, there is always an equal duty on the other. Duty is never in the Christian Ethic one-sided; it is always a reciprocal obligation. It never lays all the duty on one side, there is always an equal duty on the other. And in this case, this is to say that there is a very real sense in which the parent must honour the child, just as the child must honour the parent.

(i) There is the basic duty of nourishment, care and support. This may seem so obvious that it hardly needs stating, but it was far from always being so. When Christianity came into the world, child exposure was a normal custom, carrying with it no discredit and no stigma, and certainly not regarded as a crime. When a child was born, it was laid at the father's feet. If the father lifted it, he thereby acknowledged it and undertook the duty of nourishing it and bringing it up. If he did not do so, then the child could be abandoned and quite literally thrown out.

In a papyrus letter of 1 B.C. (G. Milligan, *Selections from the Greek Papyri*, p. 33) a certain Hilarion writes to his wife Alis during his absence from home: 'If – good luck to you – you bear offspring, if it is a male, let it live; if it is a female, expose it.' Girl babies were specially liable to be thrown out.

Stobaeus has a quotation (*Eclogues* 75): 'The poor man raises his sons, but the daughters, if one is poor, we expose.' The weak or deformed child had every chance of being thrown out. Seneca (*On Anger*, 1.15.2) writes: 'Mad dogs we knock on the head; the fierce and savage ox we slay; sickly sheep we put to the knife to keep them from infecting the flock; unnatural progeny we destroy; we drown even children who at birth are weakly and abnormal. It is not anger but reason that separates the harmful from the sound.' Tacitus notes it as unusual that neither the German tribes nor the Jews expose their children (*Germania* 19; *Historiae* 5.5).

What happened to the children who were exposed? Many, of course, simply died. In Rome they were usually exposed at the Lactarian Pillar and in the Velabrum. They were collected for various purposes. Sometimes a wealthy woman who would not herself accept the trouble of bearing a child would take one away. (Juvenal, *Satires* 6.602–609). Often the boys were trained up to be gladiators; often the girls were nourished up to stock the brothels of Rome. Justin Martyr, the Christian apologist (*First Apology* 27.1–3) says that the custom was so common that any man entering a brothel ran the risk of being served by a girl who was his own daughter. For some children there was an even worse fate. They were collected by professional beggars who deliberately maimed them and then used them to solicit alms in the street. Seneca describes the wretched children with their shortened limbs, their broken joints and their curved backs who had thus been deliberately maimed (*Controversiae* 10.4). The elder Pliny has a still more terrible picture of those who hunt for 'the brains and marrow' of infants for magical and nefarious purposes (*Natural History* 28.2).

We cannot imagine such things as these happening today in western civilization. No one owes more to Christianity than does the child. It is not that anyone would claim that even yet western civilization is fully Christian, but Christian principles have so permeated society that these things cannot happen in a society which has been touched by them.

It may seem unnecessary to speak of the duty of the parent to nourish and to care for the child today, but it was not always so. (ii) There is the equally basic duty of training and of discipline. The parent owes it to the child to bring him up in such a way that he will become a responsible citizen. The child has a mind and a character as well as a body. The child must be given the education which will enable him to play a useful part in society, and the discipline which will make him morally responsible. A

Jewish parent was bound to do certain things. He was bound to teach his son a trade. 'He who does not teach his son a trade teaches him to steal.' And he was bound to teach him the Law. It was not so easy in the Jewish world to unload parental responsibility on to others.

It is a common saying with more than a grain of truth in it, that there are no delinquent children; there are only delinquent parents. Dr George Ingle in his book *The Lord's Creed* quotes a circular issued by the police department of Houston, Texas, in the United States.

For Parents
How to make a child into a Delinquent:
12 Easy Rules

1. Begin at infancy to give the child everything he wants. In this way, he will grow up to believe the world owes him a living.

2. When he picks up bad language, laugh at him. This will make him think he's cute.

3. Never give him any spiritual training. Wait until he is 21, and then let him 'decide for himself'.

4. Avoid the use of the word 'wrong'. It may develop a guilt complex. This will condition him to believe later, when he is arrested for stealing a car, that society is against him and he is being persecuted.

5. Pick up everything he leaves lying around, books, shoes, clothes. Do everything for him so that he will be experienced in throwing all responsibility on others.

6. Let him read any printed matter he can get his hands on. Be careful that the silverware and drinking glasses are sterilized, but let his mind feast on garbage.

7. Quarrel frequently in the presence of your children. In this way they will not be too shocked when the home is broken up later.

8. Give a child all the spending money he wants. Never let him earn his own. Why should he have things as tough as you had them?

9. Satisfy his every craving for food, drink and comfort. See that every sensual desire is gratified. Denial may lead to harmful frustration.

10. Take his part against neighbours, teachers, policemen. They are prejudiced against your child.

11. When he gets into real trouble, apologize for yourself by saying, 'I never could do anything with him.'

12. Prepare for a life of grief. You will be likely to have it.

This is a warning document and for many parents it must strike home. There is literally nothing that can take the place of parental discipline and parental control. This is something that the parent owes the child. The child cannot honour the parent who is not honourable, and no parent who evades his or her own responsibility can ever expect to be honoured. Honour is something which has to be earned and deserved. It is not enough to look after the material and physical needs of the child. There is a mind and a character also to be formed, and they cannot be formed without that discipline which is the basis of all training.

(iii) But there is another side to this. Certainly the parent must give the child discipline, but equally certainly the parent must give the child encouragement. 'Fathers,' said Paul, 'do not provoke your children, lest they become discouraged' (Colossians 3:21). Or, as the New English Bible has it: 'Fathers, do not exasperate your children, for fear they grow disheartened.' Bengel's comment on this is that what Paul is warning against is that which produces 'the bane of youth, a broken spirit'. There is a discipline which breaks the spirit more than it strengthens the spirit, a discipline which drives to despondency rather than to new and greater effort. Luther hesitated to give the name father to God, because his own father had been so stern and severe with him.

One of the tragic figures on the fringe of literature was Mary Lamb, Charles Lamb's sister. She had recurring bouts of madness; she knew when they were approaching, and when she felt them coming on, she and Charles would walk hand in hand to the asylum for her to give herself up until the fit passed. When she was a girl she was very severely brought up. 'Why is it,' she used to say, 'that I never seem able to do anything to please my mother?' An atmosphere of unrelieved and unbroken criticism can break the spirit. Luther said, 'Spare the rod and spoil the child – true! But beside the rod keep an apple, and give it to him when he does well.'

It is a psychological and a spiritual truth that no human nature can ever flower or blossom without the warmth and the light of the sunshine of encouragement; a continuous east wind of criticism can blight any nature. Criticism must be counter-balanced by praise, and praise by criticism. Too much praise will produce a complacent self-conceit; too much criticism will produce a broken self-despair.

There is a real problem here, for it is often the parent who is most anxious for the child, the parent who most desires the good of the child, who will be most unrelenting in criticism. But it is almost always true that encouragement will do what criticism is powerless to do. Everyone is good at something, and a word of praise is a parental duty.

(iv) There is the duty of sympathetic understanding. There are too many homes in which parents and children are almost strangers to each other. The parent has nothing to say to the child; he is unable to communicate with his own young people. The children so often, if they want advice or guidance, do not turn naturally to their parents, but rather to someone else, to the teacher or the club leader.

This cleavage between the generations is no new thing. It seems to have been part and parcel of life all through history. Here is a well known quotation: 'The world is passing through troublous times. The young people of today think of nothing but themselves. They have no reverence for parents or old age. They are impatient of all restraint. They talk as if they knew everything, and what passes for wisdom with us is foolishness with them. As for the girls, they are forward, immodest and unwomanly in speech, behaviour and dress.' That might have been written yesterday. In point of fact, it is an extract from a sermon preached by Peter the Hermit in 1274! One generation and the generation that went before it never really understood each other very well.

On the whole, a very large part of the blame for this estrangement must lie at the door of the older generation. It may well be that the centre of the whole situation is that older people find it very hard to accept the fact that things have changed, and that time has passed, and that life has moved on. Every generation is apt to think that life must stand still as it knows it – and that is precisely what life refuses to do.

Elinor Mordaunt, the novelist, tells of a thing her own daughter said. She, the mother, had said to the child: 'I would never have been allowed to do that when I was your age.' Whereat the child immediately answered: 'But you must remember, mother, that you were then and I'm now.' It is the then and the now which cause all the trouble, unless the parent remembers that other times beget other manners, and that one generation is necessarily different from another.

The biggest step towards sympathetic understanding will come quite simply from the realization that we cannot expect our children to be the same as ourselves. This is not totally to exonerate the younger generation, for youth is characteristically impatient and intolerant, but it should be easier for those of us who are older than it is for youth out of our maturity to exercise the patience which will keep open the lines of communication between the generations.

(v) There remain two things to say, and they are by far the most important of all. The parent must give the child the respect that is due to a person. The parent of the clever and the precocious child may look on the child as something to be exhibited. The parent of the spoilt and petulant child may look on the child as someone to be placated. The stern and severe parent may look on the child as someone to be directed and controlled. The only true way to look at any human being is as a person to be respected.

The way to respect a person is to treat him as an intelligent human being, and here is one of the basic truths of the parent-child relationship. To realize this relationship and to observe it would save the parent from the 'Do it because I say so' attitude which is the ruin of the relationship.

To make life a partnership and not a dictatorship, to learn together, to act together, to ask for a reasonable co-operation instead of a blind obedience, always to be ready to explain why, to respect the child as we ourselves would wish to be respected – this is the way to the building up of a true parent-child relationship.

(vi) All that we have been saying can be summed up in the simple truth that what the parent must give to the child above all is love. This is why even a not so good home where there is love is better than a sterilized, antiseptic, hygienic institution where there is no love. All the techniques and all the medical and psychological perfection in the world will not replace a mother's love, and that is not a sentimental statement – it is a fact.

This is far from belittling the work that the great institutions for children do. It is not to criticize the work that all kinds of welfare work does for children. It is only to say that the institution cannot do the impossible; it cannot replace the personal love that the child receives within the home. Only that personal love can give the sense of belonging, which makes all the difference in life. The cleanliness of a home may be suspect, the respectability of the parents may not be all that it might be. So long as there is love even such a home, with all its imperfections, is better for the child in the long run than an institution.

The parent-child relationship must be a relationship of love. If that is there, nothing else is needed; and if it is not there literally nothing can replace it.

CHAPTER SEVEN

THE SIXTH COMMANDMENT

Life is Sacred

In the R.S.V. and the A.V. the sixth commandment reads: 'You shall not kill' (Exodus 20:13), but the modern versions in general substitute the word *murder* for *kill*; and so in Moffatt and Goodspeed and the R.V. the commandment forbids murder specifically, and not killing in general.

This is correct, for in the Hebrew the verb implies, as Driver puts it, 'violent and unauthorized killing'. Disobedience to this commandment is the sign of a depraved society. It is the complaint of Hosea: 'There is no faithfulness or kindness, and no knowledge of God in the land; there is swearing, lying, killing, stealing, and committing adultery; they break all bounds and murder follows murder' (Hosea 4:1, 2). Jeremiah hears the condemnation of God to the people: 'Will you steal, murder, commit adultery, swear falsely, burn incense to Baal, and go after other gods that you have not known, and then come and stand before me in this house . . . ?' (Jeremiah 7:9).

There is a sense in which one might say that it is hardly

necessary even to state this commandment. There is an obvious sanctity in human life, which in the very nature of things forbids the violent taking of it. But the real reason for this commandment, as the Bible sees it, is the story of the words of God to Noah after the flood: 'Whoever sheds the blood of man, by man shall his blood be shed; for God made man in his own image' (Genesis 9:6). Since man is made in the image of God, then the taking of a man's life is the destruction of the most precious and the most holy thing in the world. This commandment in itself needs no elaboration and no justification and no defence. It carries its eternal validity on its face. But out of this ancient commandment there arise three very controversial issues for modern ethics and for modern society.

(i) First, there is the question: What is the bearing of this commandment on capital punishment? Is the killing of a man ever justified, even in the interests of legitimate punishment and social justice?

It will be only fair to begin with the background out of which this commandment arose, and of the Jewish practice and law of which it was a part.

Within the Jewish legal system it was never even suggested that this commandment forbade what may be called judicial killing. In point of fact, the death penalty was exacted for many and varied crimes under Jewish law. W. H. Bennett in the article on Hebrew crimes and punishment in J. Hastings' *Encyclopaedia of Religion and Ethics*[1] conveniently lists the Jewish crimes which were regarded as being liable to the death penalty, and the particular way in which in each case the death penalty was carried out, where that way is known. The capital crimes under ancient Jewish law were as follows:

(i) Murder (Exodus 21:12; Leviticus 24:17)

(ii) Child sacrifice (Leviticus 20:2; death by stoning)

(iii) Manslaughter. Jewish law made special provision for what might be called non-deliberate killing, killing which happened by accident, or as the result of a blow or an attack which was not meant to kill. For men involved in this, six cities of refuge were set apart to which they might flee if they killed 'without intent',

1. ed. James Hastings (T. & T. Clark, Edinburgh and Charles Scribner's Sons, New York, 1921).

but, if the killer was not inside one of these cities of refuge, the avenger of blood might take his life (Numbers 35:9–28).

(iv) Keeping an ox known to be dangerous, if the ox killed a man (Exodus 21:29)

(v) Bearing false witness on a capital charge (Deuteronomy 19:18–21)

(vi) Kidnapping or stealing a man (Exodus 21:16; Deuteronomy 24:7)

(vii) Insult or injury to parents (Exodus 21:15, 17; Leviticus 20:9; Deuteronomy 21:18–21; death by stoning)

(viii) Various forms of sexual immorality.

(a) Incest, which was defined as intercourse with mother, step-mother, half-sister, granddaughter, stepsister, aunt, uncle's wife, daughter-in-law, sister-in-law, stepdaughter, step-grand-daughter, mother-in-law (Leviticus 18:6–18; 20:14; Deuter-onomy 27:20, 23; death by burning)

(b) Unchastity (Deuteronomy 22:21–24; death by stoning)

(c) Adultery and unnatural vice (Leviticus 18:23; 20:10–16; Exodus 22:19; Ezekiel 16:38, 40; John 8:5)

(d) Fornication by a priest's daughter (Leviticus 21:9; death by burning)

(e) Fornication by a betrothed woman (Deuteronomy 22:22; death by stoning; Genesis 38:24; death by burning)

(ix) Various religious and ritual offences.

(a) Witchcraft and magic (Exodus 22:18; Leviticus 20:6, 27; death by stoning)

(b) Idolatry (Exodus 22:20; Deuteronomy 13:6–11; death by stoning)

(c) Blasphemy (Leviticus 24:10–16; death by stoning)

(d) False claims to be a prophet (Deuteronomy 13:5, 10; death by stoning)

(e) Intrusion of an alien into a sacred place or office (Numbers 1:51; 3:10; 18:7)

(f) Sabbath-breaking (Exodus 31:14).

In the Tractate on the Sanhedrin in the Mishnah the different ways of carrying out sentence of death are listed and described. There were four.

(i) Stoning. The condemned man was thrown from a height twice his own height. If the fall did not kill him, stones were dropped on him until he died, the witness for the prosecution being the first to drop the stone. The killing was not by flinging stones at the man but rather by dropping boulders on him (*Sanhedrin* 6.4).

(ii) Burning. The condemned man was placed up to his knees in dried dung or in pitch. A cloth lined with softer material was placed round his throat; the two ends where then pulled until the man's mouth was forced open; then either molten lead or a lighted wick was forced down his throat (*Sanhedrin* 7.2). Herbert Loewe in his article on Jewish crime and punishment in the *Encyclopaedia of Religion and Ethics* astonishingly describes this as a speedy and a merciful death.

(iii) Beheading. This could be either by the sword or by the axe and the block. It seems that the criminal was tied to a post, so that even in death his body would remain upright, for at least some of the Jewish experts in the law had the strange idea that the collapse of the body on to the ground was an intolerable humiliation (*Sanhedrin* 7.3).

(iv) Strangling. A scarf-like cloth was wound round a man's neck and the ends pulled up until he died (*Sanhedrin* 7.3). The Mishnah even lists the crimes to which each kind of punishment is appropriate.

Those to be stoned were: the man who had connection with his mother, his father's wife, his daughter-in-law, a male, or a beast; the woman who suffers connection with a beast; the blasphemer, the idolater; the man who sacrifices his children to Molech; the man who has a familiar spirit, the soothsayer; the profaner of the Sabbath; the man who curses his father or mother; he who has connection with a betrothed girl; he who beguiles others to idolatry, the man who leads a town astray, the sorcerer and the stubborn and rebellious son.

Those to be burned were: the man who had connection with a woman and her daughter (Leviticus 18:17); the daughter of a priest, if she commits adultery.

Those to be beheaded were: the murderer and the people of an apostate city (Deuteronomy 13:15).

Strangling was not a common death and is said to be the penalty for one who was not a priest, if he served in the Temple (*Sanhedrin* 7.4; 9.1; 9.6). It is a grim story, but it would be in the last degree unfair to the nobility of Judaism to leave the matter there.

We must go on to see how the mercy of Jewish law in fact made it next to impossible to carry out the death penalty at all. The law shows the seriousness with which Judaism regards sin; the administration of the law shows the mercy with which Judaism regards the sinner. That same law which was apparently so stern in its demands is a law which was astonishingly careful to preserve the rights of even a guilty man. We may look first at the provision of cities of refuge (Exodus 21:12, 13; Numbers 35: 6–34; Deuteronomy 4:41–43; 19:1–13; Joshua 20:1–9). In the circumstances of early law such places of refuge were a necessity, if there was to be justice, let alone mercy. In the early law it was the next of kin himself who had to slay the murderer. The law gave him not only the right, but also the obligation to carry out the execution; law had not yet reached the stage in which society and not the individual was the executioner. In such circumstances an enraged and grief-stricken next of kin might go after a man and take his life rather in the spirit of a vengeful vendetta than in the spirit of justice.

To meet this kind of situation it was laid down that there should be in Israel six cities of refuge (Joshua 20:1–9). They were to be so chosen and sited that every part of the country would have its city. So there were three cities on the west of Jordan; Hebron in the Judaean mountains, Shechem in Mount Ephraim, and Kedesh in the hill country of Naphtali; and there were three cities in the east side of Jordan, Bezer in the plain belonging to Reuben, Ramoth in Gilead in the territory of Gad, and Golan in Bashan in the territory of Manasseh. The roads to these cities were kept open and perhaps even, as it were, signposted, and it has been calculated that the cities were so distributed that no one could ever be more than thirty miles from one of them.

The object of the cities was that a man who had killed another man might flee to one of them. The law and the regulations are given most fully in Numbers 35:6–34. The idea was not that entrance into one of these cities gave complete and everlasting safety and asylum. The idea was that, when a man reached one of these cities, he could not be handed over to the avenging next of kin of the dead man until the whole circumstances of the killing had been investigated.

If it was found upon investigation that the killing had been deliberate and premeditated, then the murderer had to be killed, and it was even forbidden to accept any money payment in exchange for his life. But, if the killing could be proved to have been accidental, if it came from a blow or a push or even a stab that was not meant to kill, if something had been thrown and had killed a man and there had been no intention of killing him, apparently even if the blow had been struck in a moment and an excess of passion, then the killer was given refuge. The all-important thing was the motive. If it was deliberate killing, coming from acknowledged hatred, then the killer's life was forfeit. If there was no hatred, if there was neither intention nor plan to kill, then refuge was given. The person to whom refuge had been given could not move out of the area of the city of refuge, for, if he was discovered beyond the bounds of the city, the next of kin of the dead man could kill him. This situation, it was laid down, lasted until the death of the currently officiating high priest. With the inauguration of a new high priesthood, the man who had sought refuge might safely take up life again.

Such, at least ideally, was the care of Jewish law even for a man who had committed, or who might have committed, a crime. But even when such a man was brought to justice and to trial the whole procedure of the law was designed to protect his interests and to make his condemnation very difficult indeed. The court regulations are set out in the Tractate on the Sanhedrin in the Mishnah (chapters 4–6).

No man could be condemned on any evidence less than that of two eye-witnesses (Deuteronomy 17:6; Numbers 35:30). Circumstantial evidence was not valid in a Jewish court. The precautions which the court took in order that all the evidence which could be given for the accused person should be given was extraordinary. The court was open all day to receive such evidence. A man was sent through the city in advance of the party which was taking the condemned man to the place of execution with an announcement that so and so was being led to execution upon the charge of such and such a crime and with an invitation to anyone who had any evidence in his favour to come forward with it. Even when the man was on the way to execution, a man with a white handkerchief stood at the door of the meeting-place of the court, and in the distance, but in sight, there was a man upon a horse. If any fresh evidence came in, the man waved the white handkerchief, the horseman saw it, and galloped on to stop the execution. No matter how often a man requested it, he could be taken back to the court again and again, even from the place of execution, if he could advance any further plea on his own behalf.

Such was the Jewish shrinking from the final penalty that there was a saying that a Sanhedrin which put one man to death in seven years might be called murderous. Rabbi Eliezer ben Azarya said that it could be called murderous, if it executed one man in seventy years. And Rabbi Akiba and Rabbi Tryphon said that, if they had been present, they would always have had some way of making it impossible to pass the death sentence.

It is, of course, true that in New Testament times, Palestine was an occupied country, and that therefore the Jews could not themselves carry out the death penalty, but it is clear that even if the Sanhedrin had had unlimited power to pass and to carry out the death penalty, it would not have done so, for Jewish law was determined to save life rather than to kill.

Under Greek law there were certain great crimes for which a man might be condemned to death – murder, treason, impiety, sacrilege and debasing the coinage. There were crimes against person and property. Theft by night was punishable by death, as was theft of more than fifty drachmae (about two hundred and fifty pence). Adultery was a capital crime and the injured husband could take the law into his own hands, and kill the man who had seduced his wife. Fornication on the other hand was not a crime at all. Kidnappers, burglars and highwaymen could be condemned to death. Robbers at the gymnasiums and pilferers at the harbours were liable to sentence of death. By New Testament times the Greek method of carrying out the death penalty was to give the condemned man hemlock to drink, as was done to Socrates. Under Roman law treason, corruption by governors and government officials, kidnapping, seduction and rape were all capital crimes. But in both Greek and Roman law the death penalty was very sparingly used.

It was in England itself that the death penalty was most widely used. At the beginning of the nineteenth century there were in England no fewer than two hundred crimes for which a person could be hanged; and a man could be condemned to death for stealing as little as three new pence. There has been in England an increasing mercy, but the overarching question remains: Ought the death penalty to be retained in a Christian country? Is capital punishment a proper part of the law of a Christian country?

Before we can answer this question, we must look at punishment in general. What is the aim and purpose of punishment? What is punishment meant to do? What is the place of punishment in the life of society and of the community?

(i) Society is built on law. Law is at once the foundation of society and the cement which holds society together. Without law society would disintegrate. It is law which protects the ordinary person against the strong bad man, or against the unscrupulous plots of the clever but selfishly ambitious rogue. Even in the ordinary everyday activities of life, such as motoring, house-building, buying and selling, the observance of law is essential, if life is to go on at all.

But human nature being what it is, there will always be the desire to break the law; there will be a continual danger that the law will be broken either carelessly or deliberately. The law therefore must provide itself with sanctions, and punishment is necessary for the maintenance of that law, which is the basis of society. Punishment and law go hand in hand so that there may be a fitting penalty for law-breaking.

This is not to say that there may not sometimes be bad law, law which is partial rather than impartial, law which is to favour one section of the community, and to hold down another. Nor is it to say that there are not times when the operation of law is unsatisfactory, when, for instance, those who administer it are corrupt, or when its application is so erratic and unpredictable that it produces nothing but resentment. This is to be admitted, but in a democracy it is law itself which provides the means of correcting its own misuse. But in normal circumstances it is law which holds society together, and therefore for the sake of society any breach of it, or any defiance of it, must be punished.

(ii) If a crime has been committed which has caused loss or injury to someone, there must be restoration and restitution. It would be an intolerable situation if the criminal was allowed to profit by his crime. The ultimate welfare of the criminal has to be sought, and we will look at that later, but concern for the criminal must not cause the victim to be entirely forgotten.

Punishment is necessary to conserve the interests of the person wronged.

(iii) Punishment is necessary as a deterrent. It is necessary to demonstrate to anyone contemplating a crime that crime does not pay. Punishment is intended not only to punish the wrong-doer, but also to deter others from a similar course of action.

It is this side of the matter which accounts for the element of publicity which often accompanies punishment. In Palestine it was the custom to take a criminal to the place of execution by the longest possible route, so that as many as possible might see what happened to the man who broke the law. In more modern times public executions, for instance by the guillotine in France or by the gallows or the headsman's block in Britain, were not designed simply as public spectacles to thrill the mob; they were intended to be warning demonstrations of what happened to the law-breaker. In modern times this is the justification for the newspaper publicity which attaches to crimes. In many cases the publicity is the worst part of the punishment, and in all cases it is meant to show that punishment follows crime, and so to be a deterrent.

(iv) There are two aspects of the matter at which we have not yet looked. It must be a first principle of all Christian punishment that it is not only for the sake of society, but that it is also for the sake of the criminal. From the Christian point of view, it is not enough to present the criminal in his punishment as a dreadful example, and to use him as a deterrent. It is not enough that punishment should be only retributive, that it should be no more than a penalty imposed by an outraged society to protect the all-important principle of law. The one essential additional element in the Christian view of punishment is that *it must always be remedial*. It should always have as its main aim and purpose that out of it the evil-doer should emerge a better man. It must always aim not only at retribution but also at reform, not only at penalty but also at cure.

This is so because punishment for the Christian must be dominated by love. Christian love is no easy and sentimental emotion. Love, *agapē*, means the unfailing, the unwavering, the unconquerable, the undefeatable desire for the other person's good. Clearly, this will often involve punishment, for love which exercises no discipline is not love at all; but always the punishment will be administered in order to make the wrong-doer a better person.

Obviously, you do not cure a man by killing him. Obviously, you do not seek a man's highest good by sending him to the gallows or the electric chair. The very fact that this is done is a declaration that the man is hopeless, and that neither the skill of man nor the grace of God can do anything for him. Here we have the basic reason why on Christian principles capital punishment should have no place in the law of a Christian country. On Christian principles *all* punishment should be remedial; and capital punishment is the ultimate and the blunt denial of this principle.

This does not mean the remission of punishment. It means that the criminal has to be kept confined and under treatment so long as he is a danger to society – and that could be for a lifetime. It means that he is not to be released until he is cured. It means that no sentence should be for so many years, five, ten or twenty; it should be until the person is cured and rendered fit and able to take his place in society again.

Clearly, this means far more than that capital punishment is no part of Christian law; it means that the whole prison system, as at present existing, is totally inadequate. There have certainly been advances, but the principle of imprisonment remains largely retributive. It is punishment as retribution, not punishment as cure. And it is perfectly possible as things are for a man to come out of prison a worse man than he went in. The prison should be the hospital for the sick soul. Much has been done, and is being done, in this direction, but much remains to be done. A campaign for prison reform would be a Christian crusade; somehow to strike a balance in punishment so that in it there is enough of penalty to make a man see the seriousness of the thing he has done, and enough of cure to send him out a better man is a necessary task.

(v) The second and final aspect of the matter at which we have still to look is simply the recognition of the principle that prevention is always better than cure. It is our task as Christians, and no less as citizens, to build a society in which crime will lose its attraction. The psychologists will tell us that energy has to be used, and, when it is not used in good activity, it will be used in destructive activity. The extraordinary blindness of the planners who built new housing schemes with literally no recreational facilities is both incomprehensible and unpardonable. To build a place in which people will live together without a playing-field, without even a café, with literally no place where a person young or old can find healthy activity was asking for trouble – and we got it. The energy which might have been employed in kicking a ball is employed in heaving a brick through a window; the energy which might have been consumed in athletic contest is used in gang warfare. To take the remedial view of punishment means not only to see the wrongness of capital punishment and the necessity of prison reform; it means the building up of an environment in which healthy activity will take the place of criminal action, because it has the chance to do so – if it is not already in many places too late.

Out of the sixth commandment with its prohibition of killing there further arise two related questions to which the Christian answer must be decided.

(a) The first of these questions is, *What is the Christian attitude to euthanasia?* Euthanasia is the doctrine which believes that, when a person's life has become intolerable, when it may be argued that life is worse than death, then that life may be legitimately taken away. According to this belief a person who is suffering from some incurable and agonizing disease might be killed, kindly and humanely and presumably with his own consent, if he is still able to give consent. Or, this belief might argue, a child born deformed and obviously quite unable ever to live in the real sense might never be allowed to grow up. Or, it might be held, a child mentally and incurably deficient might be deprived of life before life ever really begins. There are, however, good practical reasons as well as religious reasons for regarding euthanasia with the greatest hesitation.

(i) There is the very real difficulty of defining the area in which euthanasia might be practised. Just when does a person reach that stage when it would be better for him to have his life ended? How is the word incurable to be defined? Is it not the case that many diseases which were once incurable are curable now, and what guarantee is there that a disease which is incurable at the present moment may not become curable within the lifetime of the person who has it? It would be a task to baffle human skill to decide at just what stage of human suffering or human abnormality a person becomes a fit subject for euthanasia. A law demands a certain amount of precision in it; a law requires a certain number of uniform and applicable tests; and this is an area in which it would be impossible to achieve this precision or to devise those tests.

(ii) Even given the tests, who would make the decision as to the ending of the person's life? Would the relatives have the say? Would the person's own doctor decide? Would there be some special panel or commission which would investigate each case and then decide? What part in the decision would the person himself have? Perhaps in some ideal republic or in some Utopia in which the state is all-powerful and in which the individual has no rights at all this would be workable, but in any normal conditions the responsibility for decision would present intolerable problems.

(iii) Even given that the tests could be devised, and that the decision could be taken, who would be responsible for the carrying out of the decision? Who would carry out what in law was a kind of justifiable homicide? This obviously could not be left in the hands of the individual; the medical profession too would clearly refuse the responsibility; it would be intolerable that there should be a kind of public 'executioner'. Legally to saddle anyone with this responsibility would be an impossibility.

(iv) Any such scheme would without any doubt lend itself to enormous abuse. Once allow the right to take life under any circumstances and the circumstances may at any time be fabricated or unduly extended. The way would be open for the extermination of the aged and the infirm, or of even a whole class of unwanted citizens, as happened in Hitler's Germany. The operation of the scheme would involve and require such complicated safeguards and such unceasing vigilance that it would become impossible.

Apart from any of these practical difficulties there still remains the deep-seated conviction that it is basically wrong to give anyone the power of life and death. No state has ever legalized euthanasia, and no Chritsian state ever will. This is not to say that men and women under certain circumstances must be mercilessly condemned to agonizing and incurable sufferings. There may be times when a good and a wise physician may ease a sufferer's passing from this world, but to reduce this to a matter of laws and rights and regulations would be to take a course which would be legally indefensible, practically impossible, morally wrong, and theologically unjustifiable.

(b) The second of the questions which emerge from this commandment is: *What is the Christian attitude to suicide?* In the Bible euthanasia does not appear at all. In the Bible suicide appears as an event in both Testaments, but there is no definite teaching about it.

In the Old Testament there are at least five cases of a man taking his own life. When Ahithophel's counsel was rejected, he went off to his own city, and set his house in order. And then he hanged himself and so he died (2 Samuel 17:23). Zimri, besieged by Omri at Tirzah, went into the citadel of the king's house, and burned the king's house with fire and died (1 Kings 16:18). Abimelech, when attacking a tower, was fatally injured by a millstone thrown by a woman, and ordered his armour-bearer to draw his sword and kill him, lest men should say of him that a woman killed him. So the young man thrust him through and he died (Judges 9:54). Samson in his last tremendous effort pulled the house down on himself and his captors (Judges 16:23–31). Saul, conquered and wounded by the Philistines, fell upon his sword after his armour-bearer had refused to kill him (1 Samuel 31:4, 5). And in the New Testament Judas Iscariot flung the price of the betrayal back at the priests and went out and hanged himself (Matthew 27:3–5).

In early times suicide was rare because life was precious; but in the later times, when the Jews were scattered among the Gentiles, the prevailing pessimism entered their souls too, and for the first time the Jewish rabbinic law took cognizance of suicide. The legal proof texts forbidding it were Genesis 9:5: 'For your lifeblood I will surely require a reckoning'; Deuteronomy 4:9: 'Only take heed, and keep your soul diligently'; this commandment itself; and Job 2:9, 10 where Job in face of his disasters indignantly refuses a suggestion to put an end to his own life.

It was at this time that a suicide was legally defined as 'one who purposely destroys himself'. And it was probably at this time that it was laid down that a suicide's body should be exposed and left unburied until the evening, that there should be no mourning for a suicide, and that a suicide's body should be buried out of the line of the other graves.

The Jewish law forbade suicide; but this was not to say that there were not times when it might be necessary to lay down one's life for one's faith. Josephus has two incidents which show the two necessities. At the siege of Masada all hope was gone and Eleazar urged the garrison to slay their women and kill themselves rather than fall into the hands of the Romans. 'There is still,' he said, 'the free choice of a noble death . . . Let our wives die thus undishonoured . . . Men will testify that we preferred death to slavery . . . It is death which gives liberty to the soul, and permits it to depart free from all calamity . . . Unenslaved by the foe, let us die as free men; with our children and wives let us quit this life together' (Josephus, *Wars of the Jews* 7.8.6, 7). The result of this was that a garrison of nine hundred and sixty all killed themselves except two women and five children. So the rabbis (TB *Gittin* 57b) told of maidens who drowned themselves rather than go captive to a life of shame. To lay down life for the faith was a noble thing.

But the other side of the question is seen in the incident of Jotapata. In this case Josephus himself was involved and he pleaded with the Jews not to commit suicide. 'Why sunder such fond companions as soul and body? . . . It is equally cowardly not to wish to die when one ought to do so, and to wish to die when one ought not . . . There could be no more arrant coward than the pilot who, for fear of a tempest, sinks his ship before the storm . . . Suicide is alike repugnant to the nature which all creatures share, and an act of impiety towards God who created us.' Those who die well and nobly win eternal renown, but the darker regions of the nether world shall lay hold upon those who kill themselves (Josephus, *Wars of the Jews* 3.8.5).

So in Jewish eyes suicide itself was a sin, although on occasion it might be right for a man to lay down his life for his faith and his beliefs and his God.

In the Greek and Roman world it may be said that there never was any law against suicide; suicide was never a legal crime; but, with the exception of one period in history, suicide was never approved and it was regarded as a sin against the gods and as an injury to the state. In all ages of Greek and Roman history men did take their own lives, and for many reasons.

There was what might be called heroic suicide, when a man felt that he was involved in some kind of situation in which the demands of honour made life impossible for him. So there was the famous case of Pantites (Herodotus 7.232). One of the great battles in history was the Battle of Thermopylae at which the three hundred Spartans stood against the twenty thousand Persians. They fought until they died where they stood – with the exception of one man who was not killed, Pantites. No one blamed him for it, but when he came back home to Sparta he was so haunted with shame that he too had not died that he killed himself.

There was what might be called the romantic suicide, when a person took his own life because he could not live without some dear one who had died. 'Ere now, for human love,' says Plato, 'for dead wife, for dead son, many a man has gone willingly to the house of Hades, drawn by the hope that in the world beyond they might see and be with those whom they had loved' (Plato, *Phaedo* 68 A). As A. W. Mair beautifully put it, there were many in the Greek world too who were lovely and pleasant in their lives and who in death were not divided.

There was what might be called the pessimistic suicide, the suicide of those who felt that death was better than life – and they were many – and who felt that it was better not to be born than to be born.

The Greeks understood these reasons for suicide, as we still do, because they are universal, but the Greeks felt certain things about suicide.

They felt that suicide was a crime against the state. Aristotle is very definite about this. 'The suicide commits injustice, but against whom? It seems to be against the state rather than against himself . . . This is why the state exacts a penalty; suicide is punished by certain marks of dishonour, as being an offence against the state' (Aristotle, *Nicomachean Ethics* 5.11.3, 1138a 10).

We have already said that suicide was never illegal in Greece, and the marks of dishonour were religious rather than legal. It is the religious wrongness of suicide that Plato stresses. 'And what shall he suffer who slays him who of all men, as they say, is his own best friend (i.e. himself)? I mean the suicide who deprives himself by violence of his appointed share of life, not because the law of the state requires him, nor yet under the compulsion of some painful and inevitable fortune which has come upon him, nor because he has to suffer from irremediable and intolerable shame, but from sloth or want of manliness imposes upon himself an unjust penalty. For him what ceremonies there are to be of purification and burial God knows' (Plato, *Laws* 873). So the suicide was buried in a special place, and the right hand which had done the deed was buried apart from the rest of the body (Aeschines, *Against Ctesiphon* 244).

So in the same way the Pythagoreans and the Orphics both saw a sin in suicide. Both thought in terms of reincarnation. Therefore, in life a man is working out the cycle of life and birth that God has marked out for him. 'Life is a penitential discipline,' and suicide is an attempt to interfere with the plan and the scheme and the ordering of God.

Only at one time and in one group could suicide ever be said to be common and approved. And that was in the Roman Empire in the time contemporary with the early Church. It was the time of capricious, tyrannical emperors; it was the time of ambitious and treacherous informers; it was the time when no man's good name, no man's life, and no man's fortune was safe. It was at this time that many a man took the way of suicide as the way out of an intolerable situation. 'God gave men life,' they said, 'but God gave men the still greater gift of taking their own lives away.' 'The foulest death,' said Seneca, 'is preferable to the cleanest slavery.' Suicide, as it has been put, was 'the one refuge from tyranny, when the lancet so often offered the way to eternal freedom.' When Antisthenes was ill and in pain Diogenes came to visit him. 'Who will release me from these pains?' said Antisthenes. 'This,' said Diogenes, handing him a dagger (*Diogenes Laertius* 6.18).

This was the easier because Stoicism was the dominant philosophy, and, to the Stoic, life was something that was 'indifferent'. In itself it was neither good nor bad, neither a boon nor a blessing. In certain circumstances it could be kept; and in certain circumstances it could be laid down; but in itself it had no special value. 'They tell us that the wise man will for reasonable cause make his own exit from life, on his country's behalf or for the sake of his friends, of if he suffer intolerable pain, mutilation, or incurable disease' (*Diogenes Laertius* 7.130).

Seneca says that so long as life is tolerable he will continue to live; but if he is afflicted with an incurable and painful disease, or if age shatters his mind, he will go. 'He who dies just because he is in pain is a weakling and a coward; but he who lives merely to brave out the pain is a fool' (*The Moral Letters* 58.36). But although the Stoics regarded life as something quite indifferent, to be kept or left as the necessity demanded, they did not lightly contemplate their exit from it. When someone suggested leaving life Epictetus replied: 'Wait for God, sirs. When he gives the signal and sets you free from your service, you shall depart to him. For the present endure to live in the place where he has stationed you . . . Wait, do not depart unreasonably' (Epictetus, *Discourses* 1.9.16). The Stoic would go, but only when he felt justified in going, and never in any case would he be a deserter.

The difference between the Greek and the Christian is that the Christian would never justify suicide. Augustine forbade it on two grounds (*City of God* 1.17). First, it is a step which in the very nature of things precludes repentance. Second, it is murder, being a breach of this sixth commandment.

Thomas Aquinas forbade suicide on three grounds (*Summa* 2.2.64, 65). First, it is unnatural. Second, as Plato had already said, it is a crime against the community. Third, it is a usurpation of the prerogative of God, who alone has the right to bring life to an end. Kant condemned suicide on the grounds that it is an insult to humanity as embodied in oneself.

When we sum this up, certain things emerge.

(i) We may well say that suicide always occurs when a man is of unsound mind. H. J. Rose in his article on suicide in the *Encyclopaedia of Religion and Ethics*, Vol. xii, p. 22, drops a remark almost in the passing: 'It is questionable whether any one whose life is of normal length is absolutely sane during every waking moment of it.' And in suicide a man is, it may well be, always over the edge, for, as Schopenhauer saw, suicide is the loss of the will to live, and suicide is the denial that self-preservation is the first law of life. No one who commits suicide is in that moment of normal mind.

(ii) The fault in suicide is twofold. It involves a running away from life, and it involves, as Thomas Aquinas saw, the usurpation of that which should belong to God alone. In that act man tries to escape from life by taking the times and seasons of life into his own hands.

(iii) If there is one place where condemnation should be silent, and where sympathy should be paramount, and where self-condemnation should be in the heart, it is here. The man who commits suicide does so because he finds life intolerable and it may be, it often is, the case that that is so because no one helped to make it tolerable for him. It might well be true to say that there would be no suicides if there had been people to whom the person intent on suicide could have unfolded his mind and heart. And when people are defeated by life then we may leave them with trust to the mercy of God.

For the Christian the taking of one's own life is forbidden, but we must regard with nothing but loving sympathy the man who in his loneliness and lostness seeks this final way of escape.

Let us now consider how, from the time of Augustus, the Orthodox doctrine of the Church came to be embodied in the conception of the 'just war'.

In his commentary on Joshua 6:10 Augustine claims that only a just war could satisfy the stratagems which Joshua used. He defines a just war: 'Righteous wars may be defined as wars to avenge wrongs . . . when a nation or state has to be attacked for neglecting either to make reparations for some misdeeds committed by its own citizens or to restore what has been wrongfully seized.'

In a letter to Boniface (*Letter* 189) Augustine insists that peace is to be sought, but that war may be unavoidable: 'Peace ought to be your desire, war only your necessity . . . War is waged in order to win peace. Hence, even in warfare, be a peacemaker that you may by conquering your assailants, bring them over to the advantages of peace . . . Let it be necessity, not your desire, which slays the foe in fight.'

In another letter to Boniface (*Letter* 220.3) Augustine writes to him at a time when Boniface was depressed by the death of his wife, and was contemplating leaving the public service of the army to enter a monastery. Augustine pleads with him that he will do much more for the Church by remaining as a soldier, and defending the Church against the attacks of the barbarians.

Augustine again deals with this in the work *Against Faustus* in the eighth book. We are told to render to Caesar what is Caesar's, and this involves paying taxes for the upkeep of the army and the payment of the soldiers. 'The natural order of things, which promotes the peace of mankind, lays it down that a ruler has the authority and the ability to undertake war . . . It is wrong to doubt that war is righteous when it is undertaken in obedience to God, to overawe or crush or master human arrogance. And since there is no power except from God (Romans 13:1), a good man is justified in accepting the orders of even a bad ruler.' Love is not a sentimental thing, he says, and it may be that others for their own good have to be treated with a certain 'benignant asperity'.

Let us briefly trace the doctrine of the just war up to the Reformation when so much of our doctrine was crystallized.

Thomas Aquinas deals with objections to war alleged to be based on the teaching of Jesus. Jesus said that they who take the sword will perish by the sword (Matthew 26:25), but here *to take* means *to use without warrant*, and this forbids unauthorized or private persons from using military force. War does not agree with the commands, 'Resist not evil', and 'Avenge not yourselves' (Matthew 5:39), but these commandments are satisfied by the cultivation of a placable spirit, and cannot require us to do mischief by allowing evil to go unpunished. It may be argued that, 'If the peacemakers are blessed, then the warmakers are cursed', but war may often be the best way to make peace (*Summa* 2.2 qu. 40, art. I).

Luther never had any doubt that the gospel 'presupposes natural rights and duties', and he defends and praises the Christian soldier.

Calvin held that war is an act of retributive justice, and is to be used and waged precisely as the civil magistrate imposes penalties and punishments; it has exactly the same justification as the ordinary measures of social justice which protect the population from the criminal. 'Whether it be a king who does it on a big scale, or a scoundrel who does it on a small scale, he is equally to be regarded and punished as a robber. It is no breach of the commandment, Thou shalt not kill. The slaying of the authors of an unjust war is an execution, the judge is God, and the fighting men who defend the right are merely God's instruments. If it be objected that the New Testament does not expressly permit Christians to fight, it is to be observed that the New Testament does not undertake to legislate about civil polity, and that it presupposes the Old Testament in which the greatest men of God like Moses and David were mighty men of valour in the service of God.'

Here then is the doctrine of the just war, and this has always been the position of orthodoxy. It is true that there have been other voices, notably the voice of the Quakers. As far back as 1676 Robert Barclay wrote: 'Whoever can reconcile this, Resist not evil, with, Resist evil by force; again, Give also thy other cheek, with, Strike again; also, Love thine enemies, with, Spoil them, make a prey of them, pursue them with fire and sword, or, Pray for those that persecute you, with, Persecute them by fines, imprisonment, and death itself. Whoever can find a means to reconcile these things may be supposed to have found a way to reconcile God with the Devil, Christ with Anti-Christ, light with darkness, and good with evil.'

It may be, as Tolstoy said, that nowhere does Jesus in so many words forbid war, 'but a father who exhorts his son to live honestly, never to wrong any person, and to give all that he has to others, would not forbid his son to kill people on the highway.' Given certain principles, there are surely certain things which do not need to be said.

There can be no reasonable doubt that this is a subject in which much needs to be re-examined and this we shall now do. Once again I am indebted for source material to the article on war by W. P. Paterson in the Hastings' *Encyclopaedia of Religion and Ethics*, even if it be true that events have made many of the verdicts in that article seem fantastically unreal and even ludicrous.

Broadly speaking, a just war has always been taken to be a war in defence of that which is right, or in punishment of that which is wrong. Normally, wars of conquest have not been included in the category of just war, although even they on occasion have been claimed to be just. Before we look at any of the individual statements of great Christian writers and thinkers about just war, let us look at some of the general considerations which have been advanced as justifications for war.

There is the claim that just retribution has always been an essential part of Christian belief. There is the Parable of the Last Judgment (Matthew 25:31–46). There are the eschatological condemnations in Mark 13 and Matthew 24. There is the doom of the Revelation on all the opponents of God. Now, it is argued, if retribution on the wrongdoer is part of the very structure of the Christian Ethic and part of the very principle of the world's existence, then 'it may well be thought incredible that Christianity has made it criminal for a nation to be a fellow-worker with God in restraining the powers of wickedness and in seeing justice done upon earth.' To refuse to take part in the exercise of such retribution, it is argued, 'demands a code of morals, which, if binding, would entail grave censure upon God himself, and give ground for an indictment of the methods of his government of the universe'. It is surely relevant to answer that retribution exercised by the holy God and retribution exercised by sinful man are very different things. If there is such a thing as vengeance, that vengeance belongs to God (Romans 12:19). And it is surely difficult and even impossible to believe that those who were responsible for the bombing of Hiroshima and Nagasaki can in any sense whatever be called the co-workers of God.

It is admitted that love is the essential Christian virtue, but it is also argued that love and discipline go hand in hand, and that love must at times exercise discipline, even if that discipline involves force. No one will deny that love must exercise discipline, but it can scarcely be called discipline to blast some thousands of men, women, and children out of existence. If there is one characteristic of discipline which cannot be removed from it without destroying the whole conception of discipline, it is that discipline is remedial and curative, and it is not possible to cure a man's faults or to remedy a nation's faults by either individual or mass killing. It is a singularly odd idea to connect disciplining a man with killing him.

It is argued that no nation would ever have a right to abandon its women and its children, its aged and its weak and its defenceless to an invading enemy. No nation, it is claimed, has any right to make or demand a sacrifice like that. The reaction of chivalry to spring to the help of the weak and the defenceless is, so it is said, a much better and more honourable reaction. At the most that would justify a defensive war, and, further, it is very doubtful if any real advance has been made in history without the element of sacrifice entering into it.

It is argued that we must bring to any question the whole and the total teaching of Jesus, and that we must think of him not merely in terms of meekness and of love, but also in terms of justice, of majesty, and of power. So, it is said, 'from this stand-point it may be maintained with a good conscience that Christianity makes room for warfare in co-operation with God, in a world which teems with violence and injustice, breaks his laws, and challenges his righteous authority.' The answer which we have already given applies here too. It is extraordinarily difficult to conceive of that which is done in warfare as co-operation with God. Killing men, women and children and co-operating with God can hardly be held to be the same thing.

There are two very old pro-war arguments which must be noted, for they are still in use. There is the argument, stated by Bacon, that war is necessary to preserve the vitality of a nation, just as exercise is essential to preserve the health of the body. 'No body,' said Bacon, 'can be healthful without exercise, neither natural body nor politic: and certainly to a kingdom or estate a just and honourable war is the true exercise.'

Second, there is the claim that war is the school of all the virtues, that in war courage and heroism, loyalty and comradeship blossom and flourish as nowhere else. But there are wars of another kind, wars against want and disease and ignorance and poverty which can supply the high adventure which makes men great.

There is still another argument which is perhaps more difficult to answer than any other. It is argued, and it is true, that in many ways our debt to the state is even greater than our debt to our parents, and that to abandon the state in its time of need is just as dishonourable as to abandon a parent in his or her time of need. A country has a kind of corporate personality from which it is very difficult to divorce or isolate oneself. The only answer to this is that there can be a duty which takes precedence even of duty to parents or to country or to any earthly loyalty or relationship.

We must now turn to the views of certain of the great Christian thinkers about a just war. Thomas Aquinas (*Summa* 2.2 qu. 40, art. I) says that a just war must be waged by a prince invested with legitimate authority (this, for instance, precludes rebellion and revolution), against an enemy who has deserved punishment, and with the intention that good will be promoted and evil removed. Calvin (*Institutes* 4.20) declares that a war inspired by greed is always unjust, and that a just war is a war in which a prince, acting for God, undertakes to stop by force a nation which has embarked on a murderous and marauding enterprise. Hugo Grotius in his *De Iure Belli et Pacis* (Book 2) identifies three kinds of just war – a war in which a nation maintains and protects its own interests, a war in which it intervenes on behalf of others, and a war embarked upon in duty to God. A nation is bound, he says, to protect its own citizens, to exact reparation for injury, to insist on the fulfilling of rightful obligations and to punish the aggressor. A nation is justified in going to the help of its allies and friends, and to the general help of mankind. Any nation which denies the existence of God, or that God cares for the affairs of men, is holding a creed so dangerous that it may legitimately be forcibly repressed in the general interests of humanity.

We may note more briefly certain other views of what constitutes a just war, views which have never been widely held. It has been argued that an anticipatory war is justified, that it is just to attack a nation before it can cause the trouble that it seems set to cause. It has been argued by Hegel that a nation may at any moment be the best representative of the world-spirit of its time, and that this gives it, as an elect nation, a right to embark on a career of conquest, for in the end it will be better for lesser nations to be conquered by such a people. Rothe held that it was just to initiate an aggressive war against a nation whose lusts have made it a chronic disturber of the peace, and he held that it may be right to initiate a war to replace a lower civilization by a higher civilization, or to bring under a greater and a better power an effete and a degenerate nation. Finally, it may be noted that it has actually been held that 'aggression is a natural right, the extent of which is measured by the power which God has bestowed on the transgressor.' This is simply to say that in the last analysis might is right.

Those who believe in the doctrine of a just war have usually, at the same time, a great deal to say about the conditions under which such a war must be fought. Some of the things that it was possible to say forty or fifty years ago sound nowadays rather like grim jests.

In the article on war in the *Encyclopaedia of Religion and Ethics*, Vol. XII, p. 684, to which we have made constant reference, W. P. Paterson wrote: 'In modern times regulations for the conduct of war have been humanized to an extent that has been a welcome offset to the multiplication and intensification of the horrors due to modern inventions.' To talk to this present generation of the 'humanization of the conduct of war' sounds even fantastically unrealistic. W. P. Paterson then went on to quote what we might call the nineteenth century's ideals for war.

Benjamin Franklin was happy that the old savageries were eliminated, and saw no reason why the process should not continue. He therefore proposed that when the nations did go to war, immunity should be granted to 'cultivators of the earth, fishermen, merchants and traders in unarmed ships, artists, and mechanics working in open towns, also that rapine and privateering should be abolished and that hospitals should be respected'. The treatises on International Law of the nineteenth century expounded the doctrine that war should be a contest of states as such, and that the non-combatant citizen should rank as a neutral. This list of what we might call exemptions from the perils of war sounds to those who have seen or heard of Dresden and Hamburg, Coventry and London, like the dreams of a man who has come from another world and who has no idea what life in this world is like.

The Hague Conventions and Declarations of 1899 and 1907 made certain declarations regarding legitimate methods and weapons of warfare, and regarding the rights of occupied countries. It was laid down that the right to injure the enemy is not unlimited, that poisoning, treacherous wounding and killing, declarations that no quarter will be given, are forbidden. Attacks on, and bombardments of, defenceless towns are forbidden, as are the unnecessary destruction of edifices 'devoted to religion, art, science, and charity'.

The sack of captured cities is forbidden. Even in occupied countries the rights of private property are to be observed against individual pillage and public requisition. All this, read against the background of modern aerial bombardment, of a policy of scorched earth, of a Hiroshima or a Nagasaki, sounds like something from another world.

If the advocates of a just war think that they can control the weapons used in war and the methods of making war, they must be the most deluded simpletons that the world has yet produced. In any event, it is equally arguable that once war has been declared and engaged upon, the duty is to wage it with every weapon at a nation's disposal, so that it may be brought to an end as soon as possible. Arguments and statements like these have no relevance whatsoever in the second half of the twentieth century.

There have, of course, always been voices on the other side. Rousseau held that the only thing which stops states from holding pacifist doctrines is nothing other than sheer stupidity. 'They do not need to be good, generous, disinterested, public-spirited, humane. They may be unjust, greedy, putting their own interests above everything else; we only ask that they shall not be fools, and to this (the pacifist position) they will come.'

In our own day the question has been forced upon us. It has been said that at the present moment the nuclear powers possess in their stockpiles the equivalent of 320,000,000,000 tons of TNT, more than ten tons for every man, woman and child in the world. It has been calculated that at the present moment America alone has aerosol nerve gas to obliterate all life in an area of 455,000,000 square miles – which is eight times the total surface area of the whole world. And, as it has been grimly said, if children have toys, sooner or later they will play with them. We speak of a nuclear deterrent as if it was likely to eliminate nuclear warfare, but the stark and simple fact about a nuclear deterrent is that it is no deterrent at all, *unless its possessor is prepared to use it.* Any such discussion as this is no pleasant academic exercise in theoretical ethics; it is the most practical of practical politics.

It may be that this last sentence has raised an issue on which there can be no doubts. Is the matter of peace and war, the matter of the use or the non-use of nuclear weapons, a matter on which the Church should concern itself at all? Is this not a political issue, and should it not be left to governments and to statesmen to settle? Is discussion and action on this not a case of the Church 'interfering' in politics?

It has always to be remembered that the Church cannot be content with simply stating the truth; the Church has to use every available legitimate means to turn the truth of the word into the truth of action. 'Everything,' said Péguy 'begins in mysticism and ends in politics.' It is the wish of the world to find a Church which will not interfere. In Germany, Goebbels said: 'Churchmen dabbling in politics should take note that their only task is to prepare for the world hereafter.' It is told that Niemöller went to Hitler to tell him that he was concerned for the future of the German nation. 'Let that be my concern,' was Hitler's answer. There is nothing that the world would like so much as a silent Church.

D. H. Lawrence once wrote: 'I know the greatness of Christianity; it is a past greatness. I know that but for these early Christians, we should never have emerged from the chaos and the hopeless disaster of the dark ages. If I had lived in the year 400, pray God that I should have been a true and passionate Christian, the adventurer. But now I live in 1924, and the Christian venture is done. The adventure is gone out of Christianity. We must start on a new venture towards God.' Here is the grim thought that there is no point in looking to the Church for a lead. For a lead the eyes must be turned in some other direction. This is precisely why the Church cannot escape telling the world where it is on this question, so that men may have a lead.

In our approach to this question we can only begin from one place – we must begin from the conception of Christian love. Christian love is no easy sentimentalism. Christian love can act, and Christian love can use force. Of course, if I see a man raping or killing or maltreating someone else I will stop him, and with force if necessary. Not to stop him is to add to his crime my crime of passing by on the other side. But, if the Christian exercises force, that force must have three characteristics.

(i) *It must be remedial.* It must be exercised with the single idea of making the wrong-doer a better man. It must not only stop him; it must seek to cure him. And we will not cure a man by blasting him out of existence.

(ii) *It must be individual.* It must be directed against the person who has done the wrong. It cannot be employed completely indiscriminately. It is one thing to use force to stop a man doing a wrong thing. It is quite another to devastate a city in a night.

(iii) *It must be exercised in love.* It must be cleansed of hatred and of bitterness and of malevolence. Its desire is not for revenge; its desire is not for reparation – although that may have to be made; its desire is to make of the person punished a better person.

It would be quite wrong to say that force is forbidden to the Christian, but it must be used in order to cure and not to kill; it must be used personally and not indiscriminately; and it must be used in the love that seeks, not the obliteration of the other person, not even so much his punishment, but rather his highest good. And it is in the nature of things impossible that war should satisfy any of these conditions.

We have already seen that Rousseau once said that nothing more than common sense is needed to convince a man of the truth of the pacifist position. It is obvious that there are many who would question this. There are those who would declare that it is a gross over-simplification to argue that in no possible circumstances can we ever conceive of Jesus Christ approving the release of an atomic bomb upon any city in the world, but it is nonetheless an argument which has to be faced. It is very difficult to conceive of any possible honest argument which would support the use of nuclear weapons with their consequence of immediate devastation and with their power of cruelly affecting generations yet unborn. And yet the argument should not rest there. From the Christian point of view it is just as wrong to kill a man with a bow and arrow as it is with an atomic bomb. The principle of killing is the same; the only difference is that the vastness of the scale has nowadays forced this on our attention.

What, then, are the arguments against the pacifist position? (i) It is argued that the Christian Ethic of love is an individual ethic of personal relationships between individual people, and that it was not, and is not, meant to govern the relationships of governments and states. This would mean that there is a difference between what might be called public and private ethics.

This doctrine goes back as far as Martin Luther. Luther distinguished between two kingdoms. There is the spiritual realm, which is the *Kingdom of God's Right Hand*, and the secular realm, which is the *Kingdom of God's Left Hand*. In the *spiritual realm* we must obey, and obey absolutely, the law of Christ. The Christian as an individual is committed to an ethic of absolute love. But in the *secular world* the Christian is not an individual, he is a *man in relation*, in relation to his family, in relation to his master at work, in relation to the state. Them he must protect. Here he is not a Christian, he is a father, a master, a citizen. In this realm it is quite wrong to talk of non-resistance; he must protect property, he must defend his own and other people's rights, he must maintain the *status quo*. 'Do you want to know what your duty is as a prince or a judge or a lord or a lady with

people under you?' Luther asks, and he answers, 'You do not
have to ask Christ as to your duty; ask the imperial or the territorial law.' So Luther says definitely and bluntly that as individuals we must in the spiritual realm commit ourselves to the
ethics of love, but as citizens of the state our law is the law of the
state, and it we must accept. And that is precisely the argument
on the basis of which at least a part of the German Church was
able to accept Hitler. There can hardly ever have been preached
more dangerous doctrine.

Surely the answer to this is that, no matter where I am, I
remain I. I do not change as a person when I move from the
realm of my private life into the realm of my public life. The
state is no more than the sum total of its members and its
citizens, and, if it is possible to say that as a citizen I deliberately
accept a different code from that which I accept as an individual,
then it must mean that private and public morality will for ever
be different things; and on this argument public morality will
always be very much lower than private morality.

A Christian man is a Christian citizen. We cannot take off and
put on our Christian Ethic as we would put on and take off a coat
when we enter and leave a house. The Christian cannot agree to
do as a citizen that which he would not do as an individual
Christian. The state will only become Christian when each
member of it is Christian in every sphere of life.

(ii) There is the argument that we cannot look for, or even aim
at, perfection, because we are living in a constricting situation.
In other words, it is argued that since we are involved in a situation, we can only be as Christian as the situation will allow us to
be. In such a situation, it is said, the choice will often be, not
between that which is right and wrong, but between two alterna-
tives, neither of which is altogether right, but of which one is
more Christian than the other. In other words, what we have to
choose very often is the lesser of two evils. So, it is argued, there
may arise situations in which war is the lesser of two evils – a
statement to the consideration of which we will later return.

But it is possible to admit that there are things in a situation
which cannot at the time be changed without going on to admit
that the Christian must accept them. We might well at one and
the same time say that it is almost impossible to cleanse society
of prostitution, and also say that I personally will have nothing

to do with it. So it is possible to say, I know that society is not fully Christian, but I myself refuse to accept the unchristian things, even if my refusal to accept them means some kind of martyrdom for me. It is only by refusing to accept the situation that in the end we can change the situation. It is not true to say that our choice is between two evils; we can, if we will pay the price of it, choose the right.

(iii) This argument has certain ramifications. Another form of it runs like this. The Christian cannot expect a state which is not fully Christian to adopt fully Christian policies. The state does not claim to be fully Christian; it will therefore accept as its duty the right of protecting its citizens, safeguarding its territory, demanding and enforcing reparations for injuries received, and possibly even the prudent expansion of its territories by conquest. So, it is said, no one has any right to expect or to demand that a not fully committed state should accept the full Christian Ethic. Therefore, concludes the argument, when the state makes war, the citizen must accept war.

The danger of this argument is clear and obvious. The point of it is that it makes the state the final arbiter of the action of the Christian; it lays on the Christian the duty of acquiescing in a sub-christian or a non-christian action, because it is the action of the state. Throughout all its ages this is precisely the attitude that the Church, when it was at its strongest, has refused to accept. For the Church it is not Caesar but Jesus Christ who is Lord. And once again if enough members of the state commit themselves to the Christian way, then ultimately the state itself is committed.

(iv) The last argument against the pacifist position is the one which for very many people is the strongest. It is the argument which asks quite simply: What happens if in certain circumstances a state does not go to war? It has often been claimed that war had to be undertaken to preserve values which would otherwise have been lost. It has been claimed that what was at stake was the very existence of liberty and of freedom, of western civilization, and in the last analysis of Christianity itself.

At first sight this is a compelling argument, but there is a very real sense in which it is the supreme argument of unbelief. Do we really believe that Christianity will perish, unless it is defended by war? Do we really believe that Christianity would be obliterated, if, for instance, totalitarianism or communism came surging into the country? Do we really believe that it is possible to destroy the Christian faith?

If we do believe that, then we have deliberately passed a vote of no confidence in Christianity. If Christianity needs this kind of defence then there is little that is really divine about it. Surely the Christian faith is that Christianity has in it that which is indestructible. Surely, if Christianity is real, it must believe that its conquest must be by conversion. Surely it must have the sublime confidence that it cannot be destroyed, and that those who seek to destroy it will in the end be conquered by it. And surely this is where Judaism is our great example, because for thousands of years Judaism has never fought and Judaism, even in face of the deliberate attempt to obliterate it, has proved indestructible.

If we really believe in Christianity we would also believe that Christianity is its own defence, and it may be that we must conclude that a faith which needs the defence of modern warfare is not a faith which even deserves to survive. And because of this there is a duty on us which we must go on to face.

But before we go on to try to see the Christian duty in regard to war positively, let us take one further look at the argument that there may be times when it is necessary to defend Christian values and Christian civilization and Christian society by the use of war, and let us clearly face what that means. And we shall take our instances of what this means, not from the action of those who were alleged to be attacking the Christian values, but from the action of those who were alleged to be defending them, from the action of our own country and our allies.

In the defence of Christian values one atomic bomb was dropped on the Japanese city of Hiroshima and as a consequence 71,139 people were killed. On one night the German city of Dresden was attacked by three successive waves of bombers – first 244 Lancasters, second 529 Lancasters, third 450 Flying Fortresses. At that time the population of Dresden was about 650,000, and into the city were also packed more than 300,000 refugees from the East. The city had no anti-aircraft guns. In that one night 135,000 people were killed and 80,000 buildings were destroyed. And it is of interest to note that the British and American claim was that between 200,000 and 250,000 people had been killed. A claim was, in fact, made to even more savage destruction than was actually inflicted. If this can be called the defence of Christian values and of western civilization, then the claim is that such values and such a civilization can only be defended by destroying them. How any such action can in the remotest way be connected with the defence of Christianity is beyond all normal understanding. And that is war. It is futile to say that war could be so ordered and controlled that such things cannot happen. It is the simple fact that nothing can control war, once war is begun. No amount of argument can justify the defence of a religion said to be the religion of love by action like that.

Where, then, in view of all this, lies the Christian duty? The answer to this question is to be found along two lines.

(i) There is what we might call the negative side, and on this side the answer is that the Christian must totally, completely and absolutely renounce war, and must refuse to take any part in it.

If we then go on to ask what will happen if we do that, it has to be said that it is, in fact, the wrong question. In any situation and in any choice the Christian question is not: What will happen if I do this? It is quite simply: Is this right or wrong? This is not to say that the Christian has no interest in the consequences of anything that he does, but it is to say that his conduct is not dictated by a cautious calculation of probable consequences but by his awareness of the voice of God.

(ii) But there is a consequence in the sense of a duty which must be faced. Suppose war is renounced; suppose a country is invaded by its enemy; and suppose there is no armed resistance. In the first place, it will almost certainly be true that there will be much less physical suffering than war would entail. There will be no Dresden or Hamburg or Coventry or Nagasaki.

But, in the second place, something will immediately ensue in modern conditions. There will develop at once a quite different kind of warfare – an ideological warfare, a war between two sets of ideas, or, we may even say, a war between two religions. In its most likely form the war would then become a struggle between communism and Christianity, although at other times and in other places the particular opposing force would be different. Modern warfare is not likely to be simply a struggle for territorial expansion; it is much more likely to be an ideological conflict between two political creeds issuing in two ways of life. Such a warfare can in the last analysis only be decided by seeing which of the two ideologies, creeds, religions, ways of life provides the fullest, the most satisfactory life and the best people. Any creed or ideology or religion must be known and tested by its fruits, and its fruits are people.

We are therefore now face to face with the positive side of the answer. To plead for pacifism without at the same time pleading for the devotion of the individual Christian to his faith and for the reformation of the Church is impossible. The only weapon, the only armour, the only defence that Christian pacifism has is its Christianity. And this is why the staging of mass meetings, of marches, of passive resistance and the like are worse than useless; they are positively harmful; for they do no more than appear to demonstrate that pacifism is the enemy of law and order.

The true Christian task is much harder than that. The task is to make our Christianity such that it can not only resist any attempt to undermine or to destroy it, but that it can also itself prove so irresistible that those who began by wishing to destroy it will end by deciding to embrace it. It will be said by some that this is an impossible ideal. If that is said, those who say it would do better to admit once and for all that it is impossible to be a Christian, and that it is not worthwhile even to try.

There is one special direction in which the worth and the power of Christianity have to be demonstrated, and that is in the matter of reconciliation. It is clearly a ludicrous and a futile proceeding for Christians to preach peace and to be quite unable to live at peace among themselves. So then before the world-wide task of reconciliation can be effectively approached there are three reconciliations for which the Church must strive.

(i) There must be *the reconciliation of person to person*. There is no more tragic paradox in the world than two Christians who have quarrelled with each other. To speak of Christians at variance with each other is to use a contradiction in terms. And yet there are few congregations which do not have their explosions of anger, their personal quarrels and rivalries. The Church has still to begin with the simple initial task of trying to teach people to love each other.

(ii) There must be *the reconciliation of class with class within the community.* It is still true that society presents the spectacle of a competition rather than of a co-operation. It is still true that within society men still think of the clash of interests rather than of the identity of interests. It is still true that far too often employer and employee think of themselves as ever against each other. There can be little hope of making a fellowship of a world, if we cannot make a fellowship of a nation. The aim should be that in justice and in love we should, through the Church, make of the nation one united band of brothers.

(iii) There should be *the reconciliation of church with church.* It may well be that the Church cannot even begin its world-wide task until it has truly set its hand to this task. There are churches in which racial apartheid operates, if not in theory at least in practice. There are churches in which the snobbery of social distinctions operates, again if not in theory certainly in practice. There is the ever-heartbreaking spectacle of churches turning the table of the Lord into the table of some individual church or denomination, and refusing to recognize the ministry of any church but its own. To put it bluntly, it is a sheer impertinence for the Church, as it stands today, to preach reconciliation to the world. It cannot set the world in order before it sets its own house in order.

And here precisely is the key problem of the pacifist position. We can be absolutely sure in our minds that Christianity demands the renunciation of war, but any such renunciation is doomed to failure unless it goes hand in hand with a revival of personal religion and a rebirth of the Church as a body able to reconcile because it is reconciled. The Lord of peace must remain with his purposes frustrated until his instrument of peace, his Church, is purified and renewed – and the renewal of the Church can never happen without the total commitment of the individual Christian.

The commandment which forbids killing has a relevance for today as great as it had for the day on which it was first spoken.

CHAPTER EIGHT

THE SEVENTH COMMANDMENT

Men, Women and God

The seventh commandment reads: 'You shall not commit adultery' (Exodus 20:14). It is the paradox of human nature that there was no sin regarded in Judaism with greater horror than adultery, and there was no sin which, to judge by the rebukes of the sages and prophets, was more common.

'He who commits adultery,' said the Sage, 'has no sense; he who does it destroys himself' (Proverbs 6:32). It was laid down that not all a man's virtues will save him, if he commits adultery (*Sotah* 4b). There are three who never return from Gehenna – the adulterer, he who puts his fellowman to shame in public, and he who calls his fellowman by an opprobrious nickname (*Tan.d.b. El.* p. 29).

In the time of Akiba, after Hadrian's final destruction of Jerusalem, it was discussed how far a Jew could go in compromise to save his own life; and it was laid down that the three sins which nothing could justify were idolatry, murder, and adultery. Adultery was one of the sins for which there was no forgiveness, and which nothing could justify.

Yet the fact remains that the writings and the rebukes of the prophets make it clear that the horror that attached to the sin of adultery did not stop its committal. Jeremiah (5:7, 8) writes:

> 'How can I pardon you?
>> Your children have forsaken me,
>>> and have sworn by those who are no gods.
>> When I fed them to the full,
>>> they committed adultery
>>> and trooped to the houses of harlots.
>> They were well-fed lusty stallions,
>>> each neighing for his neighbour's wife.'

'Will you steal, murder, commit adultery, swear falsely, burn incense to Baal, and go after other gods that you have not known, and then come and stand before me in this house?' (Jeremiah 7:9). Again he says (23:14):

> 'But in the prophets of Jerusalem
> I have seen a horrible thing:
> they commit adultery and walk in
> lies.'

Destruction will come upon them, 'because they have committed folly in Israel, they have committed adultery with their neighbours' wives' (Jeremiah 29:23). Ezekiel flings his accusation against the nation in his day: 'Adulterous wife, who receives strangers instead of her husband!' (Ezekiel 16:32). 'And I will judge you as women who break wedlock and shed blood are judged' (Ezekiel 16:38).

One thing is to be noted before we proceed further with our study – it is common in modern English to use the word adultery in an extended sense, and indeed to use it almost as a collective word for sexual irregularity, but its meaning in Jewish law is clear and defined. 'Adultery is the intercourse of a married woman with any man other than her husband.' A married man is not guilty of adultery unless he has intercourse with a married woman other than his wife. Adultery is in Jewish eyes specially and uniquely the crime against the marriage bed.

There is one fact in the background of this which is more than worth noting as a factor in the situation. In the introduction to *A Rabbinic Anthology*, C. G. Montefiore has certain things to say about the position of women in ancient Judaism (p. xix). For the rabbis in particular there was no normal and natural association between the sexes. Friendship and companionship between man and woman hardly existed. Most of the rabbis were married and lived in fidelity and purity with their wives, but there was no partnership, no sharing of work and study with their wives. Repeatedly the phrase is used 'women, children and slaves'. Women were definitely inferior in station. The morning prayer was then actually used and meant: 'Blessed art thou who hast not made me a Gentile, a slave, or a woman.' Montefiore goes on to say that it is even true to say that social intercourse with a woman was actually regarded as a source of moral danger, an incitement to depravity and lust, a special invitation to the evil nature to lead it to sexual impurity. There was an almost complete lack of healthy, simple companionship between the sexes;

and this was a situation in which it was not difficult for trouble to arise. It is well to remember that too little freedom can be quite as harmful as too much.

The prohibition of adultery is clear and unmistakable. 'You shall not commit adultery' (Exodus 20:14). 'You shall not lie carnally with your neighbour's wife' (Leviticus 18:20). 'Neither shall you commit adultery' (Deuteronomy 5:18).

In primitive times it was general for the husband to have the right to kill any other man who seduced his wife, partly because adultery was a crime against property, and partly because the whole structure of society was built on the family. This explains why in the ancient codes the penalty for adultery was death. 'If a man commits adultery with the wife of his neighbour, both the adulterer and the adulteress shall be put to death' (Leviticus 20:10). 'If a man is found lying with the wife of another man, both of them shall die, the man who lay with the woman, and the woman; so you shall purge the evil from Israel' (Deuteronomy 22:22). The official punishment laid down in the Mishnah for such conduct was strangling (*Sanhedrin* 11.1).

A betrothed virgin was in the same position as a wife. If a man had intercourse with her within the bounds of a town, both were killed, because she might well have called for help and did not; if it happened out in the country, only the man was killed, for in those circumstances she could not call for help, if he attacked and violated her. In this case the penalty was stoning (Deuteronomy 22:23, 24).

In the case of adultery with a betrothed slave-girl, the woman is not blameworthy, for she is not free, and the man can atone by the bringing of a guilt-offering (Leviticus 19:20–22). If the daughter of a priest was guilty of sexual irregularity, she was to be burned (Leviticus 21:9). There is a primitive reference to the burning of an unfaithful wife in Genesis 38:24. And there is also a reference to the Egyptian custom of cutting off the nose of an adulteress (Ezekiel 23:25).

It is quite certain that the death penalty was never actually inflicted within historical times. It was superseded by divorce. When a woman was put away by her husband for any ordinary reason, she received back her dowry, but if she was divorced for adultery she lost all her rights. The guilty man was scourged. The husband of an adulteress could not legally continue to cohabit with her; he had to put her away; and even after divorce a woman could not legally marry her paramour (*Sotah* 5.1). Under Jewish law a woman had no legal rights; she therefore could never initiate divorce proceedings against her husband, however guilty he was; she could only appeal to him to take the necessary steps to give her her freedom.

In Numbers 5:11–31 there is an account of the procedure for testing a suspected adulteress, which is developed in the Mishnah tractate *Sotah*, the material of which we have in part incorporated in the account of the process. If a man, moved by the spirit of jealousy, wished to put his wife to ordeal, he brought her to the priest with one tenth of an ephah of barley flour. It was the coarsest flour and the food of animals. She had behaved like an animal and her offering was the food of animals (*Sotah* 2.1). She was brought to the Eastern Gate, which was opposite the Nicanor Gate (*Sotah* 1.5). She was clothed in black and every ornament was taken away. Her garments were rent so that her breast was exposed and a rope was put round her neck. She had exposed herself to her lover and now in shame she was exposed (*Sotah* 1.6). The priest took holy water from the laver (*Sotah* 2.2); he mixed it with dust taken from the Temple floor; the dust was taken from beneath a marble slab at the right of the entrance to the sanctuary (*Sotah* 2.2). A curse was then read to the woman which would fall on her if she was guilty, and she accepted it. The curse was then written on parchment and the writing was then washed off into the water. The cereal offering of the barley was put into her hands; she then drank the water of bitterness as it was called. If she was guilty, her body would swell and her thigh fall away, and she would become accursed. If she was innocent, she would remain unharmed, and would in time bear a child. Even if she was guilty, if she had any merits otherwise, the punishment from heaven might be delayed (*Sotah* 3.4). The ordeal would not work at all unless the suspicious husband was himself absolutely innocent (*Sotah* 2.1).

This is obviously very primitive, for it is trial by ordeal. We are told in the Mishnah (*Sotah* 9.9) that the whole ceremony was abandoned in the time of Rabbi Jochanan ben Zakkai because adultery became so common, and abandonment was justified by quoting Hosea 4:14: 'I will not punish your daughters when they play the harlot.'

So, as we said at the beginning, we can see the strange paradox of the horror of adultery, and yet the tragic prevalence of it in later Judaism.

The seventh commandment deals with adultery, which, as we have seen, is technically sexual intercourse of a woman with any other man than her husband; but we can hardly separate this from the larger issue of the whole question of sexual chastity. The wider word is fornication, which signifies sexual intercourse between unmarried persons, or of a married with an unmarried person.

The supreme importance that the Jewish mind attached to chastity can be seen from the passage in Deuteronomy which provides for the trial of a bride whom her husband suspects of not being a virgin at the time of her marriage, and for her death by stoning if the charge is proved to be true (Deuteronomy 22: 13–21).

In Leviticus 19:29 it is laid down: 'Do not profane your daughter by making her a harlot.' In Leviticus 21:7 a priest is forbidden to marry a harlot, and in Leviticus 21:9 it is laid down that a priest's daughter who becomes a harlot is to be burned. At the back of these three laws there lies a custom which is shocking to the modern mind. To examine it makes it necessary to look at customs and practices which are not pleasant, but which must be looked at if we are to appreciate the dangers which true religion encountered in its earliest days.

In the background of this there lies a custom which W. P. Paterson says 'was the most powerful and insidious force menacing the purity and permanence of Mosaism'. This custom sprang from the deification of the reproductive forces of nature. There is nothing more wonderful than the force which makes the corn grow and the grape ripen and the olive swell, for it is the life force; and that life force finds its peak and climax and its greatest manifestation in human reproduction, in sex. The result was that there were attached to many temples, especially those of Ishtar or Astarte, or, as she was known in Greece, Aphrodite, hundreds and even thousands of priestesses who were nothing other than cult or sacred prostitutes. To have intercourse with them, and for the cost to go to the temple, was regarded as an act of worship of the reproductive force.

As it has been put, the harlot was invested with sanctity as a member of a priestly and religious caste. Not only were there female priestesses attached to the temples, but there were male priests, with whom the worshipper had unnatural intercourse. This has its echoes all over the Old Testament. In Deuteronomy 23:17, 18 the use of these cult prostitutes is forbidden, and the offering of money paid to them is forbidden. They were there in the days of Rehoboam (1 Kings 14:24). Asa put them away (1 Kings 15:12). Josiah took steps against them (2 Kings 23:7). Their female counterparts are mentioned in Genesis 38:21, 22. In the days of Hosea the people were sacrificing with cult prostitutes (Hosea 4:14).

All around Israel there was this worship of the power of reproduction. In Syria the Feast Day of Attar was a day when women voluntarily prostituted themselves (Ephraem 459 C). In Hierapolis, the modern Baalbek, every maiden had once in her lifetime to prostitute herself with a stranger in the temple of Astarte (Eusebius, *Life of Constantine* 3.58; Sozomen, *Ecclesiastical History* 5.10.7; Socrates, *Ecclesiastical History* 1.18.7–9). Lucian tells how in Byblos in connection with the festival of the worship of Adonis every woman had to prostitute herself with a stranger for one day or sacrifice her hair, the proceeds being paid to the temple (*On the Syrian Goddess* 15). At Paphos in Cyprus every woman however well-born had to offer herself once as a prostitute before marriage, and Herodotus describes the scene in Babylon (Herodotus 1.199; Clement of Alexandria, *Protrepticus* 2; *Athenaeus* 12.11). In Thebes in Egypt any girl who was about to marry had to act as a prostitute in the temple for a month before her marriage (Strabo 17.1.46).

To the modern mind the connection of prostitution with religion is shocking; but it was extremely widespread in those days; and it is perfectly understandable when it is understood as the worship of the life and the reproductive force. Human nature being such as it is, it is easy to see the attraction of this form of so-called worship; and the basic purity of Jewish worship is in such an environment all the more wonderful, and we shall see later that the Christian Ethic was faced with exactly the same problem. The wonder was not that sometimes the Jews drifted into sexual irregularity; the miracle is that in such an environment the ideal of disciplined chastity ever came into being at all, and that in the end the ideal of purity won the day.

This seventh commandment invites us to look at the whole question of marriage and of the relationship between the sexes, and this we now propose to do. We shall begin by looking at marriage in the Jewish world.

To a Jew marriage was a sacred obligation. God had said: 'Be fruitful and multiply' (Genesis 1:28). It was to be inhabited that God formed the earth (Isaiah 45:18). It was not good for man to be alone (Genesis 2:18). No man may abstain from keeping the law: 'Be fruitful and multiply.' For Shammai this meant that a man must have at least two sons; for Hillel it meant that a man must have a son and a daughter, for male and female created he them (*Yebamoth* 6.6). Since man is made in the image of God (Genesis 1:26, 27), not to marry is to diminish the likeness of God in the world (*Genesis R.* 17.2). Simon ben Azzai said that a man who did not marry was like a man who shed blood, for he had as good as slain his own posterity (*Yebamoth* 63 b). A man who has no wife is without good, without a helper, without joy, without a blessing, without atonement, even without welfare and without life (*Yebamoth* 62 b). He is not even a whole man, for Scripture said he blessed *them*, and called *their* name Man (Genesis 5:1, 2).

Not only must a man marry, but he must also marry young. Eighteen was a good age for marriage, and to remain unmarried after twenty was a sin. 'Up to the age of twenty the Holy One, blessed be he, watches for a man to marry, and curses him if he fails to do so by then' (*Kiddushin* 29 b).

Eric Heaton points out in *Life in Old Testament Times* (p. 70) that it has been reckoned that on the average a man could expect to be a father at nineteen, a grandfather at thirty-eight, and a great-grandfather at fify-seven. So binding was the obligation of marriage that a man might even sell a scroll of the law to raise money in order to marry (*Megillah* 27 a).

For only one reason was it right to postpone marriage – in order to study the law, and to concentrate on being a student of it. 'A man should pursue his studies and then marry, but, if he cannot get along without a wife, he may marry first and study afterwards' (*Yoma* 72 b; *Menahoth* 110 a; *Kiddushin* 29 b). The Jewish Sages were not by any means blind or indifferent to the economic realities and necessities, when they urged early marriage. They urged a wise prudence in marriage. Arguing from

Deuteronomy 20:5-7, they held that a man should first build a house, then plant a vineyard, and after that marry (*Sotah* 44 a). The same Simon ben Azzai, who said that the man who did not marry slew his posterity, himself never married. When it was said to him that his preaching and practice did not match, his defence was to say: 'What can I do? I am in love with the Law. The population of the world can be kept up by others' (*Yebamoth* 63 b).

For a girl there was no other career but marriage. She could be married as early as twelve and a half; and, as Daniel Rops has pointed out, there is a distinct possibility and even probability that Mary the mother of our Lord was no more than fourteen years old when she bore him. Daughters were in fact not wanted, for they could be nothing but a worry when it came to finding a husband for them. Leviticus 19:29, 'Do not profane your daughter by making her a harlot,' applies, so they said, to him who delays in arranging a marriage for his daughter, when she has reached a suitable age. So much was it a parental duty to find a husband for a daughter that the later law said: 'When a daughter is an adult, free your slave and give him to her rather than let her remain longer unmarried' (*Pesahim* 113 a).

The Talmud has a passage on the worries of the man with daughters: 'It is written, a daughter is a vain treasure to her father. From anxiety about her he does not sleep at night; during her early years, lest she be seduced; in her adolescence, lest she go astray; in her marriageable years, lest she does not find a husband; when she is married, lest she is childless; and when she is old, lest she practise witchcraft' (*Sanhedrin* 100 b). At every stage the daughter brought anxiety. 'The Lord bless you and keep you' (Numbers 6:24) was expounded – Bless you with sons and keep you from daughters, for they need careful guarding (*Numbers R.*11.5).

It was held that God sits in heaven arranging marriages, and that forty days before the formation of the child a heavenly voice announces, 'This child is to marry so and so's daughter' (*Sotah* 2 a).

Theoretically, even in New Testament times, polygamy was perfectly legal, as of course it was actually practised in the time of the patriarchs. Deuteronomy 21:15 assumes it, for it begins, 'If a man has two wives...' So it is laid down: 'A man may marry as many wives as he chooses' (*Yebamoth* 65 a). Another passage limits the number to four (*Yebamoth* 44 a); the High Priest was limited to one wife (*Yoma* 13 a); and it was laid down that, if a man took an additional wife, he must give his present wife a divorce, if she asked for it (*Yebamoth* 65 a). But there is little doubt that all this in New Testament times was purely theoretical and that monogamy was the rule.

For the most part marriages were arranged either by the parents or by professional matchmakers. Ideally, it was held that marriage was much too serious a thing to be left to the emotions of young people. A girl might be engaged when she was a baby, but she did have the power of refusing to go on to betrothal when she reached the age of twelve and a day, and came of age. It was often said that love comes after marriage, and not before. Esau, for instance, followed his own wishes and brought distress to his parents (Genesis 26:34, 35). As for a son, the father was advised to have him married 'while your hand is still upon his neck' (*Kiddushin* 30 a), that is, when he is still under control.

But quite clearly in a matter of the heart, however carefully it is tried to arrange things, romance will keep breaking in. 'If a man marries a woman for her money,' it was said, 'he will have disreputable children' (*Kiddushin* 70 a). The songs in the Song of Solomon are not the songs of a couple who were doing no more than ratify a prearranged contract. There is one passage in the Mishnah (*Taanith* 4.8) which paints an attractive picture of what happened on the fifteenth day of the month Ab: 'The sons of Jerusalem used to go out in white garments that were borrowed, so as not to put to shame anyone who did not possess his own. The daughters of Jerusalem would go and dance in the vineyards crying: 'Young man raise your eyes and see whom you will choose for your wife. Pay not attention to beauty, but rather to family.' Even then careful prudence was insisted on: 'Hesitate in selecting a wife' (*Yebamoth* 63 a), and it was family which was stressed again and again.

Nothing could be more practical than the advice that the Talmud gives to those about to marry. A man was advised always to descend a step in the social scale in choosing a wife, for to choose a wife from a higher step in the social scale could lead only to trouble (*Yebamoth* 63 a). Difference in age was deprecated. 'Go marry one who is about your own age, and do not introduce strife into your house' (*Yebamoth* 101 b). A tall man should not marry a tall woman lest they have lanky children: a short man should not marry a short woman lest they have dwarfish children. A fair man should not marry a fair woman lest the children be excessively fair; nor a dark man marry a dark woman lest the children be excessively swarthy (*Bech.* 45 b). A man is advised to marry the daughter of a wise man and not of an ignorant man. In the first case, should he die or be exiled, the children will be wise, but in the other case, they too will be ignorant (*Pes.* 49 a).

In Judaism the relationship between husband and wife had a very high ideal. A man's home, it is said, is his wife (*Yoma* 1.1x). The whole of the preciousness of home is concentrated in the perfect relationship between man and wife. The word for marriage is *kiddushin*, which means consecration, sanctification, separation. And it is so called because 'the husband prohibits his wife to the whole world, like an object which is dedicated to the sanctuary' (*Kiddushin* 2 b).

There is the ideal *purity*. 'Immorality in the house is like a worm in vegetables' (*Sotah* 3 b). 'When husband and wife are faithful the Shechinah (the glory of God) is with them; when they are not worthy fire consumes them' (*Sotah* 17 a).

There is the ideal *honour*. The good man is the man 'who loves his wife more than himself, who honours her more than himself, who leads his sons and daughters in the right path, and arranges for their marriage soon after puberty.' It is to him that the text refers: 'You will know that your tent is safe' (Job 5:24; *Yebamoth* 62 b).

There is the ideal of *considerateness*. Consult and consult considerately. There was a proverb, 'If your wife is short, bend down and whisper to her' (*Baba Metzia* 59 a). 'Beware of vexing your wife, for tears are ever ready to flow' (*Baba Metzia* 59 a).

There is the ideal of *love*. 'When a man's first wife dies during his lifetime, it is as if the Temple had been destroyed in his lifetime . . . The world becomes dark for him' (*Sanhedrin* 22 a).

The Jews had a high ideal of the physical relationship between husband and wife. There are associated in the birth of every human being God, father and mother (*Kiddushin* 30 b). It was the Jewish belief that every act of conception was the work of the Holy Spirit of God. Here too considerateness was urged. They quoted the Song of Songs 4:16: 'Let my beloved come to his garden,' and they said, 'The Torah teaches gentleness. The bridegroom should not enter the marriage chamber until the bride gives him leave' (*Pesachim* 17 b). With a curiously modern touch they lay down certain laws for contraception. Three classes of women should use an absorbent: a minor, lest pregnancy prove fatal; a pregnant woman, lest abortion result; a nursing mother, lest she become pregnant again, and prematurely wean the child so that it may die (*Yebamoth* 12 b).

The ideal was the love that issues in care and consideration between husband and wife in all things. The Jews had a fixed belief that every man had two natures, the good nature which draws him upwards, and the evil nature which drags him down. And they had the idea that in marriage, when it is right, even the evil nature turns to good. 'But for his passions man would not build a house, nor marry a wife, nor beget children' (*Rabba* 9).

But for all this high ideal Judaism did not idealize women. It was laid down that a man must not covet his neighbour's wife, or his manservant, or his maidservant, or his ox, or his ass, or *anything* that is his neighbour's (Exodus 20:17; Deuteronomy 5:21). On the basis of this it was argued that women and wives are included among the *things*, and that therefore woman is to be regarded as a chattel. Women did not eat with men; they only stood and served. In the Temple and the Synagogue they were separated from men. Windows were very often grilled so that women might not be seen, and we frequently read of the lattice behind which the woman was concealed (Judges 5:28; Song of Songs 2:9). Women went veiled, and not to do so was the sign of a loose woman.

Legally a woman was a minor, not a responsible person. A husband could repudiate any agreement which she made. She was not eligible to give evidence at law. Perhaps the hardest thing was that she could not inherit from her father or from her husband, and this explains why in Scripture the widow is always the symbol of poverty and helplessness.

In religious matters a woman was excused from all commandments which begin *Thou shalt*, and from all which have to be done at a fixed and definite time (*Kiddushin* 1.7). She did not need to recite the Shema, or to wear fringes or phylacteries, or to go to Jerusalem for the compulsory Feasts, Pentecost, Passover and Tabernacles. A woman had to know the table blessings; she had to recite the Eighteen Prayers, the *Shemoneh Esreh*; she had to see to the *Mezuzah* on the doorpost; she had to light the Sabbath lamp – that was and is one of her special duties; she had to see to the *challah*, the offering of kneaded dough that had to be made from every baking. In the Temple she could not ordinarily go beyond the Court of the Women, and in the Synagogue she could not be one of the quorum of ten which was necessary to hold a Synagogue service, although theoretically she might be one of the seven people called up to share in the reading of the lesson from the Law (*Tos. Megillah* 4.11; *Megillah* 23 a).

A woman was exempt from the study of the Law. This is the reason for the Jewish prayer which is so often unfairly quoted, 'I thank thee that thou hast not made me a Gentile, a slave, or a woman' (*Menaboth* 43 b). The real meaning of the thanksgiving is that the man thanks God that he is not exempt from the study of the Law as a woman is. It is rather love of the Law than contempt for women that inspired this prayer.

It is nevertheless true that women were not educated other than in domestic tasks. 'It is the way of a woman to remain at home, and for a man to go into the market-place and learn intelligence from other men' (*Genesis R.* 18.1). On rare occasions educated women were found. For instance, in the house of Rabbi Judah the Patriarch even the maids knew biblical Hebrew and could enlighten scholars on the meaning of words (*Rosh-ha-shanah* 26 b; *Megillah* 18 a; *Nazir* 3 a). There is only one famous Jewish woman scholar in the Rabbinic Law, Beruriah, the daughter of Rabbi Channa ben Teradion, and the wife of one of the greatest of the rabbis, Rabbi Meir. On the whole the higher education of women was regarded with horror. To a learned woman who asked him a question about the golden calf, Rabbi Eliezer ben Hyrcanus answered: 'A woman has no learning except about the spindle' (*Yoma* 66 b; *Jer. Sotah* 19 a). 'Let the words of the Law be burned rather than taught to a woman' (*Jer. Sotah* 19 a). One who teaches his daughter the Law is as if he taught her lechery (*Sotah* 3.4). The Talmud objects to a pious fool, a shrewd rascal and a she-Pharisee (*Sotah* 3.4). The talkative and the inquisitive widow and the virgin who wastes her time in long prayers are heartily disliked (*Sotah* 22 a).

The rabbis often spoke cynically about women. 'Women,'

said Hillel, 'foster prejudices' (*Sayings of the Fathers* 2.7).
Women are light-minded (*Shabbath* 33 b).

But at the same time they could say: 'God endowed woman
with more intelligence than man' (*Nid* 45 b).

The shrewish wife was hated. A man with a bad wife will
never have to go to hell because he has been through his purga-
tory on earth! (*Erub.* 41 a). Among those whose life is not life is
the man who is ruled by his wife (*Baba Metzia* 75 b). Women were
notoriously talkative. God gave ten measures of words for the
whole of humanity, and woman seized upon nine of them. Any
wound, says Ben Sirach, but not a wound of the heart! Any
wickedness, but not the wickedness of a wife! (Ecclesiasticus
25:13).

Woman's love of adornment is noted. The things that a
woman longs for are adornments (*Kethuboth* 59 a), and the
adornments are listed as treating the eyes with kohl, curling the
hair into ringlets and rouging the face – and the desire is just as
great at six or sixteen or sixty! (*Moed Katan* 9 b).

Sometimes the Talmud can speak almost with ferocity about
the qualities of women. 'Four qualities are ascribed to women;
they are gluttonous, listeners at doors, lazy and jealous. They are
also querulous and garrulous' (*Genesis R.* 45.57). The final complaint is that women are often involved in witchcraft. 'Women
are addicted to witchcraft' (*Yoma* 83 b). 'The more women, the
more witchcraft' (*Sayings of the Fathers* 2.8). 'The majority of
women are inclined to witchcraft' (*Sanhedrin* 67 a). And it is a
witch (the feminine form) who is to be put to death (Exodus
22:18).

In view of the verdicts passed on women in certain of the
rabbinic writings, it will not be surprising that there were those
who looked with suspicion on ordinary social intercourse with
women. A strict rabbi would not be seen talking even to his own
wife on the street or in public. A saying of Rabbi Jose ben
Jochanan is recorded in the *Sayings of the Fathers* (1.5): 'Talk
not much with womankind. They said this of a man's own wife.
How much more of his fellow's wife. Hence the Sages have said:
He that talks much with womankind brings evil upon himself,
and neglects the study of the Law, and at last will inherit
Gehenna.' 'It is forbidden to speak to a woman in the street,
even one's own wife' (*Yoma* 240 a). Little wonder that the

disciples were astonished to return to the well to find Jesus talking with the woman of Samaria (John 4:27).

But it is obvious that there is another side to this. As Daniel Rops puts it: 'It goes without saying that in the small kingdom that is the home the wife was queen' (*Daily Life in Palestine* p. 129). A woman could acquire merit by sending her children faithfully to learn the Law in the Synagogue school, and by encouraging her husband to be a student in the schools of the rabbis (*Ber.* 17 a).

The Jews never questioned the supreme influence of the woman. The rabbis told a story of a pious man who was married to a pious woman. They were childless, and after ten years' childlessness divorce was compulsory. 'He went and married a wicked woman, and she made him wicked; she went and married a wicked man, and she made him righteous. It follows that all depends on the woman' (*Genesis R.* 17.7). The influence of the woman for good or for evil was never denied, and none ever held a more honoured place than the good wife and the good mother.

Certain pleasant stories gathered round the creation of woman. She was created from the rib taken from Adam. 'God considered from which part of man to create woman. He said, I will not create her from the head, that she should not hold up her head too proudly; nor from the eye, that she should not be too curious; nor from the ear, that she should not be an eavesdropper; nor from the mouth, that she should not be too talkative; nor from the heart, that she should not be too jealous; nor from the hand, that she should not be too acquisitive; nor from the foot, that she should not be a gadabout; but from a part of the body that is hidden that she should be modest' (*Genesis R.* 18.2). It was said that in courtship the man must pursue the woman, not the woman the man, because, since the woman was made from man's rib, man was doing no more than seek that which was already his own.

There was a famous story about how a man once said to Rabbi Gamaliel: 'Your God is a thief because it is written, The Lord God caused a deep sleep to fall upon Adam, and he slept; and he took one of his ribs' (Genesis 2:21). The rabbi's daughter said to her father, 'Leave him to me; I will answer him.' She then said to the man, 'Give me an officer to investigate a complaint.' 'For what purpose?' he said. She replied, 'Thieves broke into our house during the night and stole a silver ewer belonging to us, but left a gold one behind.' The man exclaimed, 'Would that such a thief visited me every day!' She answered, 'Was it not then a splendid thing for the first man when a single rib was taken from him and a woman to attend upon him was supplied in its stead?' (*Sanhedrin* 39 a).

There are two famous passages in praise of a good wife in Jewish literature. The first is from Ecclesiasticus 26:1–4:

> Happy is the husband of a good wife;
> > the number of his days will be
> > doubled.
> A loyal wife rejoices her husband,
> > and he will complete his years
> > in peace.
> A good wife is a great blessing;
> > she will be granted among the
> > blessings of the man who fears
> > the Lord.
> Whether rich or poor, his heart is
> > glad,
> > and at all times his face is
> > cheerful.

The other is the most famous tribute of all to a good wife (Proverbs 31:10–31), a passage which the man who possessed a good wife was supposed to read aloud every Friday evening before the Sabbath. It is too long, to quote in full but verses 25–29 run as follows:

> Strength and dignity are her clothing,
> > and she laughs at the time to come.
> She opens her mouth with wisdom,
> > and the teaching of kindness is on
> > her tongue.
> She looks well to the ways of her
> > household,
> > and does not eat the bread of
> > idleness.
> Her children rise up and call her
> > blessed;
> > her husband also, and he praises
> > her:

'Many women have done excellently,
but you surpass them all.'

So then let us turn to the actual process of marriage among the Jews. There are certain passages in the Old Testament which lay down the degrees within which marriage is prohibited (Leviticus 18:6–18; 20:11–21; Deuteronomy 27:20). The following is the list – a mother, any wife of a father, sister or half-sister, daughter, or son's daughter, or daughter's daughter, the daughter of any wife of a father, paternal aunt, maternal aunt, an uncle's wife, daughter-in-law, sister-in-law, a woman and her daughter, or her son's daughter, or her daughter's daughter.

It is to be noted that the marriage of an uncle to his niece is not actually forbidden, and it sometimes, though rarely, happened. It is also to be noted that there is no barrier to the marriage of cousins germane, and in fact that was a relationship which was considered an excellent one for marriage. In this case there was no fear of inbreeding. Neither the Talmud nor the Mishnah forbid in so many words marriage to foreigners, but the Old Testament makes it clear that such marriage was forbidden, and it was always in fact bitterly opposed. And yet Abraham's first-born child was the son of an Egyptian girl (Genesis 16:5); Moses had a Midianite and a Cushite wife (Exodus 2:21; Numbers 12:1); and Ruth, the ancestress of David, was herself a Moabite (Ruth 1:4).

We may here stop to look at another marriage custom and obligation among the Jews. It was the institution known as *Levirate Marriage. Levir* is in Latin a brother-in-law; the Hebrew word is *ysham*. The regulations governing it are to be found in Deuteronomy 25:5–10, and in the Mishnah the tractate *Yebamoth* deals with it. The rule was that, if a man died without a son, his brother must take the widow and raise up a family for his dead brother. The first-born son of such a union was regarded as the son of the dead man. We find the Sadducees posing the question to Jesus of what would happen at the resurrection to a woman who had been married to seven brothers in succession (Matthew 22:23; Mark 12:18; Luke 20:27; Ruth 4:20). In a very primitive Genesis story (Genesis 38:9) we find a certain Onan being killed because he avoided his duty.

There were occasions when a man refused to carry out this obligation, and then the ceremony of *halitzah* took place. The widow was entitled to take off one of the man's shoes and to spit in his face and to say: 'This is for the man who would not continue his brother's line.' The fact that the Sadducees asked Jesus their test question shows that levirate marriage still existed in New Testament times.

Before we look at the process of marriage in detail, we may note the broad, essential duties of husband and of wife. The husband has to feed and clothe and properly support his wife (Exodus 21:10). The wife had to grind the meal, to make the bread, to cook the meals, to nurse and feed the child, to make the bed, and to work in wool. If as her dowry she brought with her some slave girls, she was relieved of part of the work. If she brought as many as four slave girls, she could 'sit in a chair like a lady'. No matter how many slaves she had, she had always to wash her husband's feet and hands, and it was pointed out that idleness was always morally dangerous (*Kethuboth* 5.5), so that even the best dowered wife was advised to work.

In Jewish marriage there were three stages.

(i) There was the *Engagement*. This was made by the parents or by professional matchmakers. It could be made even when the couple were in infancy, and was regularly made before they had ever seen each other. It was considered far safer to arrange a marriage in this way than to leave it to the unaccountable dictates of the emotions. So serious a step had to be taken with wisdom and with care and with prudence, lest the young couple be unduly influenced by the kind of beauty which rapidly fades, and forget the importance of character and of family breeding.

(ii) There followed the *Betrothal*. This could not take place until the couple were of age. A girl came of age at twelve years and one day, and at this stage she could refuse to accept the young man. The word for betrothal is *Kiddushin*, which is really a religious word, and which means the consecration of the bride for her husband; by this act in the sight of God and of man she is consecrated to her husband, to be set apart for him.

There were three ways in which betrothal could be rendered valid (*Kiddushin* 1.1).

(a) It could be carried out by a symbolic sale in which the bridegroom handed the bride an article of value (*Kiddushin* 2.1–3). In later times it was usually a ring. The article was handed to the bride in front of two witnesses with the words:

By this ring may she be consecrated, betrothed, to me.'

(b) It could be carried out by a written agreement. The bridegroom had to give the bride her *kethubah*, her document, her *'jointure'*. In this document the bridegroom assigned a certain sum of money to the bride, which she was legally bound to receive either in the case of death or divorce. The necessity to supply this sum of money was one of the biggest controls of divorce.

In the case of a virgin, betrothal lasted for one year, 'to give her the opportunity to collect her trousseau', and in the case of a widow it lasted one month (*Kethuboth* 5.2). During the period of betrothal a young man was exempt from military service (Deuteronomy 20:5-7).

Betrothal was as binding as marriage. A betrothed girl who was unfaithful was treated in the same way as an adulterous wife (Deuteronomy 22:23, 24). Betrothal could only be ended by divorce. During that time the couple were known and regarded as man and wife. Should the man die, the girl was known as a widow, and in the law we find that curious phrase 'a virgin who is a widow'. This explains the relationship of Joseph and Mary as we find in the first chapter of Matthew. In verse 18 they are betrothed; in verse 19 Joseph is called Mary's husband, and he is said to wish to divorce her. It all happened during the time of betrothal in which the two were regarded as man and wife, and which could only be ended by divorce. Betrothal was marked by a feast, and afterwards the young couple, who may hardly have seen each other hitherto, were allowed to be alone together, in order to come to know each other better.

(c) The third way of betrothal was by way of cohabitation and intercourse, but this was considered disgraceful.

It was at this stage that what we might call the business side of the marriage was arranged and completed.

In the very earliest times the most important thing was the *mohar*. From the fact that it was a payment connected with marriage the *mohar* might be regarded as a dowry; but the *mohar* was in fact a payment from the bridegroom to the father of the bride. To put the matter at its simplest, in a primitive agricultural society, when the head of the household lost a fit and healthy and active daughter, he lost an asset; he lost, as it were, one of his staff or establishment, and he had to be compensated for the loss. So we read of the marriage present, the *mohar*, which the intending bridegroom had to give to the father of the bride (Genesis 34:12; 1 Samuel 18:25). If we put together the rulings in Exodus 22:16 and Deuteronomy 22:28, 29, we get the information that the purchase price of a daughter was fifty shekels, which is equal to about £7.50. There was further the *mattan*, which was composed of certain gifts that the bridegroom gave to the bride. Sometimes if a young man was penniless, he paid for his bride with a term of service rendered to her father. So Jacob served seven years and received Leah, and then served another seven years to win Rachel whom he really loved (Genesis 29:18–20, 30).

Certainly in later times the dowry existed in the modern sense of the term, in the sense of the property which a girl brought with her on her marriage. Rebekah brought her maids with her (Genesis 24:61); so Laban gave Leah Zilpah to be her maid (Genesis 29:24); and so Caleb gave his daughter the upper and the lower springs (Judges 1:15).

By the time of the Talmud the bride brought with her a dowry in the modern sense of the term. It is laid down that the minimum dowry that a father can give his daughter is 50 *zuz*; the *zuz* was a coin which was worth about five new pence. It was considered to be an act of 'sanctified loving-kindness' to help to provide a dowry for a bride who came from a home which was so poor that there was no dowry for her (*Shabbath* 127 a).

(iii) The third stage was the *wedding itself*. A wedding was a great day in a Jewish community and it was nothing less than a religious duty to attend it (*Pes.* 49 a). All the relations, all the friends, and the whole village would come. Autumn was the best time of all to get married, for then the grain and the grape harvests were gathered in, and there was time for relaxation and rejoicing. Virgins were generally married on Thursdays and widows on Fridays (*Kethuboth* I.I).

There was no particularly religious aspect of the events. In New Testament times there was nothing remotely like a religious service. It was rather a time of rejoicing and feasting. In the evening the bride was brought from her father's house splendidly dressed, and even crowned. She was brought in procession, carried in a litter, with songs and music, and with the friend of the bridegroom (John 3:29) – we would call him the best man – organizing the procession. When they reached the bride-groom's house, the bride was blessed by the parents and by all the guests (Genesis 24:60; Ruth 4:11; Tobit 9:46). This was the only really religious part of the ceremony. The bride was taken to her room with her bridesmaids. The rest of the guests with the bridegroom spent the early part of the evening in games and dancing. Then followed the wedding supper, at which the presents and the gifts were given. The bride was brought in veiled, and then the bridegroom withdrew the veil, as he only had the right to do. Seeds were thrown down and pomegranates crushed to ensure fertility. Up to this time the men and the women guests had been apart. Now they joined for further festivity.

Late in the evening the bride and the bridegroom departed. But there was no honeymoon; rather they stayed at home and for a week they were treated like a king and queen in joyous festivities. Then finally they settled down to the routine of life and to the making of a home and the rearing of a family.

Of the height of the Jewish ideal of marriage there is no doubt; but the tragedy was that the real fell so far short of the ideal.

Three things, it was said, a Jew will never commit – murder, idolatry and adultery. Divorce was something which God him-self regarded with horror. '. . . Let none be faithless to the wife of his youth. For I hate divorce, says the Lord, the God of Israel . . . So take heed to yourselves and do not be faithless' (Malachi 2:15, 16). Certainly the ideal was there, but the time was to come when the tenure of marriage was so insecure that it was difficult to persuade Jewish girls to marry at all.

For certain things divorce was not a matter of choice; it was compulsory. Divorce was compulsory for adultery; a woman who had committed adultery had to be divorced, whether her husband wished it or not (*Kethubim* 3.5). Divorce was compul-sory for ten years' sterility. If a Jewish wife did not bear a child within ten years, she had to be divorced. She might marry again under the same conditions. If she had a miscarriage, the ten years were reckoned from the date of the miscarriage (*Yebamoth* 6.6). It was considered to be nothing less than a duty to divorce a bad wife. 'A bad wife is like leprosy to her husband. What is the remedy? Let him divorce her.' 'If one has a bad wife, it is a religious duty to divorce her' (*Yebamoth* 63 b). There was one strangely merciful law. Insanity was never a ground for divorce. If the husband was insane, there could be no divorce, for he could not execute the deed. And if the wife was insane, it was forbidden to divorce her, because then she would have no protector (*Yebamoth* 14.1).

How then in view of the high ideal did divorce become so tragically common? Two factors were influential in the downward path.

First, in Judaism a woman had no legal rights, and, therefore, she could not ever initiate divorce proceedings. 'A woman,' says the Law, 'may be divorced without her consent, but a man can be divorced only with his consent' (*Yebamoth* 14.1). In fact, all that a woman could do was to appeal to the court to put pressure on her husband to divorce her. 'The court,' says the Law, 'may bring strong pressure to bear upon the husband, until he says, I am willing to divorce my wife' (*Arachin* 5.6). The grounds on which such pressure could be exerted were very few. It could be exerted for refusal to consummate the marriage (*Kethuboth* 13.5); for impotence (*Nedarim* 11.12); for inability or unwillingness to support the wife (*Kethuboth* 77 a); if the husband took a vow not to have intercourse for one week according to Hillel, or two weeks according to Shammai (*Kethuboth* 5.6). Pressure could be exerted if the husband developed a loathsome disease, such as leprosy, or if he engaged upon a loathsome occupation, such as that of a tanner, or a gatherer of dog's dung, used in copper smelting (*Kethuboth* 7.9, 10). Desertion in itself was not a ground for divorce; death had to be proved, but only one witness, instead of the usual two, was required (*Yebamoth* 88 a). Apostasy and migration from Palestine were also grounds on which a woman could appeal to be divorced (*Kethuboth* 110 a; *Yebamoth* 88 a).

So then in the first place it is to be remembered that the wife had no rights of divorce. All that she could do was to appeal to be divorced, and even that on very limited grounds.

Second, the ease of the process of divorce was an encouragement to divorce. The regulation governing the conditions of divorce is given in full in Deuteronomy 24:1–4: 'When a man takes a wife and marries her, if then she finds no favour in his eyes because he has found some indecency in her, and he writes her a bill of divorce and puts it in her hand and sends her out of his house, and she departs out of his house, and if she goes and becomes another man's wife, and the latter husband dislikes her and writes her a bill of divorce and puts it in her hand and sends her out of his house, or if the latter husband dies, who took her to be his wife, then her former husband, who sent her away, may not take her again to be his wife, after she has been defiled; for that is an abomination before the Lord.'

In effect, there was no legal process at all. All that was necessary was a bill of divorce, correctly drawn up and handed to the woman in the presence of two witnesses which was final. And a correctly drawn up bill of divorce read as simply as follows: 'Let this be from me your writ of divorce and letter of dismissal and deed of liberation, that you may marry any man you wish' (*Gittin* 9.3). This was the only legal step which had to be taken.

Clearly, the important point is the nature of the grounds of divorce. The ground is, 'if the husband has found some indecency in her' (A.V., 'some matter of uncleanness'). Everything will hinge on how that phrase is to be interpreted, and there was the widest range of interpretation. Shammai said it meant infidelity and nothing else. Hillel said that it could mean as little as that a wife had spoiled her husband's meal. Akiba said that a man might divorce his wife if he had found someone whom he thought fairer (*Gittin* 9.10). On Shammai's interpretation the door of divorce was closely guarded; on Hillel's the way was broad; and on Akiba's there were no limits at all to the grounds of divorce. Human nature being what it is, it is easy to see which view would prevail.

There was one thing which did in fact effectively limit divorce, and that was the purely financial side of the matter. In the case of divorce the price that the man had paid for the bride was lost. Any dowry had to be returned. We have already seen how at the arranging of the marriage the *kethubah*, the settlement on the wife in the event of death or divorce had to be paid; and many a man had to remain married, because he had spent the dowry and was quite unable to discharge the settlement.

In the event of a divorce there was nothing for a woman to do except to go back to her father's house, if he was still alive, or to eke out the wretched existence of a widow. In only one thing did the law favour the woman. Unless she was divorced for adultery, she kept the children. She kept the sons until they were six years of age, and the daughters until they were married.

At one other condition of the law we must still look, for it shows perhaps better than anything else the triviality of the grounds of divorce, and how precarious marriage could be for a woman. As we have said, normally the man had to pay the *kethubah*, if he divorced his wife. But there were certain cases in which he was exempted from this duty, which is the same as saying that there were certain things which rendered the wife a guilty party. The list of things in the case of which the law laid it down that the husband did not need to pay the *kethubah* reads as follows: these do not get the *kethubah* – a woman who transgresses Jewish law, a woman who goes about in public with uncovered head, spinning in the streets, talking with all sorts of men; a woman who speaks disrespectfully of her husband's parents in his presence, a scolding woman, who is defined as a woman whose voice can be heard in the next house (*Kethuboth* 7.6).

It is easy to see how trivial the grounds of divorce were. Of course, in Palestine there were happy marriages, and husbands and wives who were faithful and loving. But in the time of Jesus marriage in Palestine had very nearly broken down and the treatment of women was shameful indeed. It is never to be forgotten that it was against that background that Jesus made his demands for chastity, but, before we go on to look at them, we must first look at marriage in the Hellenistic world to which the gospel went out.

The tragedy of the Greek world was that the relationship between the sexes was something which degenerated rather than improved. Away back in the *Iliad* and the *Odyssey* of Homer marriage is a partnership as anyone thinking of Odysseus and Penelope can see. In that early civilization women had a real share in the life and the work of their husbands. But the breakdown had already set in with Hesiod (about 750 B.C.). By that time woman had become a thing, a situation from which in Greek society she never really escaped. Hesiod's advice to the man beginning to farm is: 'Get yourself first of all a house, a woman and a working ox. Buy the woman and do not marry her. Then you can make her follow the plough if necessary' (*Works and Days*, 405, 406). The woman and the ox are classed together as necessary equipment.

Into the Greek mind there came a kind of bitterness against

womankind. Hesiod speaks of that 'execrable breed of women, a fearful scourge upon the earth' (*Theogony*, 585–612). 'Women,' said Simonides the poet, 'are the greatest evil God ever created.' Hipponax said: 'In regard to a wife the two happiest days are the days when a man marries her and the day when he carries her out for burial.' 'A woman,' said Menander, 'is necessarily an evil thing; blessed is the man who has taken one with as moderate a degree of evil as possible.'

The dramatist Euripides was a notorious woman-hater. Would that Zeus had never created woman, 'that specious curse to man'. Would that there were some other way of producing children, then man might live in homes 'free and unvexed of womankind'. Even the fathers who begat them are willing to pay a dowry to be rid of them; and once a man has a wife he has to beggar himself decking her out. A brainless woman is most of all to be desired, and a woman of keen wit most of all to be dreaded (*Hippolytus*, 616–644). Even Plato and Aristotle, who in their ideal commonwealths would have gone a long way towards emancipating women, still held to the essential inferiority of women. Women, said Plato, are the section of humanity which owing to its frailty is most secretive and intriguing. Women are inferior in goodness to men (*Laws* 781, A, B). As between the sexes, says Aristotle, the male is by nature superior and the female inferior, the male is ruler and the female is subject (*Politics*, 1.2.12).

Of course, there are things to be said on the other side, and we shall in due course go on to say them. But Becker in his *Charicles* not unfairly sums up the Greek basic view of women: 'At this time and in the very focus of civilization, the women were regarded as a lower order of beings, neglected by nature in comparison with man, both in point of intellect and heart; incapable of taking part in public life, naturally prone to evil, and fitted only for propagating the species and gratifying the appetites of men.'

This view quite inevitably had its effect on the whole status of women, and thereby on marriage as an institution. This general attitude had three quite definite consequences for Greek women. (i) *All her life a woman remained legally a minor.* This is simply to say that a woman had no legal rights at all. Robert Flacelière writes: 'In Periclean Athens women who had been born free had no more political or legal rights than slaves.' Isaeus (*De Aristarchi Hered.*, 259) quotes a law that it is illegal for a child or a woman to enter into any agreement about anything more than a measure of barley. In his speech *Against Olympias* (1183) Demosthenes quotes a law which he attributes to Solon that anything that a man did at the request, counsel or persuasion of a woman had no legal validity and was automatically null and void. In any thing which involved any agreement or legal question a woman could only act through her *kurios*, or guardian. The necessary repercussions of this on family life, on marriage and on divorce are obvious.

(ii) *A woman was given no formal education at all.* She had to weave and spin and cook and nurse and allocate the household duties to the slaves, and for this she must have had some minimum teaching; but a girl did not ever go to school. In Xenophon's *Oeconomicus* (7–10) there is a charming picture of Ischomachus and his young wife. Ischomachus praises her housekeeping to Socrates, and Socrates asks if Ischomachus had trained her, or if she had been taught by her parents before she came to him. Ischomachus tells how when she came to him she had no knowledge at all. 'She was not yet fifteen years old when she came to me, and up to that time she had lived in leading-strings, seeing, hearing and saying as little as possible.' She knew no more than how to spin wool and to make a cloak and hand out the wool to her spinning-maids. What more could anyone expect of a gently born girl? So Ischomachus tells how he and the girl bride said their prayers together and how she became 'tame enough' to carry on a conversation, and how then he taught her bit by bit her household duties.

It is in this case a lovely picture, but we may note at this stage a basic fact to which we shall have to return, that there was little hope of a girl trained or untrained in that way ever becoming in any way an intellectual companion for her husband.

(iii) The third basic fact has already emerged in the Ischomachus story. *Greek women of the higher classes lived in absolute seclusion.* They lived in the women's quarters, which, it is not altogether unfair to say, must have been rather like a comfortable domestic prison. The Greek woman shared her husband's meals only if there were no other people present; if there were guests she remained in her own quarters. She had no public life whatsoever.

'A respectable wife,' says Menander, 'ought to keep indoors. Only good-for-nothing women frequent the streets.' A female philosopher of the Pythagorean school – a unique phenomenon – called Phyntis said that there were only three reasons for which a respectable woman would leave her house. She might participate in a festival, make purchases, or fulfil a religious duty – and even in these cases she was never unattended and never alone.

All this had one obvious consequence – the respectable Greek girl never met a man. Add to this that she was at any age still a minor, and the conclusion is clear – marriage was not a thing of the heart. It was something which was arranged, and which the young couple could do no more than accept. Naumachios, a poet, says: 'Take as a husband the man your parents prefer.' In Demosthenes' speech *Against Boeotus* (11.12, 13) one of the parties says: 'When I had reached the age of eighteen, my father insisted on my marrying the daughter of Euphemus. He wanted to see that I had children. I considered that I was bound to do whatever he pleased. So I obeyed him, and that was how I got married.' Even Ischomachus with all his tenderness explains to his child bride how he married her: 'Do you understand now why I married you and why our parents consented to our union? We could easily have found someone else to share my bed . . . But after thinking it over, I in my own interests and your parents in yours, and reviewing all the candidates for our household management and the care of our children, I selected you, and your parents myself, no doubt from a good many others.' Quite bluntly, Ischomachus chose a wife much as a man would choose a housekeeper.

Becker (*Charicles*, p. 473) quotes the, at first sight extraordinary, statement of Müller, that there is no record of any Athenian citizen ever having married a free-born Athenian woman because he had fallen in love with her. That cannot have been universally true, but it was quite certainly generally true of the Greek upper classes. Marriage was a duty and a responsibility. The state needed its citizens; the army needed its soldiers; the gods needed their worshippers; the family needed its sons. Marriage had to be undertaken. Love certainly blossomed in time in many cases, but the initial motive was the satisfying of responsibility and the obedience to duty. It was difficult soil to flourish in, if marriage was to be in any sense a partnership. That it could be a partner-

ship we shall see; that too often it could never be is obvious, and
the consequences were disastrous.

Even in a situation like this there were cases of love and of
true partnership between husband and wife. In a Greek marriage
contract we find two people marrying *pros biou koinōnian*, for
fellowship of life. Aristotle believed that in true marriage a
husband and wife shared everything in life (*Nicomachean Ethics*,
8.12). In Xenophon's *Symposium* Socrates says – true, as if it was
something unusual – 'Niceratus, they tell me, is in love with his
wife and she is in love with him' (*Symposium*, 8.3). And there is
Plutarch's charming story of Themistocles in his *Life of Themistocles* (18). Themistocles said of his own little baby at his
mother's breast: 'That child is master of the world.' 'How can
that be?' his friend asked him. Themistocles answered: 'The
Athenians are masters of the Greeks; the Greeks are masters of
the world; I am master of Athenians; my wife is the master of
me; and this little child is the master of his mother. Therefore
this child is master of the whole world!' As Plato said – perhaps
as a philosopher a little regretfully: 'In the young the constrain-
ing power of love exceeds that of geometry!' And there can never
have been a time when love did not triumph over its handi-
caps.

But in so many cases there was a formality in marriage which
kept it from being the true fellowship that it ought to be; the
status and the upbringing of the woman were all against it. There
is a fragment of dialogue in Xenophon's *Oeconomicus* which has
the essence of tragedy in it. 'Well, Critobulus,' says Socrates,
'we're all friends here and you positively must tell us the whole
truth. Are there any people you talk to less than you do to your
wife?' 'Possibly,' answered Critobulus, 'but if so, very few
indeed.' The wife was always there, but there were areas of her
husband's life from which she was largely excluded.

The result of this was inevitable. The husband sought his
satisfaction outside his marriage. The basic fact of the Greek
situation was that there was no discredit whatever in sexual
relationships outside of marriage. In the speech *Against Neaera*
attributed to Demosthenes (1386) it is laid down as the merest
commonplace, the routine of life: 'We keep mistresses for
pleasure; we keep prostitutes for the day-to-day needs of the
body; we keep wives to bear our legitimate children and to be

the faithful guardians of our homes.' Here is the Greek way of life.

Plutarch in his very beautiful essay *Precepts for Wives* draws a picture of marriage as a fellowship in which all is shared and in which the words *mine* and *yours* never occur, for everything is *ours*. But in the very same essay he actually justifies this Greek way of life by the suggestion that a man in using prostitutes pays his wife a compliment by making others the instruments of his passion and so sparing her that experience (18). There are few statements which throw so revealing a light on the position of the Greek wife. But before we go on to look at the consequences of this relationship in actual fact we must stop to look at the actual process of Greek marriage.

As we have already seen, a woman could not enter into any contract by herself, so all the arrangements were made by her *kurios*, or guardian. Normally an unmarried woman's *kurios* was her father, but, if her father was dead, her brother or her uncle or a close friend of the family could act as *kurios*. The process began with the pledging (*egguēsis*), at which matters of dowry were settled. The formula of pledging was very simple, and ran basically as follows: The *kurios* said, 'I give you this girl that she may bear legitimate children.' The suitor answered, 'I receive her.' The *kurios* said, 'I add a dowry of three talents.' The suitor answered, 'I receive it likewise with pleasure.'

As in Jewish marriage, so in Greek marriage, the regulations regarding the dowry were one of the main cements of marriage. The husband could use and administer the dowry, but under no circumstances could he appropriate it. In the event of divorce he had to return it, unless he was prepared to pay eighteen per cent interest per annum on it, and in addition pay the ex-wife alimony. Even if the wife died first, the husband still could not appropriate the dowry. He had the use of it until he died, or until he remarried, and then at his death or remarriage the dowry descended to the children of the original marriage. If there were no children, the dowry reverted to the wife's *kurios*, who in this case was held to be her nearest blood relation.

In the case of the husband dying, so long as a woman remained at home and did not remarry, she administered her own property. The sons received their share of the estate, when they came of age, subject to their proper support of the mother; the daughters had no claim on the estate at all. If the woman re-married, the dowry passed under control of her second husband. The financial obligations in connection with the dowry held to-gether many a marriage which would otherwise have broken up.

The wedding proper was in five stages, all of which had a religious significance.

(i) Both of the families involved offered propitiatory sacrifices to the gods and goddesses specially concerned – to Zeus, the king of the gods, to Hera his wife, and to Artemis, the virgin goddess. This was called *progamia*, which means the pre-marriage sacrifice.

(ii) There were then sacrifices to the local gods of the place where the families lived. This was a kind of act of dedication, and one of the ceremonies was that a tress of the girl's hair was offered to the gods.

(iii) There followed the ceremonial bathing originally in some stream which was regarded as specially sacred, in Athens in the Callirrhoe, in Thebes in the Ismenos, in Troy in the Scamander. In Troy the bride prayed to the river god to receive her virginity. In later times water from the stream was brought to the house. This was an act both of purification and of dedication.

(iv) On the day of the wedding feast offerings were made to the household gods, and the wedding cake made of pounded grain and honey was eaten.

(v) Towards evening the bride and bridegroom, accompanied by the *paranumphos*, the groomsman, set out in an ox-drawn chariot for their new home. With them there came the bride's mother, carrying a torch with a flame lit from the fire in the bride's own home. At the new home the bridegroom's mother was waiting with a torch lit from the fire of the bridegroom's own home. And so the fire in the new home was lit from a commingling of the fires from both the old homes. Flute-players and revellers accompanied the chariot. The guests wore festal crowns and the couple their bridal robes, and the door of the new home was decked with green. The bride was greeted with a shower of fruits and sweetmeats, and with a basket of loaves. The priestess of Athene carried the divine aegis round the house, thus blessing the new home. A feast was held, and even at it the men and women were in separate rooms. The bride was given a quince, the symbol of fertility, to eat. Late in the evening she was taken to the bridal chamber by an aged female relative and given to the bridegroom. The *epithalamia*, the wedding hymns were sung by the guests, and the young couple were left alone together in their new home.

There were two further ceremonies. On the next two days the wedding gifts were brought. At the same time there was the ceremony of the *anakaluptēria*, the unveiling, for only then might the bride go unveiled. Lastly, the bride was enrolled in the *phratria*, the clan of her husband, without which enrolling no marriage was legal and valid.

It was an impressive series of ceremonies with which the young couple started on their new life.

However impressive the Greek ceremony of marriage was, the Greeks nonetheless regarded it as a matter of course for a husband to have sexual relationships outside marriage. There was more than one direction towards which a man might turn to find his satisfaction.

He might turn to the temples of the gods and there he might find the priestesses who were sacred prostitutes, and to have intercourse with them was nothing less than an act of worship.

The custom of having such sacred courtesans attached to the temples came from the East. In Greece the most notorious example of it was the temple of Aphrodite, the goddess of love, at Corinth. To that temple a thousand sacred prostitutes were attached. They came down to the city streets in the evening and plied their trade in that polyglot city, until it became a proverb that not every man can afford a journey to Corinth.

It was actually considered an act of piety to present such girls as a gift to the temple. Pindar in the thirteenth Olympian Ode tells of a certain runner called Xenophon. He had won the foot-race and all the five events of the pentathlon. He had vowed that, if he was successful, he would present a group of girls to the temple of Aphrodite. And so Pindar writes: 'O sovereign mistress of Cyprus (that is, Aphrodite), Xenophon has led to your shrine a band of fifty maidens dedicated to your service, in token of his joy at your granting to him his prayers.'

So a man might even turn to the temples of the gods and goddesses to find his pleasure.

He might turn to the ordinary brothels and to the prostitutes of the streets. It was on record that Solon, the great law-giver, was the first to institute public brothels in Athens, and that Athens had more prostitutes than any other city in the world. Just at that time there was being built in Athens a temple to the goddess Aphrodite Pandēmos, and Solon financed the building of it with the proceeds of these brothels, and to the Greek there seemed nothing incongruous in building a temple and paying for its building from such a source.

The priestesses and the prostitutes were slaves, but there were, so to speak, higher class and more aristocratic establishments in which freeborn women served as prostitutes. In such an establishment it was possible to buy the exclusive rights to some girl's favours. Hipparchus and Xenocleides paid 3,000 drachmae, more than a hundred pounds, for the joint possession of the famous Neaera. We are told that Gnathaena charged a price of no less than 1,000 drachmae for one night's pleasure with her daughter.

These things might be called the normal ways of life, but in classical Greece there was one group of women who were unique. They were called the *hetairai*, which literally means *the companions*. They were easily the most brilliant, the most accomplished, and the best educated women of their day. They were much more like great ladies holding salons than anything else. It was they who were the real danger to marriage, for they could give to men the cultured and intellectual companionship which their wives could never give them. Many of them go down in fame. Lais of Corinth was the friend of Diogenes the great Cynic philosopher, and Leontion was a disciple and student of Epicurus. Herpyllis was the friend of Aristotle and it is to her son Nicomachus that the famous *Nicomachean Ethics* was written. Aspasia, the friend of Pericles, was said to have taught Pericles oratory and to have written for him the speeches which are immortal possessions of oratory. Rhodopis was so wealthy that she was said to have built one of the Egyptian pyramids at her own expense. Phryne, the loveliest of them all, was so wealthy that she offered to rebuild the walls of Thebes at her own expense if the Thebans would put up an inscription: 'Whereas Alexander demolished it, Phryne the courtesan rebuilt it.' Socrates went to visit the famous Theodota. He talked gently to her, and as he left he bade her treat her lovers as she ought. 'She ought to shut the door against the insolent, to watch her lovers in sickness, to rejoice greatly when they succed in anything honourable, and to love tenderly those who love her.'

Sometimes these *hetairai* were, paradoxically, capable of a fidelity than which none could be greater. Alcibiades was the brilliant, spoilt darling of Athens. In the end he went too far and he was sentenced to death. He was pursued from one refuge to another by those hot for his blood, as he twisted and turned in a hopeless attempt to evade capture. And in those terrible days, as Plutarch tells in his *Life of Alcibiades* (39), in the end his only friend left was his *hetaira* Timandra, and when he was in the end killed 'she took up his corpse and wrapped it in her own robes and gave him as splendid a funeral as she could afford.'

Perhaps most famous of all was Leaena, whose name means the Lioness. She had been the friend of Harmodius and Aristogeiton. Harmodius and Aristogeiton had formed a plot to assassinate the tyrant Hippias. They succeeded in killing the tyrant's son but not himself. They were arrested and killed. Leaena had been their friend, and the authorities thought that they could force out of her the names of the others who had been implicated in the plot. But under examination Leaena bit out her own tongue rather than run the risk of betraying under torture the men who had been her friends. And so the Athenians erected in her memory the famous statue of the tongueless lioness.

We have taken some time to describe the situation in Greece, for it is completely extraordinary. In the nature of things the Greek wife could hardly be a companion to her husband; it involved no stigma at all for a man to find satisfaction outside the marriage bond; and it was often with that brilliant and extraordinary race of *hetairai* that men found their real fellowship.

What was allowed to the husband was unthinkable for the wife. For the wife there was laid down the standard of utter chastity. It was in fact to ensure this that her seclusion was so complete. Aeschines in the speech *Against Timarchus* (183) describes the law as Solon laid down: 'The woman who is taken in the act of adultery he does not allow to adorn herself, nor even to attend the public sacrifices, lest by mingling with innocent women she corrupt them. But, if she does attend, or, if she does adorn herself, he commands that any man who meets her shall tear off her garments, strip her of her ornaments, and beat her (only he may not kill or maim her). For the lawgiver seeks to disgrace such a woman and to make her life not worth the living.' The man could take his pleasure anywhere, but the woman must be above suspicion.

One further salient fact must be noted. For divorce no legal process of any kind was necessary other than the dismissing of the wife in the presence of witnesses, and since the woman could not take legal action at all she could not divorce her husband at all. Divorce was compulsory for adultery and common for childlessness. In the end divorce became to all intents and purposes a matter of caprice.

It is true that there were happy marriages in Greece as in any other land. It is also true that among the humbler people there was much more fidelity. But it is also true that among the Greek upper classes at the time when Christianity emerged marriage was very near to breaking down completely.

When we turn to Roman marriage, we find it very different in its ideal from Greek marriage. True, it too was to degenerate, and the marriage bond was to be tragically loosened, but it began, and it never wholly lost its character, by being a religious far more than a civil union.

The position of the Roman woman was basically different from that of her Greek sister. We have seen that the Greek woman led a completely secluded life even in her own home, that she came to her husband with no training and no equipment for life at all, and that she was without any part in public life. The Roman matron had her full share in the life of the home and even in public life. Her place was not the women's quarters of the house, but the *atrium*, the main room round which the life of the house centred. She was in full control of the slaves; she had the keys of the store-houses; she was trained in all the arts of housekeeping; she was the mistress of the home. When her husband went to a banquet, she accompanied him; she was free to go into the streets; she could attend the games and the temples; she could be a witness in a law-suit and could even go to law herself. Compared with the Greek woman, the Roman matron was thoroughly emancipated. At a lunch or dinner party the husband looked after the male guests and the wife looked after the female guests, just as would be done in this country (Cicero, *Letters to Atticus* 5.1). The whole status of the

Roman wife was different. Let us then see the process of Roman marriage.

In Rome marriages were usually arranged. There is a charming letter of Pliny to Junius Mauricus (1.14). Mauricus has asked Pliny to find a husband for his daughter, a task which Pliny finds an honour and a privilege. He has the very man, a certain Minucius Acilianus – and the rest of the letter reads like a testimonial! Minucius' father and uncle and grandparents are all passed under most favourable review. 'You will find nothing in his family that you would not approve in your own.' The boy himself is described. 'He has great vivacity, as well as application, joined at the same time with a most amiable and becoming modesty.' His appearance is described. 'He has a genteel and ruddy countenance, with a certain noble mien that speaks the man of distinction.' Pliny hesitates to mention it, but the young man's father is 'very rich'. It is just the kind of testimonial that a teacher might well give a young man for an overseas fellowship in some college or university!

The legal age of marriage was twelve for the girl; she was growing old by the time she was nineteen; she was usually married about sixteen or seventeen. A boy could be married at sixteen, the age at which he put off the boy's toga and put on the man's; but it would probably be at about the age of twenty-five that he did in fact marry.

Betrothal had its own ceremonies. The consent of the father had to be obtained and the matter of the dowry had to be negotiated. The question was: 'Do you pledge yourself?' and the answer was: 'I do.' The couple were called the pledged (*sponsus* and *sponsa*), and the whole ceremony, which was kept as a family holiday, was called the *sponsalia*, the pledgings. Valuable articles were exchanged as a kind of security, to be returned if the betrothal was broken. The betrothal was not legally binding or enforcible, but while it was in being, infidelity by the girl was regarded, and punished, as adultery. In early Roman law, but not in later law, the girl could bring an action for damages in the case of a breach of promise.

An essential part of the ceremony was the giving of the ring, sometimes made of gold, sometimes, more often, of iron. The ring was worn on the third finger of the left hand as now and Aulus Gellius (*The Attic Nights* 10.10) tells why: 'The reason for this practice is that on cutting and opening human bodies . . . it was found that a very fine nerve proceeded from that finger alone of which we have spoken, and made its way straight to the human heart.' Since the third finger of the left hand had this direct connection with the heart it was considered natural to give it the honour of wearing the engagement ring. Juvenal says of the suitor: 'You have given a pledge to her finger' (*Satires* 6.25), and Tertullian speaks of 'the sacred pledge of the ring', and says that it was the only gold a Christian wife possessed (*Apology* 6).

When it came to the actual marriage, there were two forms of Roman marriage. In the one case the woman passed *in manum*, into the hand, the power of her husband, in the other case she did not pass *in manum*. The Roman *patria potestas*, the father's power over his children was absolute; it lasted as long as the father lived, no matter how old or how famous the child was, and it at least theoretically included the power to reduce to slavery or even to execute. When a woman was given *in manum* of her husband she became the equivalent of his daughter; she became *in potestate viri*, in the power of her husband instead of in the power of her father (Tacitus, *Annals* 4.16). She entered upon what Livy (34.7) called the *servitus muliebris*, the woman's slavery. Under this marriage form, subject to his consulting with a kind of family council, the husband under the original laws could put his wife to death for adultery. There is obviously something primitive here. This was in fact the original way of all Roman marriages. But by New Testament times, and for a considerable period before them, this form of marriage was obsolete, and the woman did not normally pass *in manum* of her husband. When she did not pass *in manum*, she remained under the guardianship of her father or of her senior male relative, but she was in fact *sui iuris*. That is to say, she could and did manage her own affairs, and her fortune and her property remained absolutely her own. She was in fact even more independent than a modern wife.

There remained one limitation in regard to marriage. A person could marry only another person with whom he or she possessed the *connubium*, the right of intermarriage, if the marriage was to be absolutely complete. In the very early days, up to 445 B.C., a patrician could only marry a patrician, and a member of the common people, a plebeian, a member of the common people.

This was widened to allow marriage between any two people who were both citizens. Such a marriage was called *justus*. Any other marriage was *non justus*. In the other kind of marriage, the *non justus* marriage, the *patria potestas* did not exist; the father did not have the usual parental power, and, more serious, the children took the status of the lower of the two parties, and were therefore not citizens. Such a marriage was otherwise morally and legally binding. Slaves could not legally marry at all. They could cohabit, and their children automatically belonged to their master, as the lambs of the sheep belonged to the owner of the flock. Marriage within the normal prohibited degrees was forbidden. By a curious principle a man might not marry a woman whom he already had 'the right to kiss'.

May was avoided as a marriage month. Plutarch (*Roman Questions* 86) speculates as to the reason for this. It is perhaps because April is sacred to Venus and June to Juno, both goddesses of marriage, so it is better to marry before May or to wait until May is past; or perhaps it is because May is the month when the Romans make offerings for the dead; or perhaps it is possible that May is derived from *maior*, which means *older*, and June from *junior*, which means *younger*, and it is better to marry in the month of the young. As for the day of the month, the calends, the ides and the nones and the day after each one of them were avoided. The calends are the first of the month; the ides are the fifth of the month, except in March, May, July and October, when they are the seventh; and the nones are eight days after the ides.

There were three main ways in which a Roman marriage could be carried out. But before the marriage ceremony proper there was the bringing of the bride from her own home (*deductio*) to the home of the bridegroom.

The procession started towards evening. The bride was dressed in a white hemless tunic, with a woollen girdle, fastened round the waist with a double knot of Hercules. Above the tunic she wore a saffron coloured cloak, and her shoes were of the same colour. Her hair had been divided into six tresses, not with a comb, but with the blade of a spear. On her head she wore a veil of flaming orange colour, and on the top of the veil a wreath, originally of verbena and sweet marjoram, but later of myrtle and orange blossom.

The procession, under the protection of Juno Domiduca (Juno who leads home), set out by torch light. The relatives and friends were there to sing along the way, especially to sing the famous song known as the *talassio*, which was so ancient that even then no one knew what the word meant. With the bride there were the *pronubae*, the matrons of honour, and no woman who had been married more than once was eligible to be a *pronuba*. There were three boys in the procession, one to carry the torch, one to hold the bride by the hand, one to carry her spindle and her distaff to her new home. When the bride reached her bridegroom's house, she wreathed the doorposts with wool and rubbed them with oil. She was always carried over the threshold.

The origin of the lifting over the threshold was lost in the mists of antiquity, but Plutarch (*Roman Questions* 29) speculates about it. Some connected it with the famous story of the rape of the Sabine women. Away back in the days of Romulus, so the legend ran, there were not enough Roman maidens for the young men to marry. So Romulus invited the Sabines to the games, and, when they were watching them, the Roman young men rushed upon them, and literally carried off and carried home all the girls of marriageable age. Just as they were carried into the homes of the young men, so was the bride. Some said it signified that the girl had to be carried in because she was unwilling to lose her virginity. Some said that it signified that she could no longer leave the home, just as in Greek Boeotia the axle of the chariot which brought the bride to her new home was burned, to show that she was never meant to leave. More probably, it was lest the bride should slip or stumble on entering, which would have been a bad omen.

Then late in the evening the ceremony began. The auspices were taken; the augurs, the fortune-tellers, killed the victims, usually birds, and judged by certain signs in the birds' entrails whether the gods were propitious or not. Then the bride made the famous and the beautiful declaration: '*Ubiter Caius ego Caia*'; 'where you are Caius, I am Caia; where you are lord and master, I am lady and mistress.' It was the sign that from that day they had all things in common, and that, as Carcopino puts it, their wills as well as their lives were one.

The bridegroom then offered the bride fire and water, to show that from then on they must share in all the essential things of life, and with the further symbolism of the fire that purifies and the water that cleanses.

Up to this point it is likely that at least two of the wedding ceremonies were the same, but now there comes the divergence. (i) By far the most sacred form of wedding ceremony was that which was known as *confarreatio*; the derivation is from *far* which means a cake of bread. This was an entirely religious ceremony. It was carried out by the Pontifex Maximus, who was the overseer of all things religious and of all public ceremonies, and by the Flamen Dialis, who was the greatest of all the priests, the priest of Jupiter. The auspices had already been taken, and the good will of the gods ascertained. The bride and the bridegroom then shared in eating the sacramental bread from which the ceremony took its name. Their hands were then joined together by the priest, who blessed them. And finally they were set to sit side by side on two twin chairs, covered by the fleece of a sheep which had been offered in sacrifice. This was the *conjugium*, literally the joining, the yoking (*jugum* is a yoke) together.

This form of marriage was for ever binding; it was indissoluble except by another religious ceremony and could never be undone. No man might put apart what the gods had joined. It was the greatest and the loveliest of Roman marriage ceremonies; at one time it had been common, but with the general laxity of the marriage bond, it had fallen entirely out of use, except for the marriage of the priests themselves. It was a truly religious ceremony.

(ii) The second type of ceremony was known as *coemptio*, which means *purchase*. This was entirely a civil ceremony; it was a civil contract, with no religious significance. It took the form of a symbolic sale in the presence of five adult male Romans to act as witnesses. In this ceremony the bride was symbolically purchased out of her own family into her husband's. Here, too, there was a question, for the bridegroom asked the bride: 'Do you wish to become the mother of my children?'

We spoke of betrothal as being carried out and arranged by parents and friends. This was so, but no marriage was valid without the definite and willing consent of both the parties.

Once the ceremony was over the feasting began, lit by the light of five torches. One of the ceremonies was the scattering of nuts among the party by the bridegroom. At the end of the evening the bride was escorted to the marriage couch by the *pronubae*, the matrons of honour. The guests gathered to sing the last of the wedding songs, some of them beautiful, and some of them traditionally ribald. Then in the dark the bridegroom went in to his bride and they were left alone.

In the morning, before the bride took over the direction of the household, she began her married life with a sacrifice to the family gods of her husband.

(iii) We said that there were three processes of marriage; *Confarreatio* and *coemptio* were the two ceremonial ways to marriage; but there was a third way, which was very like old Scottish law. The third way to marriage was called *usus*, usage, use and wont. If two people lived together for a year, and if within that year the woman was never away from home for a period of three consecutive days and nights, they were legally married. This is like the old Scottish law of marriage by co-habitation or repute. This last was clearly the least memorable and impressive way of entering into marriage, and yet it may well have been the most lasting in the end, for the two partners had a year's knowledge and experience of each other before they entered into the final state of matrimony.

So, then, the three processes of normal and regular marriage were by *confarreatio*, by *coemptio*, and by *usus*, or as we might distinguish them, by sacrament, by civil contract, and by use and wont.

(iv) One further way of living together must be noted because it was quite common. It was called *concubinatus*, a state of concubinage, but the word had not that bad sense that it has in English.

There were two ways in which this could happen. A man might wish to live with a woman with whom he had not the *connubium*, the right of marriage, and yet he might not wish to make her fully his wife. She might be an alien, a free woman, or even a slave. So he lived with her, and often such people were more faithful to each other than those who were technically or more fully married. Such a state was not morally condemned; it was legal in the eyes of the law. It was called *conjugium inaequale*, the union of unequals, or *licita consuetudo*, permitted custom.

Second, the word was used in a wider sense. It was used of the situation of a married man who lived with a mistress other than his wife, or of an unmarried man who lived not with one woman but with two. This was illegal, and was socially condemned.

So then there were four ways of marriage open to the Roman. He might marry in full religion, but that way of marriage was by New Testament times only for the priests. He might marry by civil contract, and many did. He might marry by cohabitation. And he might not undertake the marriage bond at all, but might live faithfully with one person, although he never fully married her at all.

It can be seen that there was a seriousness about Roman marriage that there was not about Greek marriage, but the time of laxity and immorality was tragically to come.

We have now seen the height of the ideal of Roman marriage, and the height of the ideal makes the death of the ideal all the more tragic.

It is commonly said that for the first five hundred years of the Roman Republic there was not one recorded case of divorce. That statement needs qualification. Even in the earliest days there were legitimate grounds of divorce. The use of poison, the substitution of a child, the counterfeiting of keys – no doubt, for the purpose of admitting a lover – and adultery were grounds of divorce. But at that time it is certainly true that there was no such thing as divorce by caprice.

Before the divorce could be carried out, there had to be a family council which gravely and seriously examined the case. The first person who simply dismissed his wife was Spurius Carvilius Ruga in the year 234 B.C. and he did so because she was childless (Plutarch, *Romulus* 22; Aulus Gellius 17.2; Valerius Maximum 2.1.4). It is true to say that for five hundred years Roman law and Roman morals were such that irresponsible divorce by caprice was impossible, and that the marriage bond was carefully guarded.

Even when Roman morals became a nightmare of shamelessness, it was still true that the old Roman spirit was never wholly lost. Tacitus (*Annals*, 15.62–64) tells of the young Paulina, the wife of the aged Seneca, the great Stoic philosopher and the prime minister of Nero. Seneca was commanded by Nero to commit suicide. He prepared to open his veins to bleed to death, as was the Roman method of suicide. He told Paulina not to grieve too much, but to take up life again, because she was young. But she chose to die with him, and with a stroke of the same dagger they both severed their veins. Nero sent posthaste to command Paulina not to die; they forcibly stopped her, and forcibly bound up her self-inflicted wounds; they would not allow her to die. And Tacitus tells how ever after she walked through life in sadness and with the pallor of death upon her face.

Pliny (*Letters* 3.16) tells the famous story of Arria. Her husband Paetus was ordered to report to Rome for having taken part in a rebellion. He was a prisoner. She asked to be allowed to go with him, not as his wife, but as his slave. They would not permit it. She hired a cockle-shell fishing boat and followed his ship. He was condemned to death and ordered to commit suicide. Arria was in his cell. She took the dagger, plunged it into her own breast, and withdrew it and handed it to her husband. 'Paetus,' she said, 'there is no pain.'

There were still in Rome husbands and wives who were faithful in life and faithful unto death, and the sight of that fidelity still stirred and moved the Roman heart. They loved the ideal even when they had lost it.

But there is the other side; and it is genuinely doubtful if there was ever such a cataract of immorality in any age as in the years when Christianity first came into the world; and the evidence for that comes, not from Christian moralists, but from the Romans themselves. Rome had become the conqueror of the world into which the world's unlimited riches flowed. 'Luxury,' said Juvenal, 'more deadly than any foe has laid her hand upon us, and avenged a conquered world' (Juvenal, *Satires*, 6.233, 234).

Rome had conquered Greece, but Greek morals had conquered Rome. It was her very victories which ruined Rome's character. Let us then examine that age, as its own writers describe it, for this was the age when the first Christian preachers were appealing to men.

(i) There came into life at that time a kind of revulsion against marriage. Juvenal is amazed that any man should marry, while he has a rope wherewith to hang himself, or a window out of which to jump, or a bridge over the parapet of which he may leap (Juvenal, *Satires* 6.28–32). The satirist sees suicide as infinitely preferable to marriage. Aulus Gellius (1.6) records the speech of a certain Metellus Numidicus: 'If, Romans, we could live without wives, we should all keep free from that source of trouble; but since nature has ordained that men can neither live sufficiently agreeably with wives, nor at all without them, let us consider the perpetual endurance of our race rather than our own brief enjoyment.' If it was possible for the human race to continue without marriage, then marriage could be happily and gratefully abandoned. It was an age when there was a cynical dislike of marriage as such.

(ii) It was an age of universal prostitution, or, at least, of universal indulgence in relations outside marriage. Cicero in a speech justifying a loose-living client (*On behalf of Caelius* 20) justifies his client by the universal practice of the time: 'If there is anyone who thinks that young men should be altogether restrained from the love of prostitutes, he is indeed very severe. I am not prepared theoretically to deny his position; but he differs not only from the licence of our age but also from the customs and allowances of our ancestors. When was this not done? When was it blamed? When was it not allowed? When was that which is now lawful not lawful?' He claims for the indulgences of his client a universal precedent and a universal permission.

Alexander Severus was one of the emperors whose face was most sternly set against vice. But when he appointed a provincial governor, it was his routine custom to provide him with a horse and with servants, and with a mistress, if he was unmarried, 'because it was impossible that he should exist without one' (Lampridius, *Alexander Severus*). Prostitution was regarded as a built-in and entirely normal feature of life, and the use of prostitutes was regarded as something with which no reasonable person could find fault.

(iii) It was an age of utter shamelessness in moral conduct. This shamelessness began in the highest places. Cicero put away his wife Terentiana after thirty years of married life in order to marry Publilia, whose trustee he was, and for no better a reason than to be able to use Publilia's fortune to pay his debts. Later Cicero's daughter by his first marriage died, and because Publilia did not seem sorry enough, Cicero divorced her. Terentiana cannot have been completely heartbroken, for she went on to marry first Sallust, and later Messala Corvinus.

Sulla was married five times, Pompey four times. Even Augustus compelled the husband of Livia to divorce her when she was already pregnant, that he might have her. Cato gave his wife to his friend Hortensius, and, when Hortensius died leaving her a fortune, remarried her. The most notorious of all instances was the instance of Messalina, the Empress, the wife of Claudius. Empress though she was, she actually went at nights to serve in the common brothels of Rome, and so insatiable was she in that trade that she was ever the last to leave, 'taking back to the imperial pillow all the odours of the stews' (Juvenal, *Satires* 6.114–132). There was an incredible coarse shamelessness about Roman society at that time.

(iv) The result of all this was a fantastic rate of divorce and the nearly complete breakdown of marriage. Seneca (*Concerning Providence*, 3.16) describes the women of his day: 'Is there any woman who blushes at divorce now that certain illustrious and noble ladies reckon the years not by the number of consuls, but by the number of their husbands. They leave home in order to marry, and marry in order to be divorced.'

Martial (6.7) has an epigram on a certain Telesilla: 'Telesilla is now marrying her tenth husband. She who marries so often does not marry. She is a legalized adulteress. I'd rather have an honest prostitute.' Juvenal says of Hiberina: 'Will Hiberina be satisfied with one man? Sooner compel her to be satisfied with one eye!' (*Satires* 6.53, 54). Jerome (*Letter* 2) records the instance of a woman marrying her twenty-third husband, whose twenty-first wife she was.

There is no doubt that even at a time like that there were happy homes and faithful husbands and chaste wives, for true love exists in every generation. But the general tone of Roman society was lax and shameless.

The moral problems which face our own generation are far from new. The fact that they are not new does not make them any less serious, but it does remind us that Christianity is not facing anything which it was not called upon to face before.

Our problems are neither new nor unique; they are part of the human situation, produced by human sin. This the Church has always to face. To this she must be ever bringing the grace of God.

We have now seen the situation of sexual morality into which

Christianity came. And Christianity confronted that situation with an uncompromising demand for purity. Immorality and all impurity are not even to be named among Christians. There must be no filthiness. An immoral or impure man has no share in the kingdom of Christ and God (Ephesians 5:3–20). Immorality, impurity, passion, evil desire must be inwardly put to death (Colossians 3:5, 6). It is only the pure in heart, and therefore the pure in life, who see God (Matthew 5:8).

We must begin with the simple, and yet far-reaching, fact that the Christian respected the body. To the Greek the body was no more than the prison-house of the soul, and from it came all the ills of life. The world at that time was deeply infected with Gnostic thought, which believed that only spirit is good and that all matter is incurably and irremediably evil.

The inevitable conclusion of this is that the body is evil. If the body is evil, two courses of action are possible. First, a man can adopt a complete asceticism in which he denies every desire and deed of the body. Second, he can say that, because the body is evil, it does not matter what we do with it, and that therefore we can sate it and glut it and it does not matter, because it is evil anyway.

But the Christian came with a new conception of the body. For the Christian the body is designed to be nothing less than the temple of the Holy Spirit (1 Corinthians 3:16). 'Do you know that you are God's temple and that God's Spirit dwells in you?' The Christian must, therefore, glorify God in his body (1 Corinthians 6:19, 20). It is not only possible, it is an obligation, to present the body as a sacrifice and an offering to God (Romans 12:1). Christianity came with a view of the body which was bound to revolutionize the ethics of sex for the Hellenistic world.

If the body is good, if the body is designed to be the temple of the Holy Spirit, if the body and all its functions and activities can be offered to God, then immediately marriage becomes a sacred and holy state. 'Let marriage be held in honour among all, and let the marriage bed be undefiled; for God will judge the immoral and the adulterous' (Hebrews 13:4). Those who forbid marriage are nothing other than pretentious liars (1 Timothy 4:3). Younger widows are far better to remarry and to rear children (1 Timothy 5:14). The general teaching of the New Testament exalts marriage. There may be reasons, and good reasons, why a person does not marry, but quite certainly the attainment of special holiness is not one of them. The New Testament as a whole would not have understood the identification of chastity with virginity; the true chastity was to be found within the married state.

There is only one passage in the New Testament which seems to teach anything else, and that is 1 Corinthians 7. All through that passage Paul seems to belittle the married state. 'It is well for a man not to touch a woman' (verse 1). A man may marry but only to avoid a worse fate, for it is 'better to marry than to be aflame with passion' (verse 9). It is better that a girl should remain a virgin. 'He who marries his betrothed does well; and he who refrains from marriage will do better' (verse 38).

It is perfectly certain that, if Paul had done the editing of his own letters for publication, he would not have included this chapter in its present form. The key to the understanding of this chapter lies in the fact that, when he wrote it, Paul was expecting the second coming at any moment. 'For the form of this world is passing away' (verse 31). He therefore wished men and women to have no distractions whatever in their intense concentration on waiting for Christ. 'I want you to be free from anxieties. The unmarried man is anxious about the affairs of the Lord, how to please the Lord; but the married man is anxious about worldly affairs, how to please his wife, and his interests are divided. And the unmarried woman or girl is anxious about the affairs of the Lord, how to be holy in body and spirit; but the married woman is anxious about worldly affairs, how to please her husband.' What Paul wants is 'your undivided devotion to the Lord' (verses 32–35).

It must be remembered that all this was written at a stage in Paul's thought when he believed that the second coming would be immediate, and that nothing must distract a man from waiting for the coming of the Lord. As time went on, he began to realize that Christ's return was not as imminent as that, and his true view of marriage is to be found in the Letter to the Ephesians, which he wrote about nine years later, and where he finds in the relationship between husband and wife the illustration of the relationship between Christ and the Church. He has come to see that the highest and the finest relationship on earth is the marriage state (Ephesians 5:21–33).

1 Corinthians 7 is a chapter which, if Paul had selected his own letters for permanent preservation, he would quite clearly have rewritten or excised; his full and considered view is in the much later Letter to the Ephesians.

There is clear and ample teaching about marriage in the New Testament, and we shall attempt to see the pattern of it. The most basic of all sayings is the saying which Jesus used: 'For this reason a man shall leave his father and mother and be joined to his wife, and the two shall become one' (Matthew 19:5; Mark 10:7; Genesis 1:27; 2:24). This shows us two basic things about marriage.

(i) On the one hand marriage is a *separation*. A man leaves his father and his mother. A person cannot continue to live the old life when he begins the new life. There is many a marriage spoiled because of the failure to realize this separation. The son or the daughter fails to realize that the centre and the focus of life must be in the new home. The parent, and it is not unfair to say specially the mother, fails to realize that the son or the daughter has grown up, that there is a new set of loyalties and a new set of priorities.

This is far from saying that, when people are married, they must turn their backs on their old homes; but it is to say that the new home is their home, and the centre of their lives is there. There is unquestionably in marriage an essential separation – and not to realize that is the way to trouble.

(ii) But there is also *union*. The two who marry become one. There is more than one way of becoming one. There is the way of domination and abdication, the way in which one partner in the marriage becomes the absolutely dominating partner, until the personality of the other is more or less completely obliterated as an independent entity. That is certainly not the biblical way. The chief biblical passages which deal with the relationship of husband and wife are: Ephesians 5:21–33; Colossians 3:18, 19; 1 Peter 3:1–7; 1 Timothy 2:9–15; 1 Corinthians 11:3. Through all these passages there runs one principle which never varies. *The principle of marriage is reciprocity*. There is never a duty and never a privilege and never a responsibility that is all on one side. Every duty and every privilege is reciprocal.

Wives are to be subject to their husbands. A home in the nature of things needs a leader and that leader is the husband

(Ephesians 5:22; Colossians 3:18; 1 Peter 3:1, 5; 1 Corinthians 11:3). It may well be noted in the passing that the husband who evades his responsibility of leadership is not blameless. But even if that leadership is there, the husband must love his wife as Christ loves the Church (Ephesians 5:23); he must love her as he loves his own body (Ephesians 5:28). The wife must respect the husband, but the husband must love the wife as he loves himself (Ephesians 5:33). The wife must obey the husband, but the husband must so love the wife that he will never be harsh to her (Colossians 3:18, 19). The wife must be submissive, but the husband must be considerate, for the wife is the weaker vessel (1 Peter 3:7). The duty is never all on the one side and the responsibility is never all on the one side. In Christian marriage every duty is reciprocal, just as every privilege is. It is not domination; it is partnership. It is not the extinction of independent personality; it is the fulfilling of personality in togetherness. It is not a tension of rights, but a partnership in rights. It is not a one-sided allocation of duties; it is a sharing of duties. It is a state in which two people are completed by each other. Neither is stifled or absorbed or dominated; both are enriched and fulfilled and completed by being together. Marriage for the Christian is the perfect partnership of two people in love.

We have now to come to a question which is a real problem for the Christian Ethic, and it is a problem rendered doubly difficult by the fact that it is not only a theological problem, but also a human problem. What is the Christian attitude to divorce?

We have studied the background out of which Christianity came. Unquestionably, the Jewish ideal of marriage was very high, whatever the practice may have been. Equally unquestionably, there was in the Hellenistic world of Greece and Rome an almost unparalleled laxity in sexual ethics, so that divorce was normal rather than exceptional. It is clear that these two factors, apart from anything else, would combine to produce in the Christian Ethic an uncompromising demand. The uncompromising demand would be in line with the highest ideals of Judaism, and it would be an inevitable reaction against the shameless immorality of the pagan world.

In this matter the New Testament teaching is laid down for us. The Pharisees questioned Jesus as to the legality of divorce. He asked them what Moses himself had said about it. They replied that Moses had allowed divorce. Jesus' answer was that the action of Moses was no more than a concession to the hardness of the hearts of the Jewish people. He then took the matter back behind Moses to the Genesis story (Genesis 2:24; 1:27), and to the saying that for the sake of marriage a man would leave father and mother and be joined to his wife, and that the union would be so complete that they would be one person. Therefore, said Jesus, what God has joined man must not put asunder.

In private the disciples questioned him further about this, and he laid down the principle: 'Whoever divorces his wife and marries another, commits adultery against her; and if she divorces her husband and marries another, she commits adultery (Mark 10:2-12). Luke transmits the saying thus: 'Every one who divorces his wife and marries another commits adultery, and he who marries a woman divorced from her husband commits adultery' (Luke 16:18). Matthew tells exactly the same story as Mark about the question of the Pharisees and the inquiry of the disciples and then transmits the saying thus: 'Whoever divorces his wife, except for unchastity, and marries another, commits adultery' (Matthew 19:3-9). Matthew also has the saying in Matthew 5:32: 'every one who divorces his wife, except on the ground of unchastity, makes her an adulteress; and whoever marries a divorced woman commits adultery.'

It can be seen that this saying of Jesus exists in two forms. It exists in Mark and in Luke in a form in which the prohibition of divorce is absolute, without any exceptions at all; and it exists in Matthew in a form in which divorce in general is forbidden, but one exception is made. It is allowable in the case of infidelity.

Mark is the earliest gospel, and therefore nearest to the actual spoken words of Jesus, and there is little doubt that the original form is the absolute form, which allows no exceptions whatsoever. Even on general grounds, the stricter saying is much more likely to be the original, for the tendency is always to relax and not to intensify the demand. Does this then mean that for the Christian divorce is absolutely and completely and without exception forbidden? Before we can evaluate this saying, there are certain things to be remembered.

(i) Matthew adds something still further to this. According to Matthew, when the disciples heard this saying of Jesus, and when they realized how absolutely indissoluble Jesus believed marriage to be, they said that, if this was the case, it was surely better not to marry at all. Jesus' answer was: 'Not all men can receive this precept, but only those to whom it is given', or, as the N.E.B. has it, 'That is something which not everyone can accept, but only those for whom God has appointed it' (Matthew 19:10, 11). This is to say, the acceptance of the absolute prohibition of divorce is something which not everyone can accept. To put this completely simply and directly, it means that *Christian marriage is only possible for a Christian.* It is only a Christian who can understand and accept and achieve the standards of Christian marriage.

It may well be that we ought to think of marriage in terms of two different standards. It may be that we ought to think of marriage, on the one hand, in terms of the kind of contract and agreement into which two people enter, and which is terminable, as any contract may be; and, on the other hand, as an indissoluble bond into which two people enter with full knowledge of what they are doing. The analogy is that in the Church of Scotland we put the baptismal vow only to parents who are members of the Church, that is, pledged Christians, because we believe that only pledged Christians can take and keep a vow and a pledge to bring up children in the knowledge and the love and the fear of God. We might well hold that no more can the marriage vow, which demands unaltering fidelity until the parting of death, be put to anyone except to a pledged Christian. Perhaps there is a case for holding that the Church can only marry those who regard marriage in the way that the Church regards it, and who have the help of Jesus Christ to carry it out in that way, and that those for whom marriage is no more than an agreement should be married by civil marriage, always with the proviso that, if and when they come to pledge themselves to the Christian faith, the blessing of the Church willingly awaits them. It is very difficult to get away from the fact that it is a strange proceeding to allow all and sundry to take a vow and to make a pledge which in the last analysis only the true Christian can keep with the help of Jesus Christ.

But does this mean that, when a man enters into Christian marriage knowing what he is doing, there can be no such thing as divorce?

It is perfectly obvious that, whether or not *divorce* is allowed, there are cases where *separation* must be allowed. No two people can live together, if one of them is guilty of flagrant and open infidelity. No two people can live together when one of them is guilty of a cruelty which can actually endanger either the mental or the physical health of the other, or place a child's life in danger. No one can forecast what is going to happen when two people decide to live together in marriage, and there can arise a degree of incompatibility which makes life a hell for the husband and wife and a danger for the children. It is impossible to argue that there can never be *separation*; to refuse to allow separation would be to be guilty of an incredibly callous inhumanity.

But is there anything possible for the Christian beyond separation? Let us remind ourselves of certain things. Let us remind ourselves of the fact that Jesus laid down principles and not laws, and to make his principles into laws is in fact to de-christianize them. It is sometimes said that the marriage vow is made in the presence of God; let us remember that every promise is made in the presence of God, and no pledge ought to be more or less serious than any other.

Let us remember that there are many of the commands of Christ to which we do not in fact demand a literal obedience. The word of Jesus that he who calls his brother a fool will go to hell, we do not take literally (Matthew 5:22). We do not in fact pluck out the offending eye (Matthew 5:29). We do not in fact abolish all pledges upon oath (Matthew 5:33–37). We do not always give to him who begs from us and we do turn away from him who tries to borrow from us (Matthew 5:42). We do not love our enemies (Matthew 5:44). We are anxious about the needs of life (Matthew 6:25). We do judge others in spite of Jesus' prohibition of judging (Matthew 7:1).

It is a very odd thing that we have literalized Jesus' command about marriage in a way that we have not literalized any other commandment. Above all let us remember that the supreme value and the supreme principle of judgment is love. And let us remember that talk of guilty and innocent parties can be sadly misleading. The elder brother in the parable was innocent and the younger was guilty, but it may well be that it was the elder brother, and what he was, that drove the younger brother from home, and the technically innocent party in a broken marriage may well be the one who was responsible for the break.

We cannot help feeling that we must lay down as the Christian principle the indissolubility of the marriage bond, but that we must also remember the principle of love. If two people cannot live together, if the help of the priest or the minister, the help of the doctor, the help of the psychiatrist have all been called in and the situation is incurable, then it cannot be an act of Christian love to condemn these people and their children to a life of misery, which can do nothing but injure themselves and their family. If we are to think in terms of Christian love rather than in terms of Christian law, then there are cases when divorce is justified. Nor is it right permanently to despoil such people, who have failed once, of the possibility of happiness for ever; it is not right to insist that the child of such a marriage shall be for ever without a father and the partner for ever alone. There may be times when remarriage is right and justified.

Of course, there is a danger here. Law is always easier to administer than love. Of course, these cases and occasions must be rare, and, of course, no one justifies irresponsible and selfish divorce, but, if we are to be truly Christian, we shall have to temper the inflexibility of law with the sympathy and the understanding of love.

Before we leave this subject there are certain things at which we must look. The first is the question of sexual intercourse prior to marriage.

Not to look at this subject is to close our eyes to the facts. According to a recent estimate, of boys of seventeen one in four has had sexual experience, and of girls of the same age one in eight; of boys of nineteen, the number is one in three, and of girls of the same age one in four. It is the statistical fact that of all babies born in this country about one in twelve is illegitimate, that is, born to an unmarried mother. In the case of girls under twenty, it is estimated that two out of every three babies born to them were conceived before marriage, although in many cases born after marriage. It is estimated that in certain parts of the country two out of every three girls who have reached the age of twenty-five, and who are unmarried, are no longer virgins. There are now more than three times as many abortions as there were in the year after abortion was in certain cases first legalized. There are about 180,000 known abortions per year in the country.

The Christian Ethic must look at this, and must make its views known on this, because sexual intercourse before marriage is well on the way to being, not the abnormal, but the normal practice.

It is not too much to say that there is from some quarters a deliberate attack on the accepted standard of morality in the sexual sphere. In 1959 the British Medical Association published a book by Eustace Chesser and Winifred de Kok entitled *Getting Married*. In it the sentence occurred: 'Chastity is out-moded, and should no longer be taught to young people.' True, public reaction was so hostile that the book had to be withdrawn, but the significant fact is that it did get itself published, and in the first place with the approval of the British Medical Association. Noel Tovey, the choreographer-director of the notorious show *Oh! Calcutta!* said that playing in that piece was ex-hausting because, 'It's a constant battle every night against all those standards we were brought up with.' This is to say that we have here a deliberate challenge to the accepted standards of sexual morality.

Mrs Thatcher, the Minister of Education, asked school authorities to refuse to show children the sex education film *Growing Up*, in which naked teachers are shown in twos and threes in sexual acts, including masturbation. Thereupon the National Council for Civil Liberties produced a Children's Sex Charter, demanding the right for children to have sexual ex-perience 'as soon as they wish'.

We might not be totally surprised at an attack on accepted sex standards emanating from these sources, but the matter becomes very much more serious when we hear Joseph Fletcher, a Pro-fessor of Christian Ethics in an American seminary, saying: 'The cult of virginity seems to me to be making its last stand against the sexual freedom which medicine has now made possible.' We are bound to pay attention to this matter, when the attack is coming not only from outside but also from inside Christian circles. Malcolm Muggeridge has said: 'Our artists may safely be left to destroy art, our writers to destroy literature, our scholars to destroy scholarship, and our clergy to destroy religion. We breed our own barbarians.'

The extraordinary thing about this ever-accelerating revolution is that it has come upon us in one sense almost unawares. As I said in the preface to this book, the book began as a series of articles in the *British Weekly* in 1964–5. When I began to revise the material on the seventh commandment in June 1972 I discovered that the situation had completely changed. Within that comparatively brief period the contraceptive pill had arrived; abortion in certain cases had been legalized; and homosexual practices between consenting adults had become legal.

In *No No Calcutta* which tells the story of how the showing of that musical was banned in South Australia, Dr John Court the psychologist uses a significant illustration. He tells of what he calls a classical psychological experiment. A frog was placed in cold water. Then the temperature was slowly and imperceptibly increased. Eventually the temperature reached boiling-point, yet the frog made no effort to escape. Because the change occurred so slowly, there was no recognition of danger and the frog died, making no attempt at self-preservation. It is like the possible effects of smoking. If the effects of smoking were immediately visible, then the smoker would stop smoking. But, we are told, the effect is going to take twenty years to arrive, and it works so gradually that the damage is done all unawares. So, it is suggested by analogy, there can be what might be called a moral desensitization which happens so gradually that one day all unexpectedly we wake up and find the standards destroyed and the damage done. And that is precisely why we are bound to look at this matter, and to look at it most carefully.

Those who support the abandonment of the old standards and the acceptance of the new standards would, at least in some cases, say that they believed in, and practised, free love. And they would go on to argue, at least in some cases, that it was this free love that, for instance, Plato advocated in the *Republic*, his picture of the ideal state (469–471). But the truth is that no one could have been further from advocating free love than Plato was. Plato began from the principle that, if it is right to take the greatest care in the breeding of animals so that the finest beasts are produced, it is surely even more necessary to take the greatest care with the breeding of human beings. So in the case of the guardians, the rulers of the state, the best men and women were selected to have children, the women from the age of twenty to forty, the men from the age of twenty-five to fifty-five. Of the children only the physically perfect were to be kept; the others were to be destroyed. At birth the child was to be handed over to the state nurses. Mothers would come to feed the children with their milk, but it was strictly laid down that no mother might ever know which child was hers, and no child might ever know who his parents were. This, of course, meant that unless care was taken there might later be intercourse between men and women of the forbidden degrees of relationship, for a man would never know what girl might be his own daughter, or what woman might be his own sister. Plato solved the problem by enacting that weddings were only to be held at special seasons of the year, and a man would be bound to regard every child born from seven to ten months from his own marriage as his own son or daughter, and all such children would call him father. Marriage was thus arranged by the state, and all children belonged to the state. Nothing could be further from free love than all this. Anyone who married outside the limits that the state imposed was said to act 'in darkness and strange lust'. Marriage was regarded simply and solely as a way of producing the finest possible children for the sake of the state. The sexual act was never thought of as an act of lust or even of love, still less of pleasure; it was an act of duty. So far from being free love, it was love utterly disciplined.

It was something like this in Sparta, as Plutarch in his life of Lycurgus tells (chapter 15). The noble, the good and the brave were encouraged to produce children for the sake of the state. A man with a good and beautiful and noble wife did not mind it, if an equally noble man sired children from her – he welcomed it. A wife with a wise and gallant husband did not mind, if he produced children from an equally splendid mother. It was the Spartan boast that there was no such thing as adultery, in the low and the lustful sense, in all their land.

Plato's *Republic* and the state of things in Sparta are often cited as examples of what is called free love; but in both cases more self-control was called for than in any other system, and the whole matter was for the good of the state, never for the satisfaction of individual desire. It is in fact true that pre-marital intercourse has never been regarded as right and natural and proper. Of course, it happened, for human nature is weak, but it has never been approved, or conceded as a right. We are today faced with a new situation.

There is a further complication here. There are few who are

likely to argue in favour of prostitution. To have intercourse with a prostitute is to use a person as a thing. Normally, her client will not even know her name. Normally, he has never seen her before, and he will never see her again. Sexual intercourse with a prostitute is sex without love, and even without respect for human personality. For a few moments a man uses a woman to gratify an animal desire, and, having used her, passes on. It is true that there can arise a kind of relationship between a man and a prostitute in which the man regularly turns to the same woman; but the element of using the person for self-gratification is never wholly absent.

The complication does not arise with loveless sex; the complication rises from what is claimed to be love. There are four situations in which the problem may arise.

(a) There is sexual intercourse by what we might call anticipation. This is a situation in which two people claim that they love each other so much, and that they are so certain to marry, that they can anticipate marriage by having sexual intercourse before they are actually married. There is no question of promiscuity, or of what one might call deliberate immorality. There is simply the anticipation of that which will, as they believe certainly, be some day a right.

There are two things to be said here. The first is that it would be equally possible to say that they love each other so much that they will not have sexual intercourse until they are totally and irrevocably committed to each other, that the boy loves the girl too much to take that which is not yet his to take, and the girl loves the boy too much to come to him less than completely, that love has taught them that self-control, self-discipline and self-giving are very closely connected. The second thing is that nothing is certain in this life, and it is not certain that they will marry. All of us have seen two people who seemed utterly certain to marry, but who in the end did not. The human heart is not so completely predictable that anyone can take its future movements for granted. It is not wise to anticipate that which we have neither the right nor the power to anticipate.

(b) There is sexual intercourse for the reason of trial or experiment. Sometimes two people argue that they will not commit themselves to marriage until they find out by experiment whether or not they are suited to each other. The error in that attitude is that it is not possible in that way to simulate the conditions of marriage. Let us take an analogy. A man may wish to know what it is like to live in a slum. He may go and live there for a time to see. But he has not really simulated or experienced the conditions, for the difference between him and the real slum-dweller is that he can walk out at any time, while the real slum-dweller cannot. Clearly, no one is really experiencing the depth of a situation, if it is possible for him to escape from it at any time. The very essence of the situation is that there is no escape from it. When two people speak about a trial marriage, in which they live together without being married, they are not really reproducing the conditions of marriage, for they are not in a binding situation, which is the very essence of marriage, but in a quite impermanent situation out of which either may walk at any time. They are in a situation in which at any moment they can freely walk out of their problems instead of a situation in which they have to solve their problems, or wreck the situation. The whole point about marriage is that marriage can never be an experiment; it has to be a commitment; no one can experiment with a commitment; a commitment has to be accepted or refused.

(c) There is the case of those who choose to live together, but who, as they say, see no necessity for any marriage ceremony, either civil or religious. They say that they cannot see what any such pledge or ceremony could add to their relationship. They hold that without any marriage ceremony of any kind they are just as really married as those who have accepted some form of promise.

It is relevant and reasonable to say that in every sphere of life there is some way of marking a binding obligation. This is so in industry and in business and in employment and everywhere agreements are entered into. There are few people who refuse to enter into a binding contract. To take it at its very lowest marriage is a contract; and to take it at its highest marriage is a promise made in the presence of God. It is perfectly true that a man can keep an agreement without any ceremony or contract of promise; but, human nature being what it is, there come times when the agreement is difficult to keep, and when there is every temptation to break it; and at such a time it is of very great value to be able to look back to some moment when we pledged ourselves unbreakably to the keeping of it.

I would never wish to be unfair or unjust, or to take a cynical view of what for some people is regarded as a matter of principle, but I sometimes wonder if those who say that they can live together with no ceremony or pledge are in reality rationalizing a reluctance to commit themselves fully and irrevocably to one another, and subconsciously wish to leave the door of 'escape' still open. It seems to me that marriage is either a contract in the eyes of men, or a union in the sight of God, or that it includes something of both; and if that is so, some moment and act of pledge is a necessity.

(d) There is one last form of this which can be serious. Sometimes a girl will say, especially if she is lonely, or if she has no family of which she forms a part: 'What I want above all is someone of my very own, someone who is bone of my bone and flesh of my flesh. Therefore, what I want is a baby of my own. I do not want a husband. I want a man, whom I can respect and admire, to father my child, but that is all.' It is not difficult to understand this, and to understand the deep longing which lies behind it. But anyone who thinks like that should remember two things. The first is the quite practical matter of the support of herself and the child. True, she can work for the support of the child, but a little child brought up with a working mother and no father is going to lose a great deal. And second, what we have already said includes a still greater objection. A child brought into the world like that, and brought up like that would never know what it is to have a father – and that is a loss which nothing could replace. A girl who thinks like this may well ask herself if she is not thinking too much of herself and too little of the child.

It is argued that modern discoveries have changed the whole significance of the sex act in such a way that it is no longer necessary to confine it within marriage. We have a new situation, so it is said, which demands a radical rethinking of the whole matter. It is said that in the older days the whole situation was dominated by three fears – the fear of conception, the fear of infection, and the fear of detection. But, the argument runs, these three fears have been removed, and so sexual intercourse can be used, not only for baby-making, but also for love-making, whether in marriage or before marriage. The pill has removed the fear of conception; or, if a child is conceived, it can be removed by abortion. Infection can be cured by modern treatment

and drugs. And, since the whole attitude towards sexual intercourse is changed, detection is no longer a problem, for the right
to sexual intercourse before marriage is accepted and conceded.

Have we then to accept all this? Have we to accept the position
that sexual intercourse before marriage is to be regarded as right
and normal for a Christian?

We may well accept the fact that the danger of conception is
very largely done away with, and that the pill is very largely
effective and in the vast majority of cases without injurious
effects on the person who takes it. But the same cannot be said
of the danger of infection. A doctor whom I know will give an
unmarried girl the pill, because – and I think rightly – he feels
that if the girl is determined to have sexual intercourse, it is
better that she should have the pill than that she should have a
baby. He will not give her the pill willingly and he will do his
best to dissuade her from doing what she intends to do, and he
will say to her: 'I have most likely enabled you to shut the door
on having a child, but I also have enabled you to open the door
wide to venereal disease.' In England and Wales alone cases of
venereal disease rose by nearly 60,000 cases in one year. In one
large English town the medical officer of health reports treating
a girl of twelve for venereal disease. The danger is there all right,
and the danger is intensified by the fact that there are strains of
venereal disease which have developed an immunity to the drugs
normally used to cure them. As for abortion, there are few who
will declare that abortion must never be used, although that is
the Roman Catholic position. Most Protestants will agree that
there are cases in which for the sake of the mother and even of
the unborn child abortion is to be accepted. But to use abortion
as simply a convenient means of getting rid of an unwanted
child irresponsibly conceived can surely seldom or never be
right. There will be endless argument as to when the unborn
foetus becomes a person, for at that stage irresponsible abortion
is murder; but abortion is always at least the bringing to an end
of a potential life, and surely that can only be done after the most
careful consideration, and cannot be made into a service which
can be had on demand. And in any event the psychological effect
on the mother is something that can neither be forecast nor
calculated. The dangers are by no means eliminated. As for the
fear of detection, the day has not yet come when pre-marital

sexual intercourse is regarded with equanimity as the accepted thing, and therefore it has to be practised in conditions of secrecy and concealment, which surround it with a conscious or subconscious anxiety, and under circumstances which turn what ought to be a thing of beauty into a tawdry thing.

But we are in danger of sending the argument down the wrong road. If we proceed on the lines on which we are at present thinking, we might come to the conclusion that, if it was possible to eliminate all danger from pre-marital sexual intercourse, then it could be accepted as quite legitimate for a Christian. But the basic and the ultimate argument of the Christian must be, not that such sexual intercourse is dangerous, although that may be used as a secondary argument, but that it is wrong, and, even if it was completely safe, it would still be wrong. What then are the basic and fundamental arguments against it?

(i) If sexual intercourse before – and outside – marriage is accepted as normal, then the whole institution of the family is radically altered. The very essence of the family is that in it two people take each other to have and to hold all the days of their life. It is precisely this exclusive relationship which gives marriage its security. The family is the one stable group in a fluctuating world; it is the one permanence in the middle of impermanence. It is the one unchanging thing in a child's life. Take away the family and the very foundations of society are undermined. The basic security would be turned into insecurity – and the ultimate consequences of that on life and on people are terrifying. It is the sense of security which keeps people sane and healthy; it is the sense of insecurity which makes them anxious and neurotic. Remove the central stability of the home, and the whole life of the nation would be wounded. It is from broken homes that delinquent young people usually come. And the stability of the home depends on the exclusive relationship of the two people round whom it revolves.

(ii) To demand pre-marital sexual intercourse is to demand privilege without responsibility. It is to demand from someone the gift of something which can never be replaced without any corresponding acceptance of responsibility for the welfare of the giver. For a woman to surrender her virginity is for her to surrender something which can never be replaced; she is a literally changed person. To accept such a gift as if it were something given, as it were, in the passing, is the essence of irresponsibility. To demand all and to give nothing is not the act of an honourable or responsible person.

(iii) To demand pre-marital intercourse is to demand rights without commitment. Sexual intercourse should not be the beginning of a relationship but the consummation of it. The natural end of sexual intercourse is a child; it is for the begetting and the bearing of children that this instinct is primarily put into human nature. It is therefore the simple rule that sexual intercourse is wrong in any case in which it would be a disaster for a child to result from it. It is only two people who are totally committed to each other who have the right to bring a child into the world, for on their commitment the welfare of the child depends. To demand a right without a corresponding commitment cannot be other than wrong.

It may well be that we must look at this in a wider context as well. Freud has written: 'We believe that civilization has been built up by sacrifice in gratification of the primitive impulses, and that it is to a great extent for ever being recreated as each individual repeats the sacrifice of his instinctive pleasures for the common good.' This is to say, it is precisely the disciplined control of impulse and instinct which makes a man a man and not an animal. It was this disciplined control which built up civilized society and on which civilized society depends. If there is a general refusal to continue this discipline, if the satisfaction of the primitive instincts comes to be regarded as right, then the breakdown of society may be anticipated. John H. Court says that the historian J. D. Unwin studied eighty-eight different civilizations, and from the study discerned the following pattern: 'Every civilization is established and consolidated by observing a strict moral code, is maintained while this strict code is kept, and decays when sexual licence is allowed . . . Any human society is free to choose either to display great energy or to enjoy sexual freedom; the evidence is that it cannot do both for more than one generation.' It may well be that the lesson of history is that the loosening of sexual standards threatens the welfare of not only the individual, but also of the nation.

The second great problem at which we must look is the problem of homosexuality. It is estimated that perhaps six per cent of men are practising homosexuals and the same percentage of women are lesbians. Here then is a problem of some magnitude and a situation within society which cannot be disregarded.

We begin with the biblical attitude to this way of sex. In the Bible there are three things that we must note.

(i) The old story in Genesis 19:1–11 gives the origin of the other name for homosexuality, sodomy. To Lot there came two angel visitors, but when he brought them into his house the men of Sodom surrounded it with threats and even with violence, demanding that the two visitors should be handed over to them to satisfy their lust. The story shows the ancient existence of this practice, and the loathing of Old Testament religion for it.

(ii) The A.V. speaks rather misleadingly in certain places of the sodomites. We have seen how in the temples of the Baals there were sacred prostitutes with whom to have intercourse was an act of worship. This was part of the worship of the life force which was at the back of so much ancient religion. But the fact is that in these ancient temples there were not only female prostitutes; there were male prostitutes too. The temples were the scene of homosexual activity. There is in Deuteronomy 23:17–18 what is to us an obscure passage:

> There shall be no cult prostitute of the daughters of Israel, neither shall there be a cult prostitute of the sons of Israel. You shall not bring the hire of a harlot, or the wages of a dog, into the house of the Lord your God in payment for any vow; for both of these are an abomination to the Lord your God.

The payment to these sacred prostitutes was regarded as an offering to God, and the male prostitutes were commonly called 'dogs'. This verse is a reference to the female and the male prostitutes who were to be found in ancient temples.

There are fairly frequent references to these male prostitutes. Among the evils of the reign of Rehoboam it is said that 'there were also male cult prostitutes in the land' (1 Kings 14:24). It is said of Asa, as an act typical of a good king that 'he put away the male cult prostitutes out of the land' (1 Kings 15:12). It is said of Jehoshaphat that 'the remnant of the male cult prostitutes who remained in the days of his father Asa, he exterminated from the land' (1 Kings 22:46). It is said of Josiah that 'he broke down the houses of the male cult prostitutes which were in the house of the Lord' (2 Kings 23:7). It can be seen how deeply rooted this practice was in Jewish religion.

(iii) Homosexuality as such is unsparingly condemned in the Old Testament. Leviticus has it: 'You shall not lie with a male as with a woman; it is an abomination' (Leviticus 18:22); and in a later passage it prescribes the death penalty for such practices (Leviticus 20:13). In the New Testament Paul cites homosexual practices as part of the moral rot of the pagan world (Romans 1:26, 27); and in the Letter to the Corinthians he lists homosexuality as one of the sins from which the Christians have been saved and purified (1 Corinthians 6:9).

Let us look at the practice of homosexuality in the Greek and Roman worlds to which Christianity came.

Homosexuality was something with which Greek society was permeated and riddled from top to bottom. It was woven into the very fibre of Greek life. Although it is in fact an unfair description, it is not difficult to see how it has been possible for someone to describe ancient Greece as 'a pervert's paradise'. One writer has said that homosexuality was 'ingrained into the Greek character'. Another has said: 'The whole people inhaled the pestilence with the air they breathed.' Still another has said that the degeneration was 'not personal but social, a thing indigenous and ingrown'.

Let us look quite simply at the facts. In Greece this practice was given the name not of homosexuality but of pederasty, which is the literal Greek for love of boys. The reason for choosing this other word in the case of Greece is that homosexuality has an unvaryingly bad connotation; pederasty, while it could become bad, had its noble side as well as its degenerate side. In Greece it could describe something which was beautiful and not ugly. It could describe a relationship between an older man and a youth of fifteen to nineteen which was closer and more spiritually intimate than that between even father and son. It is only fair to remember that in Greece there were two sides to this, and there was only one word to describe both. The good and the bad we shall go on to see.

We have said that pederasty or homosexuality was ingrained into the Greek character. And yet it is worth noting that it does not exist in Homer. It was a comparatively late development. The Greeks themselves often traced it to the gymnastic training which became so typical of Greek education. It was the gymnasium with its physical training and its nudity which, as the

Greek saw it, was the beginning. Ennius the old Latin writer has it: 'It is the beginning of vice to bare the body among citizens' (Cicero, *Tusculans* 4.34); and no less a person than Plato himself makes a character say: 'Pederasty is the price paid for the nude gymnasia' (*Symposium* 634). The worship of the body and its beauty had its dangers.

Nor does it seem that pederasty in Greece really reached the common people in anything like the same degree as it reached the upper classes. It was, if you like to put it so, the sin of the intellectual and the aristocrat. Lucian, who hated this practice, writes bitterly (*Am.* 51): 'The marriage bond was made for all other men, that philosophers might indulge their passion for boys.' It was a fact that the headship of the philosophic schools had a way of passing from lover to loved one. In the Academy Xenocrates was succeeded by Polemon; Polemon by Crates; Crantor by Arcesilaus; Aristotle by Hermias; and in every case there was a homosexual relationship between the teacher and his successor. It may not be altogether unfair to say that the open supporters of homosexuality have usually been drawn from what may be regarded as the intellectual and the cultured classes.

There were certain spheres in Greek life in which homosexual relationships had notable effects. It has often been held that homosexuality began among warriors, that it is the result of what the Germans call *kriegskameradschaft*, the comradeship of warriors. Socrates once said: 'The most formidable army is composed of pairs of lovers inspiring each other to deeds of heroism and sacrifice' (Plato, *Symposium* 178 E: Xenophon, *Symposium* 8.32). It was certainly true that one of the most famous fighting bodies of troops there has ever been in history was the Theban band, and the Theban band was essentially a homosexual society of comrades (Plutarch, *Pel.* 18). Valour and courage and the love of man for man went hand in hand.

One of the strangest things is the way that homosexual relationships had an extraordinary effect on Greek politics. One of the greatest blows for freedom in history was when Harmodius and Aristogeiton led the revolt against Pisistratus, although it ended for them in disaster. The beginning of the whole matter was that Aristogeiton was in love with the young Harmodius, and Pisistratus tried to take him away; and thus the revolt happened. Plutarch, who also hated homosexuality,

comments in amazement that even love of liberty can be quies-
cent, 'but as soon as a tyrant sets out to seduce the boy they
loved, the lovers rebelled at the peril of their lives, as though it
were a question of defending an inviolable sanctuary' (Plutarch,
Erot. 929). Such was the force of homosexual love that it drove
men to rebellion, even when they had accepted the tyrant's sway.

But the real centre of homosexuality in Greece lay in education.
We must understand the situation. Educationally the home was
useless, for the mother was quite uneducated, and the father was
far too busy on the business of the city and the state to look after
his own son. The schools were looked down on, for the Greek
had an ingrained antipathy to the man who taught for pay.
What regularly happened was that a boy attached himself to
some fine man and was with him everywhere for the five years
from fifteen to twenty, learning to be a man. This is exactly where
the diametrically opposite possibilities emerged. It has been quite
correctly said that the essence of this kind of pederasty, the love
of youths, had nothing sexual in it at all. It produced a situation
where the youth admired the man and the man strove with all his
heart to be worthy of the admiration. But the trouble was that in
Greece, as Marrou puts it, such a relationship was always in
peril of degenerating into something murkier and more carnal.
Of course there were relationships which were noble, but such
was the state of Greek education that the Greek laws – even if
they were honoured more in the breach than in the observance –
officially banished adults from the school and the gymnasium
and allowed no teacher to be with a pupil after dark (Aeschines,
Against Timarchus 9.II). The disaster was that Greek education
was homosexual through and through.

The result was that the homosexual theme runs blatantly
through Greek literature. It is always said that Plato's *Symposium*
is one of the greatest works on love in all literature, but it must
be remembered that the love is homosexual love. Right at its
opening it begins: 'I know not any greater blessing to a young
man who is beginning life than a virtuous lover, and to the lover
than a beloved youth.' Aeschines says quite openly and bluntly:
'To be fond of good-looking and well-behaved lads is a natural
tendency of all sensitive and liberal minds.' In the *Feast of the
Lapiths*, Lucian writes – it is popular opinion that he is summariz-
ing, not his own – 'It were better not to need marriage, but to

follow Plato and Socrates and to be content with homosexual love.' In Lucian's *Hermotimus*, Socrates is asked: 'What is your attitude to pretty boys?' and the answer is: 'Their kisses shall be the guerdon for the bravest after they have done some splendid reckless deed!'

Even so pious a character as Sophocles was involved in a homosexual scandal. He met a youth. The youth laid his worn old shabby cloak on the ground for them to lie on. Sophocles covered them with his new and expensive cloak. When they rose, the youth ran off with the rich cloak of Sophocles and left him with his own rags (*Athenaeus* 605). And even after that Sophocles was still regarded as a model of piety.

Plato describes the conduct of homosexual lovers: 'They do everything that lovers do for boys they cherish, the prayers and the entreaties with which they support their suit, the oaths they swear, the nights they spend on the doorstep of the beloved one, the slavery they endure for his sake, which no real slave would put up with.' He describes their agitation at 'the sight of a lyre, a garment or any other object in constant use by their loved one, any of which is sufficient to call up the image of their darling even if he be absent' (*Symposium* 183 A, 73 D).

Plutarch is horrified at the whole business: 'Homosexuality resembles a son born late, of parents past their maturity, or a bastard child of darkness seeking to supplant his elder brother, legitimate love. For it was only yesterday that the homosexual came slinking into our gymnasia to view the games in which the youths first began to strip for exercise. Quite quietly he at first started touching and embracing the boys. But gradually in those arenas he grew wings and then there was no holding him. Nowadays he regularly insults conjugal love and drags it through the mud' (*Erotikos* 751 F). There were even male brothels and boy prostitutes walking the streets, although such youths were held in contempt.

It is a grim and dreadful picture, and this is the world into which the Christian Ethic came. But there is one thing to remember – and it is the most astonishing fact of all. In spite of everything, to the end of the day, in Greece, homosexuality might be universal but it was regarded as abnormal, *and it was never legal*. We have seen what Plato could say, and how he could act, but just about the last book that Plato wrote was the

Laws, and in it he banished homosexuality from his ideal state.

More than once in that work he attacks homosexuality. 'The intercourse of men with men, or of women with women is contrary to nature, and the bold attempt was originally due to unbridled lust' (636). 'How can we take precautions against the unnatural loves of either sex, from which innumerable evils have come upon individuals and cities? How shall we devise a remedy and a way of escape out of so great a danger?' (836). 'We must abolish altogether the connection of men with men' (841). It is altogether significant that Plato, himself a homosexual, writes: 'Who would ever think of establishing such a practice by law? Certainly no one who had in his mind the true image of law' (836). It is one of the most significant facts in this whole matter that the most homosexual society in history regarded it as the act of a madman to legalize homosexuality. The Greek was enslaved by homosexuality, but he knew he was a slave.

We turn now to the Roman world, that world of which Paul delivered his tremendous indictment in the Letter to the Romans (Romans 1:18–32). There was a time when homosexual practices were regarded with such horror that the centurion Laetorius Mergus, who had been guilty of them, committed suicide; but there came a time when in this as in so many other things Rome conquered Greece, and was then conquered morally by those whom she had defeated.

Homosexuality became worse in Rome than it ever became in Greece. In Rome it never had any good side to redeem it. As one writer has said of Roman homosexuality, it was naked, crude, coarse and filthy. It was even known for beautiful boys to be offered by their owners to bribe judges and to win the votes of influential people (Cicero, *To Atticus* 1.16).

The Roman victims of homosexuality were even worse treated than in Greece. They were castrated and made into eunuchs. Their physical development was deliberately retarded and halted so that they might remain with the soft bloom of youth upon them. Such slaves, Seneca tells us, were kept beardless by having their hair smoothed away or even pulled out by the roots.

There were in certain households such droves of them that they were classified by race and colouring, with care that the different classes might not get mixed up, and for instance, the straight-haired mingle with the curly-haired. You might meet them in some great man's travelling party with their faces covered or smeared with protective cosmetics lest the sun and the wind and the rain should destroy the bloom of their youth (Seneca, *Moral Letters* 47.95.123). Sometimes these men became so feminized that they were decked out in flounces, with a train and veil like a bride (Juvenal, *Satires* 2.124).

There is no better way of seeing the grip that homosexuality had on Roman society than to remember, as Gibbon notes, that fourteen out of the first fifteen Roman emperors were practising homosexuals, the one example of normality being Claudius. Nothing will show the state of Roman society better than simply to take some glances at that imperial catalogue of perversion.

Julius Caesar was notoriously the lover of King Nicomedes of Bithynia. 'The queen's rival,' Dolabella called him, 'and the inner partner of the royal couch.' When a general was given a triumph, the soldiers were permitted to sing rude and insulting songs, doubtless with the idea of keeping the conqueror humble. So the soldiers sang at Caesar's triumph: 'All the Gauls did Caesar vanquish; Nicomedes vanquished him' (Suetonius, *Caesar* 49).

Julius Caesar was succeeded by Augustus, perhaps the greatest name in Roman imperial history, and, so it was said by the scandal-mongers, Augustus persuaded Julius Caesar to adopt him and to nominate him as his heir by allowing Caesar to become his lover, and, again so it was said, he acquired a fortune of 300,000 sesterces by allowing Aulus Hirtius to possess his body (Suetonius, *Augustus* 48). Tiberius had his boys literally in droves and the things he practised with them were so perverted that they cannot even bear translation (Suetonius, *Tiberius* 43).

With Nero the thing reached its peak, or rather plumbed its depth. He took a boy called Sporus and had him castrated. He then publicly 'married' him, with all the ceremonies of an imperial wedding, leading him home in procession through the streets. He himself was 'married' to a freedman called Doryphorus, again with all the ceremonies of a true wedding, and later 'went so far as to imitate the cries and lamentations of a maiden being deflowered' (Suetonius, *Nero* 28, 29).

Even a good Emperor like Titus was notorious for 'his troops of catamites and eunuchs' (Suetonius, *Titus* 7). Hadrian had his favourite Antinous whom he took with him everywhere. When Antinous was drowned, Hadrian 'wept like a woman', and persuaded the Greeks to enrol Antinous among the gods (*Life of Hadrian* 14).

It is a dreadful catalogue of imperial perversion, and Roman society from the highest to the lowest was equally affected. This was the moral atmosphere and climate into which Christianity came.

But, once again, as in the case of Greece, we must note that the Romans never tried to legalize homosexuality. The law which forbade it was never repealed, and was used by Domitian at the end of the first century.

Homosexuality has always been a problem, and is very much in the foreground of problems at this present time.

What are we to say about it?

We may start with the fact that on the biblical evidence homosexuality is forbidden for the Christian. Those who seek to justify it will have to begin with the fact that there is no justification for their advocacy of it in the teaching of either the Old or the New Testament. But the matter is not just as simple as that. We have to do more than simply state a blunt and direct negative.

There are certain problems here. In the first place, there is a certain difficulty in discussing homosexuality at all. There is in homosexuality for most people a quality of 'unnaturalness', and of perversion. Fornication and adultery are 'natural' things, into which any person will very probably admit that he or she might conceivably fall. But at the mention of homosexuality many people wil¹ at once say: 'That is one thing – or even one sin – which I cannot understand.' The aura of unnaturalness makes discussion difficult.

But, in the second place, there is something which makes discussion even more difficult. There is more than one kind of homosexual. There is the homosexual who is a homosexual because he is so constructed; he did not choose to be so; he *is* so, through no fault of his own. He was, it can only be said, made that way. There is in him an abnormality which he did not acquire, but which is part of the essence of his being. It is not part of the things which he voluntarily chose; for him it is part of the given.

But even this kind of homosexual varies in his attitude. There are some homosexuals whose condition is an agony to them;

they know their difference from ordinary men. They know the desires which move them; and they are deeply distressed and desperately unhappy that they are as they are. Often in this kind of case a man knows his condition but in spite of it never practises homosexuality. To this kind of person his condition is a heart-break and his life a loneliness. But there are other homosexuals who welcome their condition as completely natural for them. They feel nothing wrong with it; they have no desire to be 'cured'. Homosexuals they are; they have no intention of con-cealing the fact. They do not regard themselves as abnormal; they practise homosexuality as for them the natural thing, and in certain cases they will even try to persuade others to become as they are. In the case of the first kind of homosexual, we might meet the man or woman and never know or guess his condition. In the case of the second kind of homosexual there will be no concealment. In the one case there is a deep and torturing sense of abnormality; in the other case there is no awareness that there is any abnormality at all, or, if there is awareness of difference, there is no admission of abnormality.

But there is a second kind of homosexual, and it is he who presents the problem. This kind of homosexual is not homosexual by nature, but by choice. He is the kind of person who, so to speak, has exhausted the thrill of the ordinary experience, and who quite deliberately sets out to find new experience in what for him is perversion. He is a homosexual 'for kicks', and there are cases in which such a person finds a further thrill in corrupting someone else into his own perversion. It would be difficult to find any justification for this kind of person, or to feel any sympathy for him. For the homosexual who is a homosexual because he cannot help it, there can be nothing but sympathy and nothing but the attempt to understand; for the person who practises homosexuality simply to extract a new thrill from the unusual and the perverted there can be nothing but condemna-tion.

As things are, as a result of the Wolfenden Report, homosexual practices in private between consenting adults are legalized. At least part of the reason for this legalization was the ease with which homosexuals were previously blackmailed. It was com-mon for the homosexual to be inveigled into homosexual practices by unscrupulous persons, who then used the relationship so engaged in as a means of blackmail. The person so black-mailed was in an impossible position, because he could not seek the protection of the law without admitting that he himself was a breaker of the law, and without the most distressing publicity. By legalizing homosexuality between adults this open door to blackmail was closed; but the report never at any time intended a general legalization of homosexual practices, and for the homosexual to interfere with young boys is still illegal.

What are we to say about this, not so much from the point of view of the law of the land, as of the Christian Ethic? And in whatever we say we must remember the difference between the man who is essentially a homosexual and the man for whom homosexual practices are a deliberate perversion of themselves and a corruption of others.

I do not think that we can escape from beginning with the fact that, if the authority of the Bible is to be accepted, homosexual practices are forbidden as wrong. This would seem to mean, from the biblical point of view, that even if it is impossible to blame a man for *being* homosexual, it is still necessary to blame him for *practising* homosexuality.

Two things are clear. The homosexuality of deliberate perversion must remain illegal and condemned. And secondly the deliberate propagation of homosexual practices, the attempt to persuade people to become homosexuals, what one may call the advertising of homosexuality, must remain forbidden. Up to this point there can be no real doubt as to what the Christian attitude must be. But the question of what the Christian Ethic has to say about the action of the man who is essentially and by nature homosexual is much more difficult. The law has now provided for this man; but that which is legal is not necessarily Christian. There is no law which legally forbids a man to live with a mistress, but the Christian Ethic would not accept such a situation.

We may begin by saying three things. The first we have already stated. If we accept the authority of the Bible, homosexual practices are forbidden. The person who accepts the authority of the Bible cannot begin by appealing to the fact that homosexual practices are legal under the legal code of this country; he will have to begin by putting himself right with the ethic of the book which, if he is a Christian, he accepts as the supreme rule of faith and life. Second, it seems both wrong and unreasonable to condemn a man for being that which he cannot help being. But it could be answered that to condemn homosexual practices is not to condemn a man for being what he cannot help being; it is to condemn him for doing that which he can help doing, even being such as he is. The normality of life is only guaranteed by not allowing those who have abnormal tastes to gratify them. And yet to take this point of view means that the homosexual is debarred from the fellowship and the companionship which are the very foundation of life, even with people like himself. Thirdly, if a person is found guilty of the homosexual practices which are still forbidden, a prison sentence seems an entirely inappropriate punishment, for, as someone has said, to send a homosexual to prison is like locking up an alcoholic in a distillery. This is a case in which not punishment but cure must surely be the aim. What then shall we say of this? Whatever we say, we must say tentatively, not so much as a solution, as the sketch of the way to a solution.

(i) We have to begin with the admission that homosexuality is an abnormal condition. This in the first place has to be accepted.

(ii) If it is an abnormal condition, the practices which it involves must be strictly controlled. It is not something which can be freely practised or propagated. The abnormal must always be controlled. It must not be allowed to become an increasing part of life.

(iii) In cases in which it is deliberate perversion and in which it involves deliberate corruption, it must never be legalized, and it must be dealt with as any other crime against society is dealt with.

(iv) In cases where it is part of a person's being three things may be said. (a) The homosexual must be helped to see that his is an abnormal condition. (b) He must be persuaded that no one is condemning him for being as he is, but at the same time he must be encouraged to seek a cure, by physical or by psychiatric treatment, or by both. (c) Already treatments exist, and research towards the discovery of more effective treatment must continue to be sought.

(v) In the cases in which no cure is possible homosexuals who associate for the only human relationship they know must be regarded with sympathy and understanding, in the awareness that those of us who have never known this problem must be hesitant to condemn something which is outside our experience, and which we cannot understand.

It would not be possible to leave the discussion of the sexual and the marriage relationships of men and women without some mention of birth control and family planning, especially in view of the very different ways in which the Protestant and the Roman Catholic Churches regard this matter.

As far as the Protestant Church and the practice of ordinary people is concerned, it may well be claimed that we are dealing with a *fait accompli*, with something whose legitimacy is not questioned and with something which in one form or another is universally practised.

In 1921 a voluntary, privately run clinic was opened in London. There were patients who had had as many as thirteen children with miscarriages in addition. A woman of thirty-three had had seven children and four miscarriages. But in 1881 the birth-rate in Hampstead was 30 per thousand; in 1911 it was 17.5. The Royal Commission on Population Report, presented to Parliament in 1949, has some very interesting statistics. The national birth-rate fell from 35 per thousand in 1878 to 14.9 per thousand in 1933. The size of the average family fell from 5.71 children per family in 1841 to 2.19 children in 1929. The Report has a comparative table of the number of children in marriages which took place about 1860 and in marriages which took place in 1925:

Number of children born	In marriages which took place about 1860 Per cent	In marriages which took place in 1925 Per cent
0	9	17
1	5	25
2	6	25
3	8	14
4	9	8
5	10	5
6	10	3
7	10	2
8	9	1
9	8	0.6
10	6	0.4
Over 10	10	0.3

The drop in the size of families is clear and obvious.

It is clear that more and more birth control of some kind was being practised; and yet it is the fact that even as late as 1878 the very mention of birth control, even in medical journals, was something which was regarded as intolerable. But there were factors in the situation which forced this matter on the attention of the country. A good account of the situation and the way in which things moved is given in *The Fight for Acceptance, a History of Contraception*, by C. Wood and B. Suitters. I am indebted to this volume for very many of the facts that I have quoted, although the conclusions are my own.

(a) There was the insistence of Malthus that 'the realization of a happy society will always be hindered by the miseries consequent on the tendency of population to increase faster than the means of subsistence.' Malthus underlined the threat of a too quickly growing population.

(b) There was the growing emancipation of women. The situation in which up to middle age a woman's life was entirely occupied in carrying, bearing or feeding a child could not for ever be tolerated. There was bound to be a feminine revolt. Under the conditions of unlimited child-bearing a woman by the age of forty could be an old woman, with strength and beauty gone from her.

(c) There were the social conditions under which the poor, who had the greatest number of children, were forced to live. Wood and Suitters quote passages from the reports of London's first Medical Officer of Health. Here is his description of London housing:

> 'Courts and alleys with low, dark, filthy tenements, hemmed in on all sides by higher buildings, having no possibility of any current of air, and (worst of all) sometimes constructed back to back, as to forbid the advantage of double windows or back doors, and thus to render the house as perfect a cul-de-sac out of the court as the court is a cul-de-sac out of the next thoroughfare.'

It was, the report goes on,

> 'no uncommon thing, in twelve feet square or less, to find three or four families styed together (perhaps with infectious diseases among them), filling the same space night and day – men, women and children in the promiscuous intimacy of

cattle. . . . Whatever is morally hideous and savage in the scene – whatever contrasts it offers to the superficial magnificence of the metropolis – whatever profligacy it implies and continues – whatever recklessness and obscene brutality arises from it – whatever deep injury it inflicts on the community – whatever debasement or abolition of God's image in men's hearts is tokened by it – these matters belong not to my office. Only because of the physical suffering am I entitled to speak, only because pestilence is forever within the circle; only because Death so largely comforts these poor orphans of civilization.'

He goes on to describe others, even worse off 'renting the twentieth straw-heap in some lightless fever-bin . . . squatting among rotting soakage . . . breathing from the cess-pool and the sewer'. In a world like that it was inevitable that it should be asked if children should be brought into it at all.

(d) There was the apparent disregard of the child. It was, for instance, not until 1875 that Parliament made it illegal to use small boys as living brushes to sweep chimneys. Incredibly, in the year 1839 Parliament allocated £30,000 for national education and £70,000 for the building of royal stables and kennels at Windsor. It was no kind of society into which to bring a child.

One of the earliest pioneers was Francis Place. He had been born in a debtor's prison, of which his father was keeper. He had known unemployment and near-starvation, but he had become successful and self-educated. Malthus had had nothing to suggest, except to delay marriage and to practise moral restraint, as he called it. Place in print advocated the use of the vaginal tampon; but the medical and the social establishment branded the leaflets he published as 'The Diabolical Handbills'. His main contribution was made in his *Illustrations and Proofs of the Principle of Population*, published in 1822. At the age of seventeen John Stuart Mill was arrested for distributing birth control leaflets in a market-place.

The real clash came in 1877. In that year Charles Bradlaugh and Annie Besant published an English edition of Charles Knowlton's American production *Fruits of Philosophy*. The book had been in circulation for forty years. It was, as Wood and Suitters say, already a rather old-fashioned and boring book; but the prosecution went on. The indictment is in amazing terms:

The Jurors for our Lady the Queen, upon their oath present that Charles Bradlaugh and Annie Besant unlawfully and wickedly devising and contriving and intending, as much as in them lay, to vitiate and corupt the morals as well of youth as of divers other liege subjects of our said Lady the Queen, and to incite and encourage the said liege subjects to indecent, obscene, unnatural, and immoral practices, and bring them to a state of wickedness, lewdness and debauchery, therefore, to wit, on the 24th day of March, 1877, in the City of London, and within the Jurisdiction of the Central Criminal Court, unlawfully, wickedly, knowingly, willfully, and designedly did print, publish, sell, and utter a certain indecent, lewd, filthy, and obscene libel, to wit, a certain indecent, lewd, filthy, bawdy, and obscene book, called 'Fruits of Philosophy' thereby contaminating, vitiating, and corrupting the morals as well of youth as of other liege subjects of our said Lady the Queen, and bringing the said liege subjects to a state of wickedness, lewdness, debauchery, and immorality, in contempt of our said Lady the Queen and her laws, to the evil and pernicious example of all others in the like case offending, and against the peace of our said Lady the Queen, her crown and dignity.

Such was the horrified voice of the establishment against anything that had to do with birth control. Charles Bradlaugh and Annie Besant were found guilty, but the verdict was reversed and the sentence was never carried out because of a technical error in the indictment.

The opposition to birth control based itself on two charges. First, there was the charge that to teach and to provide methods and means of birth control was to open the way to unchastity, and even to invite it. As a certain Dr Routh said: 'It must tend to demoralize women. If you teach them vicious habits, and a way to sin, without detection, how can you assure yourself of their fidelity when assailed by a fascinating seducer, and why may not even the unmarried taste of forbidden pleasures also; so that your future wife shall have been defiled ere you knew her?' As for men, it will give them 'general nervous prostration, mental decay, loss of memory, intense cardiac palpitations, mania and conditions which lead to suicide'. So then in the first place methods of birth control were held to be calculated to destroy chastity and in the second place were regarded as ruinous to health.

But the conventions were fighting a losing battle. By 1913 the members of the Malthusian League were preaching birth control at the street corners, and distributing leaflets. By 1921 private clinics were opened in London by the Malthusian League, and by the Society for Constructive Birth Control and Racial Progress, led by the famous Marie Stopes and financed by her husband H. V. Roe, famous in the world of aviation. By 1925 the movement first reached the provinces in Wolverhampton. In 1921 the supporters of birth control received powerful support. The famous doctor, the king's physician, Lord Dawson of Penn was invited to address the Church Congress in Birmingham. He told them bluntly that artificial birth control was desirable on social, medical and personal grounds. He called on them to break with the old traditional views in the light of modern knowledge and conditions. 'Birth control,' he said, 'is here to stay.'

The early providers of private clinics never meant the private clinic movement to be extended. They meant it to be no more than an introduction to the time when the state would take over. And soon the battle was won and the opposition was defeated, and in 1930 the Ministry of Health itself began to provide clinics with instruction and treatment, at least, in the first place, in necessary cases. It can be seen how long and often how bitter the fight was, and how very recent the acceptance of birth control has been.

The methods of birth control have been many and varied. There have been those which were the products of sheer magic and superstition. Pliny the Elder says that the best method he had found was to wear as an amulet the worms taken from the body of a hairy spider. Aetios of Amida writing in the sixth century speaks of amulets such as a cat's liver worn in a tube on the left foot, or the testicles of a cat worn in a tube around the navel, or part of the womb of a lioness encased in an ivory tube. There were methods of primitive medicine, which were half magic. Willow leaves beaten small and taken in water were said to prevent conception, as was asparagus, either eaten or worn as an amulet. Aristotle recommended the use of oil to cover the cervix and to coat the inside of the vagina. Dioscorides recommended pessaries made of herbs, pepper, sword-shaped sickle wort, and peppermint juice. Aspasia recommended a wool tampon soaked with herbs, pine bark, nut galls, myrrh and wine.

There were what might be called natural methods. There was simple continence and self-control. There was withdrawal, coitus interruptus, which goes right back to Onan and biblical times (Genesis 38:7–10), and which is therefore sometimes called Onanism. There was the method of the Oneida community, founded in 1844 by John Humphrey Noyes. The Oneida community was an experiment in group marriage. In it a method of intercourse was practised in which the man and the woman remained in union for an hour and more; and in this union the woman had her orgasm, but the man was so disciplined in self-control that he never had his orgasm; and detumescence took place in the vagina. Using this method, such intercourse was allowed between any members of the community. When it was decided that a couple should from their physical and mental and characteristic excellence produce a child the normal method of intercourse was used, so that the begetting and bearing of children was closely controlled. It is said that the Roman Catholic Church allows this method of birth control, when it is exercised between man and wife.

There have been violent and unnatural methods of achieving birth control. The Russian sect of the Skoptzies took such texts as Matthew 19:12 which speaks of those who made themselves eunuchs for the sake of the kingdom of heaven, and Luke 23:29 where there is pronounced a blessing on the sterile, the barren. On the basis of these texts they practised self-mutilation, calling the male genital organs 'the keys of hell', and the female 'the keys of the abyss'.

In due time there came developments of the tampon, the pessary, the cervical cap, the vaginal diaphragm, the condom. In modern times, in our own day, there has been a very considerable increase in voluntary sterilization, the tying of the Fallopian tubes in the case of women, vasectomy in the case of men. But by far the most important event in modern times was the arrival of the oral contraceptive pill. The pill very rarely has its dangers; still more rarely it fails in its effect; in some cases its psychological effects have been unhappy; but broadly speaking it opened the way of contraception to all.

Before we end by asking what the Christian attitude to this whole question is, it will be wise to ask how the oral contraceptive pill came into being, and to ask just what it does.

The idea of the pill was born in 1950. Margaret Sanger was one of the dynamic forces in the struggle for birth control in America. In that year she met Gregory Pincus, the Director of the Worcester Foundation for Experimental Biology. She wanted him to devise some method of birth control which would be both safe and universally effective. Gregory Pincus saw that the real answer was not, so to speak, to block conception, but effectively to limit fertility. How could that be done? It could be done by the prevention of ovulation in the woman by the use of some substance taken by the mouth. If the eggs can be prevented from leaving the ovaries, they cannot be fertilized.

He began with the fact that a pregnant woman does not ovulate. Now a pregnant woman's blood contains large quantities of a hormone called progesterone. So the answer seemed to lie in progesterone. The difficulty was to obtain progesterone in anything but minute quantities. It was literally true that it took tons of sows' ovaries, obtained from the slaughter-houses, to produce some hundredths of an ounce of progesterone. But with the little which could be produced it was found that progesterone did work with animals, with rabbits and rats.

It so happens that the steroids occur in plants as well as in animal tissues; and it might be possible, so it was believed, to extract progesterone from plants. And now comes the extraordinary story of Professor Russell Marker. He found a way of extracting progesterone from a certain plant, but the plant itself was very rare. He set out to search the world for it. In the jungles of Veracruz in Mexico he found a plant which the Mexicans called 'the black-headed one', which could be a source for his material. No drug firm was interested; so he set up his own factory in Mexico City, and set out to extract progesterone with such labour as he could obtain. Within three years he had produced four pounds of it, which is very much better than hundredths of ounces. So experimental work with progesterone became possible. It had still to be proved that progesterone, given by mouth, effectively limited fertility. It so happened that Dr John Rock of Harvard was engaged on an experiment in which progesterone was being given to a group of a hundred women in conjunction with another female sex hormone, oestrogen. The oestrogen was withheld from certain volunteers, and the effect of progesterone was studied. It was found to be largely but not universally effective.

During the 1950's the chemists had been busy producing not only progesterone, but also a large number of substances – more than two hundred of them – chemically closely related to it. These substances were called gestagens. Three of these, when taken by mouth, proved to be very powerful in limiting fertility. One of them called norethynodrel became the basis of the first oral contraceptive pill. Its one drawback was that it disturbed the cycle of menstruation, and erratic menstruation was an awkward problem. The problem was solved by combining the synthetic gestagen with synthetic oestrogen. And it was this combination which was so spectacularly effective in the Puerto Rican experiment of 1956. There have been refinements in the process, but that is a simplified account of how the scientists found a combination of synthetic drugs which prevented ovulation, and which therefore also prevented conception.

What then is the Christian to say to all this? Let us for the moment leave the principle on one side and look at the method. The Christian will not accept self-mutilation. The Christian will accept necessary abortion, but will not accept abortion as the normal method of merely getting rid of an unwanted child. There may be times when sterilization is almost a necessity. It is far better to sterilize than to allow people to produce more and more children who are defective in mind or in body. If people are living in difficult circumstances, or if they are of such low intelligence that they cannot be depended on correctly to take the pill or to use any other means, then sterilization is perfectly justified. There are cases when the pill produces in women such physical or psychological disturbances so that some form of sterilization either of husband or of wife may well be preferable. Mechanical means of contraception have the disadvantage that people may forget to use them. Sheer self-control or the confining of intercourse to the 'safe' period in the woman's cycle both demand a self-discipline which not everyone has, and which in anyone may on occasion fail. For most people the pill will be the easiest and the best and the most effective method. But is any method right for the Christian? Apart from anything else, the attitude of the Roman Catholic Church demands that we ask this question.

(a) On only one ground can contraception be regarded as essentially wrong. It is only wrong if the only function of sexual intercourse is to produce a child. I do not think that that view can be held. It is true that the ultimate reason for the existence of the sex instinct is to ensure the continuance of the race; but it is also true that sexual intercourse is the deepest and the most fundamental expression of love; it is literally consummation. It can surely express the ultimate union of love as well as the desire to beget a child.

(b) To provide the means of contraception and to approve of them has in this and in every other generation been declared to be an opening of the door to immorality. It has simply to be answered that any drug and any process can be misused; but that is no reason for not using it at all. If everything in life which has a risk in it was removed, there would be very little left. But it is to be laid down for the Christian Ethic that contraception must be within marriage.

(c) There can be no doubt that the limitation of families is a duty in a world which is in serious danger of over-population. Some means of population limitation is essential.

(d) There is no doubt that for parents to produce more children than they can provide with a proper chance in life is an act of grave irresponsibility. The limitation of the family to the number which we can afford is a reasonable action.

(e) The one thing which we must guard against is a purely selfish limitation of the family. A limitation of the family in the interests of increased luxury and increased 'freedom' is a selfish thing, and therefore a wrong thing.

On the balance it may well be that we should thank God for the scientific and medical discoveries which have made possible both family planning and the expression of love.

CHAPTER NINE

THE EIGHTH COMMANDMENT

The Condemnation of the Thief

The eighth commandment is: 'You shall not steal' (Exodus 20: 13). This is what might be called a basic commandment. It is not only a necessary part of the Christian Ethic; it is a necessary part of any agreement to live together. It is part of the foundations of any society, and without obedience to it any society would be impossible.

It is frequently quoted and repeated in the Bible. It is there again in Leviticus 19:11 and in Deuteronomy 5:19. When the prophets are rebuking the sins and the disobedience of Israel, theft and stealing again and again come under their condemnation. The curse is on him who steals, and he will be cut off (Zechariah 5:3). If the wicked wishes to live, the first thing he must do is to restore that which he has stolen (Ezekiel 33:15). It is a terrible thing to have begotten a son who is a robber (Ezekiel 18:10). The condemnation is that the people of this land have practised extortion and committed robbery (Ezekiel 22:29). Amos condemns those who store up violence and robbery (Amos 3:10). Isaiah speaks of the princes who are the companions of thieves (Isaiah 1:23). Prophet and lawgiver alike show the prevalence of stealing and the horror of it.

The law of the Old Testament does not simply condemn stealing: it has much to say about the penalty for it. The law of the Old Testament never fails to insist that restitution has to be made; in fact, the restitution is usually the punishment. One of the notable features of the Old Testament law is that it is just as eager to see that the victim is compensated as that the criminal is punished.

If a sheep or an ox is stolen and is then killed and sold, the thief must pay back five oxen or four sheep and, if he cannot, he himself will be sold to pay the debt. If the animal is recoverable alive, the thief must pay back double (Exodus 22:1–4). According to the Proverbs (6:30–31) that which is stolen must be restored sevenfold. If a thing is taken fraudulently from anyone, it must be repaid in full plus one-fifth of its value (Numbers 5:7).

There are similar detailed regulations regarding restitution in connection with the damage or the loss of personal property. If a man damages another man's vineyard or field by allowing his animals to break into it or to graze on it, he is bound to make restitution of the best that he has (Exodus 22:5). If anything has been entrusted to a person, or deposited with a person, and that thing is either lost or stolen, then the person with whom it has been deposited must restore twice its value, if he is to blame (Exodus 22:7). In one particular instance the punishment for theft is death. That is in the case of the theft of a human being. It did sometimes happen that a person was kidnapped or abducted, that is, so to speak, 'stolen', and then sold into slavery; and the penalty for stealing a person is death (Exodus 21:16; Deuteronomy 24:7).

The Jewish law regarded theft as a serious offence, and everywhere it is concerned equally with the punishment of the criminal and with the restitution of the thing stolen.

In Rome and Greece the law dealt very severely with theft. There were three places where theft was very prevalent – in the gymnasia, in the public baths, and at the docks. The stealing of the clothes of people who were in the baths or the gymnasia, or the theft of their belongings at such a time was very common. Pilfering from the docks and warehouses was as big a problem then as it is now. And Greek and Roman law punished such theft by death. In both classical law and Jewish law theft by night was considered doubly criminal; and in Jewish law it was laid down that, if a robber by night was killed by a householder in defence of his property, no guilt attached to the householder (Exodus 22:2).

In our present situation theft is still a serious and an antisocial crime. Burglary and robbery, breaking into houses, what may be termed brigandage on the roads and on the railways, are things about which there is no argument. No one is going to dispute that these are crimes, that those who commit them are criminals, and that punishment is necessary, and must for the sake of society be justly inflicted. But there are today certain new elements in the situation.

(i) It is certainly true that today the temptation to theft has become very much greater, and the chances to steal are very much more numerous. This is so because of the 'open' shop and market. Instead of goods behind a counter, asked for, and supplied by a shop assistant, there is the open shop in which the goods are displayed, and in which the shopper takes what he or she wants, and pays on leaving the shop. This system proves an overwhelming temptation to a large number of people. And it is certain that more of this kind of theft goes undetected than is detected.

In close connection with this is the attitude which regards theft in such places as kleptomania rather than theft. The kleptomaniac is under compulsion to take, and will often collect things, quite independently of their use or value. Thus the thief is regarded as a person abnormal and psychologically ill rather than as a criminal. It is perhaps neither unkind nor unjust to say that a good deal of such theft is just plain theft, even if it be disguised under another name, although this is not to say that there are not genuine cases of compulsive taking, which have been caused by the new shopping conditions.

(ii) What is much more serious is that there is a kind of theft today which is regarded as clever, and which brings hardly any social stigma with it. This is the kind of theft which regards public authorities as fair game for anyone who can outwit them.

There are, for instance, people who regard it as clever to travel by bus or by rail without paying the fare. If they were called thieves, they would be shocked and offended – but theft it is. There are people, and there are probably even more of them, who regard the evasion of the payment of income tax as something which is perfectly natural. They would not hesitate to falsify their returns and to misstate their expenses. The state is regarded as an enemy which any man may outwit, if he can. But again, this, to give it its real name, is nothing other than theft. A swindle remains a swindle no matter against whom it may be carried out, and no matter how heavy tax conditions may be. In the same category is the kind of so-called cleverness which seeks to evade the payment of customs duty on articles brought in from abroad. The concealment of articles brought into the country is a common thing. But that too is theft.

But perhaps the most serious thing is theft from an employer. Thefts at the docks, thefts in factories and in shipyards and in public works, are notoriously common. Nor is this confined to industry. In an office an employee may use the notepaper, take the stamps, use the telephone of his employer for private and personal purposes. There is a kind of creeping dishonesty in all kinds of work; and the person who is scrupulously honest in these things may well find himself in a small minority and an unpopular minority too. Very often the young person who goes to work after being brought up in a Christian home and in the Church and in Christian organizations finds himself shocked by what he sees going on. He sees it as almost the normal thing for employees to take what they want for their own purposes, when and where they can.

The trouble about this is that the things involved may be small things. The things may look unimportant and hardly worth worrying about. But it is symptomatic of a situation in which strict and scrupulous honesty is out of fashion. One of the rarest things in modern society is to carry out the Christian Ethic of absolute honesty in a society in which strict honesty has almost ceased to be a virtue. Many a person who would be shocked at being identified with people who rob banks, or burgle houses, or steal from shops, is, in fact, daily guilty of the fault of annexing property, even if it be small and apparently unimportant, to which he has no right. There are few areas of conduct in which the Christian example is more important and more difficult to give. The Christian witness in this is clamantly necessary if this wave of petty dishonesty is to be halted.

There are thefts other than the theft of material things, and many a person who would never be guilty of material theft is frequently guilty of them, and they are such that they are the most serious thefts of all.

(i) There is the theft of *time*. When a man enters into employment, he also enters into a contract, be it written or be it understood, in which he undertakes to give his employer so much of his time in return for so much pay. He may, for instance, engage to work for eight hours a day. It may well be that, of all thefts, the theft of time is most common. It is a commonplace for people to start late; it is an almost universal custom to finish early; and the number of people who do not waste at least some part of the time during which they are supposed to be working is very small indeed. And, even when most of us are working, we put nothing like our maximum effort into the work.

There are very few people who are not guilty of the theft of time and of effort from the people to whom they have contracted to give their time and their effort. Although it is far from being true of every worker, it is true of many that their aim is to do as little as possible and to get as much as possible.

One of the problems which confront the Christian at work is precisely the fact that, if he did work as hard, as conscientiously and as fast as he could, he would almost certainly find that he had caused far more trouble than anything else. Restriction of work is much more common than encouragement of work, and there is here a problem for a Christian which is not easy to solve.

(ii) There is such a thing as the theft of *innocence*. There is a kind of person who seduces others into sin. When Robert Burns went as a young man to Irvine to learn flax-dressing, he fell in with a certain man who taught him a good deal about reckless living. Afterwards Burns said of him: 'His friendship did me a mischief.' There are those whose alleged friendship does others a mischief.

It is the simple and the tragic fact that the invitation to sin often, perhaps oftenest of all, comes from the invitation of some fellow human being. It is by some so-called friend that a young person may receive the initial push that sets him on the pathway whose end is ruin. The teaching of Jesus is clear about one thing in regard to this – it is serious to sin oneself, but it is still more serious to teach someone else to sin. Jesus said: 'Whoever causes one of these little ones who believe in me to sin, it would be better for him to have a great millstone fastened round his neck and to be drowned in the depth of the sea' (Matthew 18:5; Mark 9:42; Luke 17:1–2). To rob a person of his or her innocence is one of the most serious sins in the sight of Jesus Christ.

(iii) There is such a thing as the theft of a person's *character or good name*. The recklessness with which people repeat stories about other people without ever checking them is an astonishing thing. There seems to be in human nature something which takes a delight in hearing and repeating that which is discreditable to others. Many a person's good name is stolen away in gossip over the teacups, and harm done in such a way is almost impossible to undo, for it is easy to start a story and almost impossible to stop it. As the proverb has it, there are three things which never come back, the spent arrow, the lost opportunity and the spoken word. And it is further true that there is no more serious wrong that we can do to any man than to rob him of his good name. As Shakespeare wrote in *Othello*:

Good name in man and woman, dear my lord,
Is the immediate jewel of their souls,
Who steals my purse, steals trash; 'tis something, nothing;
'Twas mine, 'tis his and has been slave to thousands;
But he that filches from me my good name
Robs me of that which not enriches him,
And makes me poor indeed.

To listen to the malicious story is almost, if not quite, as bad as to repeat it. It might be well that if, when we were told some discreditable story of someone, we were to say; 'Let us go straight round and ask the person involved if this is true.' It might well be that, more often than not, the story-teller would be unwilling to accept the challenge.

(iv) There remains one thing to say. It has sometimes been said that all private property is theft. The saying, 'Property is theft', occurs in the works of Pierre Joseph Proudhon. The idea is that no man has any right to possess anything, and that everything belongs to the community. For the Christian there is a sense in which this is true and a sense in which it is not true. There are very many parables of Jesus in which the whole point and the whole standard of judgment is the way in which a man uses such possessions as he has. It is assumed that he will have them; he is not in the least condemned for having them; the praise or the condemnation comes from the way in which he uses them.

The only occasion when Jesus said that a man must divest himself of all his property was in his encounter with the rich young ruler. This young man claimed to have kept all the commandments. And Jesus told him that the one thing he still needed was to sell all that he had and to give the proceeds to the poor (Mark 10:17–22; Matthew 19:16–30; Luke 18:18–30). Ever since that parable first became known, there has been argument as to whether or not Jesus was laying down a universal rule.

The real meaning of Jesus' command can be seen in the version of this incident which appears in the lost Gospel according to the Hebrews. That Gospel's version of this story is preserved in

Origen's *Commentary on Matthew*. The story begins in the same way with the rich man claiming to have kept the commandments. Jesus answers him: 'Go, sell all that you have, and distribute it to the poor.' The rich man began to scratch his head, for the answer displeased him. And the Lord said to him: 'How can you say, I have kept the law and the prophets? For it is written in the law, You must love your neighbour as yourself. But, as you can very well see, many of your fellowmen, who are descendants of Abraham, just the same as you are, are clothed in rags and dying of hunger, and your house is packed with good things, and not a single thing goes out of it to them.' This man is commanded to sell his goods, because he has been using them absolutely and completely selfishly, with never a thought for anyone less fortunate than himself.

Here, then, is the point. Private property is not in the least wrong, when the owner of it remembers that he posseses it, not only to use it for himself, but also to use it for others. But private property is a kind of theft when a man uses it for nothing but his own pleasure and his own gratification, with never a thought for anyone else. It is not the property but the selfishness which constitutes the theft.

So then, all theft is forbidden. And even if we never steal any material thing, we may still be guilty of breaking this commandment by stealing time which rightly belongs to someone else, by stealing someone's good name with a gossiping tongue, and by using selfishly that which we should share with those who have less than we have.

There are still certain other things which arise in the day-to-day dealing of men with each other which are in principle theft. (i) In the first place there is *debt*. 'Owe no one anything,' says Paul (Romans 13:8), and that is in fact a Christian principle.

Debt is theft in this sense – it is a withholding from a man that which is his due. There may be times when this is not, as it were, fatally serious; but it happens again and again in modern circumstances that a small tradesman has been driven out of business altogether simply because there are customers who will not pay their debts. I have myself known of a skilled craftsman with a small business who had to give up his business and take much less skilled employment in someone else's business, while there were people who, collectively, owed him more than £2,000.

This kind of debt is theft, because there are times when it can take a man's livelihood away from him.

The Bible is always supremely interested in the rights of the man for whom life is a struggle, the man who is living almost on the borderline of starvation. Twice the Bible lays down the rights of such a man. 'You shall not oppress a hired servant who is poor and needy, whether he is one of your brethren or one of the sojourners who are in your land within your towns; you shall give him his hire on the day he earns it, before the sun goes down (for he is poor, and sets his heart upon it); lest he cry against you to the Lord, and it be sin in you' (Deuteronomy 24:14-15). 'The wages of a hired servant shall not remain with you all night until the morning.' And that commandment is prefaced with another commandment: 'You shall not oppress your neighbour or rob him' (Leviticus 19:13). In James it is said of the rich who failed to pay their workmen their wages that they will find that the money they did not pay will be evidence against them when they are judged (James 5:4). The failure to pay a man that which is his due, especially if he is a poor man and the payment means much to him, is a kind of robbery.

There was a time when debt was much more disgraceful than it now is. There is a change – and a dangerous change in emphasis now. The emphasis was once on the obligation of earning what one wanted; the emphasis is now much more on the right to possess what one wants. And in such a state of society the fact that debt is a kind of theft needs to be stressed.

(ii) There is in the Law of the Old Testament a three times repeated prohibition of lending money at interest, at least to a fellow Jew. It occurs in Exodus (22:25): 'If you lend money to any of my people with you who is poor, you shall not be to him as a creditor, and you shall not exact interest from him.' It is repeated in Leviticus (25:36–37): 'Take no interest from him (that is, your brother who is in poverty) or increase, but fear your God; that your brother may live beside you. You shall not lend him your money at interest, nor give him your food for profit.' It is repeated again in Deuteronomy (23:19–20): 'You shall not lend upon interest to your brother, interest on money, interest on victuals, interest on anything that is lent for interest. To a foreigner you may lend upon interest, but to your brother you shall not lend upon interest; that the Lord your God may bless you in all that you undertake in the land which you are entering to take possession of.' The Deuteronomy version of this particular law is one of the less happy developments of the law, for it allows the Jew to do to the Gentile what he may not do to a fellow Jew. When Jews have selfishly interpreted a passage like this, it has inevitably gained them unpopularity, for it has seemed to give them the right to use one law to each other and another to the Gentile. But the purely selfish interpretation is not in accordance with the highest spirit of Jewish law.

Is this a total prohibition of lending money at interest? The real principle of this goes much deeper than that. It is not simply a prohibition of lending at interest; it is the commandment of God that no man must ever take advantage of his brother's misfortune. No man must, to put it in modern language, cash in on his brother's need. There are times when it is possible to drive a hard bargain, or to charge a high price, simply because someone desperately needs something. The law of the Bible is that no one must ever take advantage of another man's need, and use that need for his own profit and enrichment.

In this the conduct of the medical profession is an example to all. If any doctor or surgeon or scientist discovers a cure for, let us say, cancer or leukaemia, he could, if he so chose, make his fortune of it. But if ever such a cure is discovered, the man who discovers it will certainly not cash in on it. It will immediately become available for all – and available free. To make profit from the need of another is forbidden.

(iii) There is one further frequently repeated commandment in the Law of the Old Testament – the commandment to have just scales and balances and measurements. It is an extraordinary thing that no fewer than, at least, five times, the Old Testament states this law. We get it in Leviticus (19:35–36): 'You shall do no wrong in judgment, in measures of length or weight or quantity. You shall have just balances, just weights, a just ephah, and a just hin.' (The last two are cubic capacity measures.) It is repeated in Deuteronomy (25:13–15): 'You shall not have in your bag two kinds of weights, a large and a small. You shall not have in your house two kinds of measures, a large and a small. A full and just weight you shall have, a full and just measure you shall have; that your days may be prolonged in the land which the Lord your God gives you. For all who do such things, all who act dishonestly, are an abomination to the Lord your God.' The injunction is repeated twice in Proverbs (11:1; 20:23): 'A false balance is an abomination to the Lord, but a just weight is his delight.' 'Diverse weights are an abomination to the Lord, and false scales are not good.' It is part of Amos' condemnation of those who are forsaking God that they 'make the ephah small and the shekel great, and deal deceitfully with false balances.' (Amos 8:5).

It may seem a quite extraordinary thing that the Bible should take up so much space to speak about weights and measures, and the accuracy of scales and containers and units of measurement. It is intensely significant that the assumption is that God is interested in these things, and that careful justice and meticulous honesty in these things is the natural and essential expression of true religion.

The Bible lays it down that there is something badly wrong with the religion of the man who will worship on the Sunday and who will then go out to be a careless or a dishonest tradesman, robbing others by offering less than his best, or a man in any kind of business indulging in smart practice to make a quick profit, or a clever opportunist using someone's need as a chance to make more for himself, or an employer who is blind and unsympathetic to his employees' needs.

Perhaps we regarded the commandment which forbids stealing as having no relevance to us in our respectability. Perhaps now we may have to open our eyes to the fact that it applies to us too.

CHAPTER TEN

THE NINTH COMMANDMENT

The Truth, the whole Truth, and nothing but the Truth

The ninth commandment runs: 'You shall not bear false witness against your neighbour' (Exodus 20:16), and it is repeated in the same form in English in Deuteronomy 5:20. Although the

English form is in both cases *false* witness, the Hebrew is different. In the Exodus version the meaning is *lying* or *untrue*; in the Deuteronomy version the meaning is *insincere*, *empty*, *frivolous*. The meaning is not essentially different, but it might be said that the Exodus version thinks rather of the nature of the evidence and the Deuteronomy version thinks rather of the spirit in which it is given.

This, of course, was originally a forensic commandment and dealt with the obligations of a witness in a court of law. The Hebrews had a horror of false witness, and again and again it is grimly and seriously condemned.

For the Psalmist the bitterest thing of all is that false and malicious witnesses rise up against him (Psalm 27:12; 35:11). Repeatedly the wise man in the Proverbs condemns this sin. One of the six things which God abhors is 'a false witness who breathes out lies' (Proverbs 6:19). The man 'who speaks the truth gives honest evidence, but a false witness utters deceit' (Proverbs 12:17). 'A faithful witness does not lie, but a false witness breathes out lies' (Proverbs 14:5). 'A man who bears false witness against his neighbour is like a war club, or a sword, or a sharp arrow' (Proverbs 25:18). 'A worthless witness mocks at justice' (Proverbs 19:28). 'Be not a witness against your neighbour without cause, and do not deceive with your lips' (Proverbs 24:28). 'A truthful witness saves lives, but one who utters lies is a betrayer' (Proverbs 14:25). Not only is the false witness condemned; he is also threatened. 'A false witness will not go unpunished, and he who utters lies will not escape' (Proverbs 19:5; 19:9). 'A false witness will perish' (Proverbs 21:28). God's vengeance, says the prophet, is against those who swear falsely (Malachi 3:5).

In the New Testament false witness is one of the sins which come out of the evil heart of man (Matthew 15:19). And the false witnesses appear at the trial of Stephen (Acts 6:13), and of Jesus himself (Matthew 26:59–60).

One of the most interesting facts about the Jewish law is that the man who refuses to give evidence, when he has evidence to give, is condemned as severely as the man who gives false evidence. 'If any one sins in that he hears a public adjuration to testify and though he is a witness, whether he has seen or come to know the matter, yet does not speak, he shall bear his iniquity' (Leviticus 5:1). It is an important principle that a cowardly or a careless and irresponsible silence can be as serious a crime as false and lying speech. The sin of silence is as real as the sin of speech.

We shall not be surprised in view of all this to discover that the Jewish law took the greatest pains to see that testimony was reliable and true. Three times it is laid down that the evidence of one witness is never enough; no man is to be condemned on the strength of uncorroborated evidence. In two of the cases this principle is stated in regard to crimes involving the death penalty. 'If any one kills a person, the murderer shall be put to death on the evidence of witnesses; but no person shall be put to death on the testimony of one witness' (Numbers 35:30). 'On the evidence of two witnesses or of three witnesses he that is to die shall be put to death; a person shall not be put to death on the evidence of one witness' (Deuteronomy 17:6). In the third case this principle is extended to cover any crime. 'A single witness shall not prevail against a man for any crime or for any wrong in connection with any offence that he has committed; only on the evidence of two witnesses, or of three witnesses, shall a charge be sustained' (Deuteronomy 19:15). The law of the necessity of the two witnesses is often referred to in the New Testament (Matthew 18:16; 2 Corinthians 13:1; 1 Timothy 5:19; Hebrews 10:28).

It is to the Mishnah that we must go for even more detailed and careful regulations. The two witnesses are to be examined independently, and hearsay evidence is absolutely excluded. A man can only testify to that which he has actually heard or seen (*Sanhedrin* 3.6). Any contradiction between the witnesses renders the whole evidence invalid (*Sanhedrin* 5.2). In a case involving the death penalty the witness is to be solemnly warned that he is responsible for the life of the man on trial, and for his unborn posterity (*Sanhedrin* 4.5). The more a judge cross-questions the witnesses and the more he tests the evidence, the better a judge he is (*Sanhedrin* 5.2).

There is a careful listing of those who are eligible and ineligible to give evidence. Any man who is under the least shadow of suspicion himself can neither give evidence nor judgment in any case (*Bekhoroth* 7.3). If any witness takes payment for his evidence or any judge for his sitting in judgment, then the testimony and the verdict are both invalid (*Bekhoroth* 4.6).

No relation of the man on trial is eligible to give evidence, and the disqualifying relationships are carefully listed – kinsmen, father, brother, father's brother, mother's brother, sister's husband, father's sister's husband, mother's sister's husband, mother's husband, father-in-law, wife's sister's husband, together with all their sons and sons-in-law. A stepson may not give evidence, but his sons can. In general, no one qualified to be the heir of the person on trial can give evidence (*Sanhedrin* 3.3, 4; *Makkoth* 1.8). Neither a friend nor an enemy can give evidence. The friend is described as one who had been the accused's groomsman and an enemy as one who has not spoken to him for three days, because of a difference (*Sanhedrin* 3.5).

People following certain trades and professions are barred – a dice-player, a usurer, a pigeon-flyer, a slave, a trafficker in the seventh year produce (*Rosh ha-Shannah* 1.8; *Sanhedrin* 3.3). (In each seventh year the ground was supposed to lie fallow and the crops that did grow were not reaped; the trafficker in the seventh year produce was the man who failed to observe this law which is in Leviticus 25:1–7.) In general a man who follows a discreditable trade or profession is barred. It is assumed that gamblers and the like will not make satisfactory witnesses.

There are still further laws to control the witness. The most interesting is that a man convicted of false witness must pay the same penalty as the man on trial would have paid, if the charge had been true. 'If a malicious witness rises against any man to accuse him of wrongdoing, then both parties to the dispute shall appear before the Lord, before the priests and the judges who are in office in those days; the judges shall inquire diligently, and if the witness is a false witness and has accused his brother falsely, then you shall do to him as he had meant to do to his brother; so you shall purge the evil from the midst of you. And the rest shall hear, and fear, and never again commit any such evil among you. Your eye shall not pity; it shall be life for life, eye for eye, tooth for tooth, hand for hand, foot for foot' (Deuteronomy 19:16–21). The false witness, says the Mishnah, shall pay the whole penalty (*Baba Kamma* 7.3). If this punishment is impossible, as, for instance, in the case where a witness might give false evidence as to the legitimacy of a child, then the false witness shall be given the forty stripes, and, if the penalty itself was forty stripes, the false witness shall be given eighty stripes (*Makkoth* 1.1, 3). The law was so arranged that a false witness would think twice before he offered false witness, for the penalty, if he was convicted, was severe.

There was one other law which would make a false witness hesitate. In a capital case where the penalty was stoning to death, in the case of conviction, it was the leading witness for the prosecution who had to push the victim down the precipice and roll the first great stone upon him (*Sanhedrin* 5.4; cf. Acts 7:58–59). The Jewish law was so arranged that a witness was compelled to think of his responsibility for the truth. Jewish thought hated false witness; Jewish law condemned false witness; and Jewish regulations did everything to make a witness hesitate to tell anything but the truth.

The matter of false witness must be seen against the background of falseness in general. False witness is a kind of lie, and it has to be seen in the context of the whole attitude of the Bible to lies and to falsehood. The many condemnations of lies and lying in the Old Testament show both the prevalence of that particular sin and the horror that men of God had of it.

(i) We find prophetic condemnations of it. Hosea (10:13) says of his generation: 'You have ploughed iniquity, you have reaped injustice, you have eaten the fruit of lies.' Isaiah (59:3–4) has the same charge to make: 'For your hands are defiled with blood and your fingers with iniquity; your lips have spoken lies, your tongue mutters wickedness. No one enters suit justly, no one goes to law honestly; they rely on empty pleas, they speak lies, they conceive mischief and bring forth iniquity.' It is the same in the time of Jeremiah (9:3): 'They bend their tongue like a bow; falsehood and not truth has grown strong in the land.' Lying is the sin of every age and every generation.

(ii) Lying can become something that is ingrained and inborn, second nature to a man. From their very birth the wicked speak lies; it is in falsehood that they find their pleasure (Psalm 58:3; 62:4). The wicked may well say: 'we have made lies our refuge, and in falsehood we have taken shelter' (Isaiah 28:15). This is something which has got into the very centre and core and essence of life.

(iii) And yet the result of all this can be nothing but delusion and the loss of the way. 'You have uttered delusions and seen lies,'

says Ezekiel (13:8). It is their lies that have led the people astray
(Amos 2:4). And nowhere is condemnation more fierce than for
the prophet who speaks and teaches lies, with his lying divina-
tions (Ezekiel 13:9; 21:29; 22:28; Isaiah 9:15; Jeremiah 14:
14; 23:25, 26, 32; 27:10, 14, 16, 18; Zechariah 10:2). 'You
speak lies in the name of the Lord' is Zechariah's accusation
of the false prophets (13:3). Their own lies and the lies of their
false leaders have deluded the people into taking the wrong
way.

(iv) One of the most interesting and the most significant things
in the prophets is to see the things in company with which lying
is mentioned and rebuked. Hosea says: 'they multiply falsehood
and *violence*' (12:1). Jerusalem is full of lies and *booty*, or
plunder (Nahum 3:1). Lying is the source of *misgovernment*. 'If a
ruler listens to falsehood, all his officials will be wicked' (Proverbs 29:12). The false prophets *commit adultery* and walk in lies
(Jeremiah 23:14). Violence, plunder, misgovernment, adultery –
these are the companions, and at one and the same time the be-
getters and the consequences of lies. Falsehood brings its own
deadly companions in its train.

(v) Lying is a sin which profanes God. They profane God by
lying and listening to lies (Ezekiel 13:17–19). The Psalmist has
the vivid phrase: 'The godless besmear me with lies' (Psalm 119:
69). Lying dishonours God and man alike.

(vi) There are frequent threats and warnings to those who
practise falsehood and lying. Isaiah has it (28:17): 'Hail will
sweep away the refuge of lies, and water will overwhelm the
shelter.' The Psalmist says: 'The mouths of liars will be stopped'
(Psalm 63:11). 'No one who practises deceit shall dwell in my
house; no man who utters lies shall continue in my presence'
(Psalm 101:7). In the New Testament Revelation it is said that
abomination and falsehood debar from the presence of God, and
everyone who loves or practises falsehood will be shut out
(Revelation 21:27; 22:15).

(vii) Finally we may note that the prayer of the wise man is:
'Remove far from me falsehood and lying' (Proverbs 30:8); and
the picture of the golden age is of an age when 'they shall do no
wrong and utter no lies, nor shall there be found in their mouth a
deceitful tongue' (Zephaniah 3:13).

So then, when we set out the biblical evidence, we see how

prevalent this sin must have been, and how the heart of the prophets and the wise men was set against it.

It will be of interest to try to see from where lies come, to try to see what makes men tell lies.

(i) There is the lie which comes from malice. Among the instructions of Exodus there is the injunction (23:1): 'You shall not utter a false report. You shall not join hands with a wicked man, to be a malicious witness.' There is nothing commoner than the story maliciously repeated, or even maliciously invented. More than once the Bible speaks of the whisperer. The sage in the Old Testament said: 'A perverse man spreads strife, and a whisperer separates close friends' (Proverbs 16:28). This sin of whispering malicious gossip is said by Paul to be one of the sins of the godless contemporary world to which he preached (Romans 1:28–29), and it was also one of the sins of the trouble-beset church at Corinth (2 Corinthians 12:20).

There are three closely interconnected New Testament Greek words. There is the word *diabolos*, which means a *slanderer*, which is one of the things which women are forbidden to be (1 Timothy 3:11). There is the word *blasphēmia*, which, when it is used in regard to God, means *blasphemy*, and when it is used in regard to men means *insulting slander*. It is one of the sins which are forbidden to the Christian in Ephesians 4:31. There is *katalalia*, which the A.V. translates *backbiting* and *evil-speaking* (2 Corinthians 12:20; 1 Peter 2:1), but which the R.S.V. once again translates *slander*.

It is significant that there are so many Greek words for this kind of sin, whispering, slandering, backbiting. The number of different words shows how prevalent the thing was – and is. And there can be few sins which are more terrible in their effect, for this sin of the malicious lie can destroy character and kill friendship. As Coleridge wrote in 'Christabel':

> Alas! they had been friends in youth;
> But whispering tongues can poison truth.

In the A.V. the word *gossip* does not occur, but in the R.S.V. it and its kindred words occur five times. Ezekiel tells how Israel has been so crushed by her enemies that she has become the talk and evil gossip of the people (Ezekiel 36:3). Gossip is one of the sins that Paul both fears and expects to find at Corinth, and he joins it with slander, conceit and disorder (2 Corinthians 12:20).

The sage of the Old Testament says: 'He who goes about gossiping reveals secrets; therefore do not associate with one who speaks foolishly' (Proverbs 20:19). In Romans 1:29 Paul joins gossip with deceit, and malignity and in 1 Timothy 5:13, gossips are joined with idlers and busybodies. So we can see that in the newer translation the fact emerges that gossip and gossips are sternly rebuked.

Many a person who enjoys gossip, who repeats gossip, and who initiates gossip would be shocked to be called a malicious liar, but that is precisely what he or she is. The malicious lie is something which all Scripture sternly condemns.

(ii) Perhaps the first of all lies in a man's life, and to the end of the day the commonest of lies, is *the lie of fear*. A man departs from the truth to escape the consequences of something he has done. He denies that he has said or done something; he blames someone else for not having done something; in his own defence he makes an excuse which is in fact untrue. This is the kind of lie that we begin to tell in childhood and go on telling all our lives.

The trouble about this kind of lie, even to look at it from the most practical point of view, is that all the probability is that it will sooner or later catch up with us. 'Be sure,' said Moses, 'your sin will find you out' (Numbers 32:23). Epicurus was not a religious man; he did not believe in the gods at all, and he believed that religion was a delusion. But he always held from the sheer point of view of practical politics that truth must be told, for once a man tells an untruth there is always at the back of his mind the nagging fear that he will be found out – and there is no happiness that way. The lie of fear simply begets another fear. To tell the truth and face the consequences may be difficult, but better the immediate ordeal than the long unhappiness.

(iii) We have said that the lie of fear is the commonest lie, but perhaps even commoner is *the lie of carelessness*. A man can become almost chronically inaccurate in his statements. He tells a lie, or makes a false statement, not so much deliberately as carelessly. This was one of the things on which Dr Johnson had the strongest ideas, especially in regard to the bringing up of children. 'Accustom your children,' he said, 'constantly to this; if a thing happened at one window and they, when relating it, say that it happened at another, do not let it pass, but instantly check them; you do not know where deviation from the truth will end.' Strict accuracy of statement can be a discipline, and a difficult discipline, and it is a discipline which very few people in fact accept.

(iv) There is *the lie of boasting*. Very few people, for instance, in relating a personal experience can resist the temptation to tell it in such a way that it shows them in a better light than the facts actually warrant. Often even the best of us in relating some incident make ourselves say and do, not what we did, but what we would like to have said and done!

There is an odd aspect of this. Young people especially often tend to make themselves out *worse* than they are. They exaggerate their own exploits and their own wildness, for, as Augustine long ago said, when we are young, we fear to seem better, more respectable, more innocent than our contemporaries.

To put it quite simply one of the hardest kinds of truth to tell is the truth about ourselves.

(v) There is the *lie for profit*. This is the kind of lie at which the high pressure salesman is an adept, and of which so much advertising is an example. It is the kind of lie which a man tells in the hope of gaining something by it.

Closely allied with this is what we might call *the lie of propaganda*, the kind of exaggerated claims which a person or party may make in order to win support. It has always been said that in war 'truth is the first casualty.' One side becomes the shining example of honour and gallantry; the other becomes the aggressor and the committer of atrocities. In war there is no such clean-cut division. The trouble about this kind of lie is that in the end it defeats itself, for, unless we are very simple-minded, we come to a stage when no one believes what a salesman says, and no one expects to find the claims of an advertisement justified. The Christian wishes to succeed in business and in life as any other man does, but he cannot accept a success which is based either on the twisting, the suppression or the falsifying of the truth.

(vi) There is *the lie of silence*. Silence can often be a lie. It is often the case that the easiest way to avoid trouble is to do or to say nothing. By remaining silent we may indicate support for something which we know to be wrong. By remaining silent the martyrs could have avoided martyrdom. All they needed to do was simply nothing, but this is the very silence that they refused. By remaining silent we can avoid ridicule at least in certain companies, but, as Lord Chesterfield once said, ridicule is the best test of truth. It is seldom that silence and inactivity will get a man into serious trouble. But there is a silence which is the coward's refuge and which is a lie.

(vii) There is *the lie which is a half-truth*. It is often very easy to give the truth a twist and a slant to suit ourselves, and there is no greater danger than a half-truth. A half-truth is often more dangerous than an out-and-out falsehood.

There were those, for instance, in the early Church to whom Paul refers in Romans 6, who twisted the doctrine of grace. They argued that since grace is the loveliest and the greatest thing in the world, and since grace is wide enough to cover every sin, then the natural conclusion is that we should go on sinning to our heart's content, for all that sin does is to give this wonderful all-sufficient grace more and more opportunities to operate. So Christian freedom can be turned into an excuse for unchristian licence; Christian love can be turned into the weakness of escapist sentimentality; Christian discipline can be turned into prechristian legalism.

(viii) *There is the lie to self*. There is no harder thing in this world than to be strictly honest with oneself. Burns prayed for the power to see ourselves as others see us. It is not that we do not know ourselves; we do. But even the best of us can avert our eyes from the reality and look at the idealized picture. We often justify in ourselves what we would condemn in others. We often demand from others standards which we ourselves never even attempt to satisfy. We are often blind to things in ourselves that are painfully obvious to others. We often fail to see how much we hurt and fail other people.

If it is hard to see ourselves as we are, it is still harder to see our motives as they are. There is nothing more bitter than to see oneself as one is and to see one's heart as it is. And yet the fact remains that we cannot start on any process of reformation and cure until we face ourselves as we are. We so often build a picture of ourselves which has little basis in fact, and we so often bask in a glow of self-satisfaction which has no foundation. To be honest with ourselves is the way to self-humiliation, but self-humiliation is the way to grace.

(ix) The final lie that we may tell is *the lie to God*. We can lie to God by trying to conceal things from him, and we can lie to God by asking for the conventionally correct things even when we do not really want them. But it is obvious folly to try to deceive him who searches the hearts of men and who knows our thoughts as well as he hears our words and sees our deeds.

CHAPTER ELEVEN

THE TENTH COMMANDMENT

The Wrong Desire

The tenth commandment runs: 'You shall not covet your neighbour's house; you shall not covet your neighbour's wife, or his manservant, or his maidservant, or his ox, or his ass, or anything that is your neighbour's' (Exodus 20:17; Deuteronomy 5:21). With the tenth commandment the commandments enter a new world. Up to now the commandments have dealt with *outward actions*; but this commandment deals with *inward thoughts*. This commandment lays by far the hardest task upon man. To control one's actions is one thing. To control one's thoughts and feelings and emotions is quite another.

It was a breach of this commandment which produced one of the grimmest stories in Jewish history, the story of Achan (Joshua 6 and 7). At the siege of Jericho the order was that, when the city was captured, everything in it was to be devoted to the Lord for destruction (Joshua 6:17). Men and women, young and old, oxen, sheep and asses were destroyed with the edge of the sword (Joshua 6:21). All the silver and the gold, the vessels of bronze and of iron, were to be sacred to the Lord and were to go to the treasury of the Lord (Joshua 6:19). No Israelite was to take anything that was in Jericho as spoil.

Jericho was triumphantly captured, and the next city to be taken was Ai. It should have fallen to the Israelites without difficulty, but the first attack upon it issued in totally unexpected disaster (Joshua 7:2–5). It was revealed to Joshua that this disaster had happened because some Israelite had disobeyed the command that everything in Jericho had to be devoted to destruction and to God, and had kept for himself some of the spoil (Joshua 7:6–15).

It was discovered that the guilty man was Achan. Achan admitted his guilt: 'Of a truth I have sinned against the Lord God of Israel, and this is what I did; when I saw among the spoil a beautiful mantle from Shinar, and two hundred shekels of silver, and a bar of gold weighing fifty shekels, then I coveted them, and took them; and behold, they are hidden in the earth inside my tent, with the silver underneath' (Joshua 7:20–21). As a punishment Achan and all his family were stoned to death in the valley that is called the Valley of Achor, or the Valley of Trouble (Joshua 7:22–26). It was Achan's covetousness which brought disaster to his nation and the terrible death of himself and all his family. In the Achan story the sin of covetousness stands branded for ever.

In the New Testament covetousness is regarded as equally terrible. To Paul covetousness was the sin of sins; it was the sin which begat every other sin; and the terrible paradox of this commandment was that it begat the very sin it forbade. 'I should not have known what it is to covet,' said Paul, 'if the law had not said, You shall not covet.' It was in and through this very commandment that sin found its opportunity. It was this commandment which awakened the very sin that it sought to suppress (Romans 7:7–12). Here Paul is speaking of an experience which is part and parcel of human nature. Whenever a thing is forbidden it becomes desirable. The command not to covet something begets the desire which covets it. That which a man must not have becomes the very thing that above all he desires to have.

The classic expression of this is Augustine's description in his *Confessions* of his boyhood escapade:

'There was a pear-tree near our vineyard, laden with fruit. One stormy night we rascally youths set out to rob it and carry our spoils away. We took off a huge load of pears – not to feast upon ourselves, but to throw them to the pigs, though we ate just enough to have pleasure of forbidden fruit. They were nice pears, but it was not the pears my wretched soul coveted, for I had plenty better at home. I picked them simply in order to become a thief. The only feast I got was a feast of iniquity, and that I enjoyed to the full. What was it that I loved in that theft? Was it the pleasure of acting against the law, in order that I a prisoner under rules might have a maimed counterfeit of freedom by doing what was forbidden? . . . The desire to steal was awakened simply by the prohibition of stealing. The pears were desirable simply because they were forbidden.'

This is in fact the pattern of the first of all sins as the Bible tells the story (Genesis 3:1–7). It is as psychologically true today as it was in the beginning of time.

In the Old Testament the covetous man is consistently condemned. 'All day long,' says the Sage, 'the wicked covets, but the righteous gives and does not hold back' (Proverbs 21:26). The prophet calls down woe on those who devise wickedness, and then goes on to say: 'They covet fields, and seize them; and houses, and take them away' (Micah 2:2). To him covetousness was the first example of wickedness.

It so happens that the word *covetousness* occurs far oftener in the Authorized Version than it does in the Revised Standard Version. The word translated *covetousness* in the A.V. is the Hebrew word *betsa*, which basically means *dishonest gain*. And the various translations of it in the R.S.V. go far to show the real meaning of the word *covetousness*.

In Exodus 18:21 there is a description of the men whom Moses is to take as his helpers and assistants in the ruling of the people. The A.V. says that they must be men *hating covetousness*; the R.S.V. has it that they must be men *who hate a bribe*. In Psalm 119:36 the A.V. has it that the heart of a man must not be inclined to *covetousness*: the R.S.V. that a man's heart must not be inclined to *gain*. In Proverbs 28:16, as the A.V. has it, the Sage says that 'He that hateth *covetousness* shall prolong his days,' while the R.S.V. has 'he who hates *unjust gain*'. In Jeremiah 6:13 and 8:10 Jeremiah's charge in the A.V. is that everyone is *given to covetousness*, and in the R.S.V. it is that everyone is *greedy for unjust gain*. In Ezekiel 33:31 the A.V. has 'Their heart goeth after their *covetousness*', and the R.S.V. has, 'their heart is set on their *gain*.' In Jeremiah 22:17 the A.V. has 'thine eyes and thine heart are not but for thy *covetousness*', while the R.S.V. has 'you have eyes and heart only for your *dishonest gain*.' Isaiah 57:17 is one of the few places where the A.V. and the R.S.V. agree to retain *covetousness*: 'Because of the iniquity of his *covetousness* I was angry.'

Light is thrown on the true meaning of covetousness by these various translations. To covet something is to desire something which is not one's own and which belongs to someone else. But that is not in itself a bad thing, for one might honourably covet the great qualities which belong to someone whom one has made one's hero and pattern and example. So we have to add something to this.

To covet something is to desire something which one has no right to have or to possess. We have no right either to the possessions or to the person who belongs to someone else. So to covet is not merely to desire something which one does not possess; it is to desire something which one has no right to possess. But the examples we quoted from the Old Testament go further than that in some cases. There are some of them which show that covetousness, when it has reached full growth, means to desire that which belongs to someone else and that which one has no right to possess and to be willing to use dishonest and dishonourable means to attain it. For it is true that covetousness is a feeling and emotion of the mind and heart, but it is also true that that feeling and emotion, being themselves wrong, are always liable to issue in action which is also wrong. The wrong desire will in the end almost inevitably become the wrong action.

When we turn to the New Testament we find covetousness condemned, if possible, even more sternly. As in the case of the Old Testament, so in the case of the New Testament, we find that the actual words *covetous* and *covetousness* occur more often in the A.V. than they do in the newer translations; but the new translations and the variety of translations are helpful, for they fill out the meaning of the word.

In the New Testament there is more than one word for *covetousness*. The word most often translated *covetousness* in the A.V. is *pleonexia*. To the Greek and the Roman this word described a detested quality. It comes from two Greek words which taken together mean *to have more*, and it is the spirit which always wants more, and wants it in the ugliest way. Polybius says that the man who has this quality of *pleonexia* in his soul uses methods which are not fitting for a man to use. It is used to describe over-reaching ambition, shameless cupidity, conscienceless rapacity. The Romans described it in two vivid phrases. They called it *amor sceleratus habendi,* the accursed love of having, and they called it *iniuriosa appetitio alienorum*, the baneful desire for that which belongs to others. It is the hungry desire for that which a man has no right to have.

It occurs in the New Testament in Mark 7:22; Luke 12:15; Romans 1:29; 2 Corinthians 9:5; Ephesians 5:3; Colossians 3:5; 1 Thessalonians 2:5; 2 Peter 2:3. The A.V. consistently translates *covetousness*. The R.S.V. often keeps *covetousness* but has *greed* in 1 Thessalonians 2:5 and 2 Peter 2:3. The N.E.B. is more vivid. It has *ruthless greed* in Mark 7:22; Luke 12:15; Ephesians 5:3; Colossians 3:5, and it has *rapacity* in Romans 1:29. In the New Testament it is a particularly ugly quality. In Romans 1:29 Paul lists it as one of the characteristics of the heathen and the godless world, the quality which is the very opposite of the generosity of the love of God. In Luke 12:15 Jesus uses it for the quality of the man whose only yardstick of measurement is material things, and who sees the value of life in the number of things he has amassed. In 1 Thessalonians 2:5 and 2 Peter 2:3 it is the quality of the man who uses his position 'to make merchandise of' the people he ought to be serving, and to exploit those who are in his charge.

Closely connected with *pleonexia* there is the word *pleonektēs*, which means *the covetous man* (1 Corinthians 5:10, 11; 6:10; Ephesians 5:5; 2 Peter 2:14). The A.V. in all these passages translates *covetous*. The R.S.V. has *greedy* four times and retains *covetous* in Ephesians 5:5. Once again the N.E.B. is more vivid. In Ephesians 5:5 it has *greed which makes an idol of gain*. In 2 Peter 2:14 it has *mercenary greed*. In 1 Corinthains 5:11 it has *grasping*, and twice, in 1 Corinthians 5:10 and in 1 Corinthians 6:10, it calls the *pleonektēs* the *grabber*.

The word *philarguros* occurs three times in the New Testament (Luke 16:14; 2 Timothy 3:2; Hebrews 13:5). It is composed of two Greek words which literally mean, taken together, *a lover of money*. In all three cases the A.V. has *covetous*. The R.S.V. and the N.E.B. keep closer to the Greek by speaking of *love of money*. The translation of Hebrews 13:5 well shows the difference between the three translations. The A.V. has: 'Let your conversation be without covetousness.' This is a seventeenth-century use of the word *conversation*; in modern English conversation means *talk*, but in seventeenth-century English it meant *a way of life* and conduct. The R.S.V. has: 'keep your life free from love of money.' And the N.E.B. has succinctly: 'Do not live for money.'

The word *oregomai* occurs once in this sense in the New Testament (1 Timothy 6:10). It literally means *to reach out after*. The A.V. translates it by the idea of *covetousness*, the R.S.V. by *craving for*, and the N.E.B. by *reaching for*. It describes the action of a man reaching and stretching out to take.

Still another Greek word is translated to covet in the New Testament. It is the verb *epithumein*. This is the verb which is used in Acts 20:33, when Paul says: 'I *coveted* no one's silver or gold or apparel,' and still more important it is the word that is used in the New Testament to translate the word *covet* in the tenth commandment itself (Romans 7:7; 13:9). Its meaning may best be seen in the accompanying noun *epithumia*, which is very common in the New Testament. The regular New Testament translation of it in the A.V. is *lust* or *lusts* in the plural (Mark 4:19; John 8:44; Romans 1:24; Galatians 5:16; 1 Peter 1:14; 1 John 2:16–17). It occurs in the New Testament about thirty times. The modern translations usually use the word *passion* or *desire*. Of all the words it best shows the passionate craving which is the basis of covetousness. It implies an almost overmastering desire to get and to possess, whether the object of desire be a person or a thing.

One thing about the word *covet* as a word remains to be noted. The A.V. can and does use the word *covet* in a good sense, translating the word *zēloun*. In 1 Corinthians 12:31 the A.V. has: '*covet* earnestly the best gifts,' and in 1 Corinthians 14:39 it has: '*covet* to prophesy.' In both places the R.S.V. has *earnestly desire*. In the first, the N.E.B. has *aim at*, and in the second *be eager to*. This is an interesting sidelight on the word. The word *zēloun* is perhaps connected with the verb *zeō*, which means to *boil*. It denotes a fervent and even passionate desire, a desire kindled to a flame, for something. And here is a notable illumination of the whole question.

We are so built and so constructed that we must desire something; and we are so built that these instinctive desires of ours are the strongest part of our natures. They constitute the real dynamic force and driving power within us. Now the value of any powerful force depends entirely on the use that is made of it. For instance, as we well know, nuclear power could be used to provide a source of power which would drive machines and light cities and make life easier for all the world, but that same nuclear power can be used, as it has been used, and as its use is continually threatened, to bring destruction and death throughout the world, so that by its use mankind may well end in a kind of mass suicide. To this must be added the further truth that the use of any power will depend on the character and the heart of the man who possesses it. To return to our illustration, if nuclear power is in the hands of those who wish to benefit and to help mankind it can be a very great blessing. If it is in the hands of those who are moved by personal, national, or racial ambition, it can ruin and destroy mankind.

Here is the perfect analogy to the nature of man. Man's desires will drive him to long for things, and to take such action as he can to get them. If he is driven by selfish ambition and by the desire to get, then the desire will issue in the covetousness which cannot be other than an evil thing. If in his heart there is love of God and love of man, then he will, as the A.V. has it, covet the best gifts; and his desire, his covetousness, his driving power will be for the things that are high and holy and good and true and lovely.

The conclusion is clear. Desire cannot be eradicated from the heart of man. Man will always covet something. And it is only when Jesus Christ reigns within his heart that the desire for the wrong will be eradicated and the desire for the good will be the dynamic of life.

We must now turn to look in more detail at what we might call covetousness in action. We must look at the areas of life in which covetousness operates, and at the things which men desire, when they have no right to desire them.

(i) The simplest form of covetousness is *covetousness for material things, covetousness for money and for the things which money can buy*. The Bible is never in any doubt that the love of money is the root of all evils (1 Timothy 6:10). The commandment itself forbids the coveting of house, of ox, of ass (Exodus 20:17). The Pharisees are branded as lovers of money (Luke 16:14), and the Christian leader must be no lover of money (1 Timothy 3:3). Covetousness is something of which every man must beware (Luke 12:15).

The danger of covetousness is the danger of so many wrong

desires, for so many wrong desires are essentially good and legitimate things gone wrong, or things which ought to be in life but which have got out of proportion in life. Acquisitiveness is an instinct, for it is by the wise acquiring of things that a man can support his own life, and the life of those dependent on him. Without any instinct of acquisitiveness a man might and would become an improvident and shiftless creature. But when acquisitiveness gets out of proportion, then it becomes covetousness, and then it is wrong.

(a) Covetousness can lead to *dishonesty*, or, if not to actual dishonesty, to that sharp practice which may be legally within the law, but which is morally wrong.

If the desire is nourished long enough, and if it is allowed to grow unchecked and to acquire strength uncontrolled, then the likelihood is that the desire will become action, and the desire to take will become the action of taking. The making of unjust gain is repeatedly condemned (Psalm 119:36; Proverbs 28:16; Jeremiah 6:13; 22:13–14; Ezekiel 33:31). Covetousness will lead to that sharp practice in business which is more concerned with personal profit than with a fair deal for the customer. It will lead to that attitude in industrial relationships which demands more, without a thought for the consequences for the community and for the equal rights of other workers. Covetousness will issue in that action which does not care what methods it uses in order to get.

(b) Covetousness issues in *exploitation*. 'In their greed,' says the writer of 2 Peter, 'they will exploit you with false words' (2 Peter 2:3). Richard Collier in his life of William Booth, *The General Next to God*, tells of working conditions less than one hundred years ago. A woman with the help of two children had to work sixteen hours per day to make one thousand matchboxes for a pay of seven and a half pence per day. People had to work with phosphorus, tipping matches, until the phosphorus quite literally ate their jaws and gums away, so that in a dark room you could see the gleam of the corrosive phosphorus in their very flesh. At no time can anyone have believed that such conditions were right or even reasonable, but for long they were allowed to continue for the reason that employers, covetous for money, were adamant against changing them. Prostitution was and is supremely difficult to root out, because there were and are those who live on the immoral earnings of the prostitutes. Under no conditions could anyone call this right – but it was and is profitable.

The basic cause of all exploitation is quite simply that some-one wants to make money out of his fellowmen.

(c) There can be little doubt that basically covetousness is at the root of the *gambling fever* which has society in its grip today. At the bottom of this there is the desire to get money, money which will give life a new material standard. It comes from a desire for a material way of life higher than the standards which a man enjoys.

Human nature being such as it is, life is inevitably shot through with covetousness, and covetousness begets action which is on any grounds indefensible. The dope addict is deliberately created, in order that someone may make money out of him. The advertisement is deliberately designed to awaken a desire, so that someone may make money out of satisfying an artificially stimulated need. Almost any invitation to gamble will find a response because of the basic covetousness of human nature. The share-pusher and the confidence trickster would vanish to-morrow if there was no covetousness in human nature to play upon. In truth we have here the root of all evil.

(ii) There can be a more subtle form of covetousness than this. There is the covetousness *for status and for place*. Jesus knew how this desire for prominence was also a part of human nature, especially in the scribes and the Pharisees of his day, although far from only in them (Matthew 23:5–7; Mark 12:38–39; Luke 11:43; 14:7–11; 20:46). This kind of covetousness invaded even the apostolic band. James and John coveted the chief places in the coming kingdom (Mark 10:35–45). As Luke tells the story, even at the end of the day, with the twilight of tragedy closing in on them, the disciples were still disputing about who should be greatest (Luke 22:24–27).

This kind of covetousness can beget the most corrosive of sins, envy and jealousy. One of the new phrases of our generation is the phrase *status symbol*. A man covets the house, the car, the holiday which will show visually to his neighbours and to the public the particular height to which he has risen, and he will bitterly grudge them to those who have attained them when he has not.

It is an odd fact that there is no place where this is more common than within the Church. There are unfortunately few congregations in which there has not been trouble because some-one did not get the place or the prominence to which he or she thought himself or herself entitled. There is a kind of social covetousness, which is one of the present-day diseases of society and which exists even in the Church.

(iii) There is a last and a very serious form of covetousness, the covetousness for *people*. The commandment forbids a man to covet his neighbour's wife; the Deuteronomy version of the commandment (Deuteronomy 5:21) actually puts that kind of covetousness at the head of the forbidden things. And Jesus in the Sermon on the Mount forbids the look of lustful desire (Matthew 5:27). It is this kind of covetousness which produced one of the most tragic stories in the Bible, the story of David's illicit love for Bathsheba and his arrangement for the inevitable death of Uriah, her husband (2 Samuel 11).

To covet a person whom one has no right to desire is the way to tragedy, and to the worst of all tragedies, the kind of tragedy which involves many more than the person who is originally guilty. The moral state of society today and the prevalence of divorce and sexual infidelity and immorality is the proof of the strength of that covetousness in our present situation.

(iv) The last word about covetousness as a quality is said in the Letter to the Colossians (3:5), for there covetousness is identified with *idolatry*. Idolatry basically and essentially simply means putting something else in the position which God alone should occupy. If a man's desire is solely for God, and for obedience to God, then he will not covet the wrong things. If God is given his proper place, then all other things will take their proper place. The heart which is occupied by God is thereby cleansed of the wrong desires, and so the love of God will banish all false loves, whatever they may be.

We must bring our study of covetousness to a conclusion by trying to see just what the roots and the foundations of covetous-ness are, for we are better able to avoid a physical or a spiritual illness if we know its basic conditions.

(i) The basis and foundation of covetousness is the idea that to get what we have not got will bring happiness. The feeling in the mind and heart is: 'If I had this or that, I would be happy. If only I could get this or that I would be satisfied.' All life, from childhood to old age, proves what a delusion that idea is. It is quite true that when we get the thing on which we have set our hearts, there is a brief thrill, but the thrill does not last. It loses its interest; it ceases to give enjoyment; and all that happens is that we transfer our desires to something else, and the whole process begins all over again. It is like a child with a new toy. For an hour or two, or a day or two, he is engrossed with it, and then it is tossed aside, and he is standing looking in at the shop window and setting his heart on something else. It is like the drug-taker who takes his drug and has his moment of uplift or of serenity; then the moment passes; and he needs another dose. It is like the rhythm of hunger and of thirst. There is the desire, the temporary satisfying of the desire, and the rise of the desire again.

It is, in fact, worse than this. Let us go back to the analogy of the drug-taker. It is characteristic of the drug-taker's situation that he needs more and more of the drug to produce the same effect. When we try to satisfy covetousness by the acquisition of that which we have not got, as more and more is possessed, covetousness becomes more and more complicated and sophisticated and developed. It takes more and more elaborate things to produce the temporary lull in desire.

It was for this reason that Epicurus, the ancient Greek philosopher, laid down his prescription: 'If you want to make a man happy, add not to his possessions, but take away from his desires.' In other words, covetousness cannot be satisfied by the acquisition of anything; it can only be cured when the desire to acquire is eliminated. In a sentence, the cure for covetousness is content. Obviously, this is only to ask still another question – where is content to be found? But the answer to that question we must for the moment postpone.

(ii) All that we have been saying can be stated in another way. We could put it this way: *covetousness comes from the idea that things can bring happiness*, for covetousness as we have said, says: 'If I had this thing, I would be happy.' Now it is true that things have their place in happiness. Hunger and poverty and a constant struggle against insufficiency are never enjoyable things. It is not true to say that things do not matter. To have enough to eat, to have a good home, to have reasonable comfort are not things which are of no importance. But though things have their place in happiness, theirs is not the only place. If it were, it would simply mean that the wealthiest person would be the happiest, which is obviously very far from being the case.

Everyone knows the often quoted story of the king who was dying of melancholy. After he had tried all the doctors and wise men in vain, he was told that, if he could get the shirt of a perfectly happy man and wear that, he too would be happy. So there was a search for a perfectly happy man. He was found at last, but he was a tramp on the road – without a shirt to his back.

If the possession of things brought happiness and content, then this would be the happiest and the most contented age in history, for never was there such material well-being, and never were this world's goods more widely distributed in western civilization. Things which were once the possession of the privileged few, things like motor cars and television sets and continental holidays are the possession of the many – which in itself is an excellent thing; but it is also true that there never was a more neurotic and dissatisfied age in history. Unrest and unease are the marks of the affluent society. Content is certainly not to be found in the possession of things.

(iii) But before we try to find a solution to all this, we turn to the other kind of covetousness, the covetousness for a person, the desire for someone whom we should not desire, who does not and who ought not to belong to us. Here the feeling is that, if we could only possess the person who is forbidden to us, then happiness would come. Suppose we take the person whom we ought not to take. There may be the thrill of the moment; there may even be a period of time when we are lost in the forbidden relationship. But unless a man is lost to conscience, there can be no ultimate happiness that way. If the thing is kept secret, there is the constant fear of discovery, which in the end must poison pleasure. If the thing is openly admitted, and the person is taken, the memory of the other people who have been involved in the situation, the thought of their shame and their sorrow, the memory of how they have been wronged, is always in the background, and when passion dies and there is time for thought, there can be no happiness in a situation which has caused someone else's tragedy.

The taking of that which is forbidden is in the old Garden of Eden story the first of all sins and the begetter of the tragedy of the human situation, and that story is true to life.

(iv) What then is to be said in face of this situation? Where is the contentment which will end this covetousness to be found?

It has been said that there are two kinds of relationships in this world. There is the 'I-it' relationship, which is our relationship to things; and there is the 'I-thou' relationship which is our relationship to persons. We do not need to argue any more that contentment cannot be found in the 'I-it' relationship, for happiness can never be founded in the possession of things. Contentment must therefore be found in the 'I-thou' relationship. This is to say that contentment must come from personal relationships. Now a man has three personal relationships – a relationship to himself, a relationship to his fellowmen, and a relationship to God. In Shakespeare's *Henry the Sixth* the king is asked the question:

'But, if thou be a king, where is thy crown?' and he answers:

> My crown is in my heart, not on my head;
> Not deck'd with diamonds and Indian stones,
> Nor to be seen. My crown is call'd content;
> A crown it is that seldom kings enjoy.

In the first case, any situation which causes a man to lose his self-respect, or which involves him in his own self-condemnation, cannot be productive of happiness. In the second case, any forbidden relationship, which requires concealment, or which is the cause of tragedy for others, cannot be productive of happiness. In the third case, anything which estranges a man from God, and which he would wish to hide from God, cannot be productive of happiness.

So then there are three things which lead to perfect satisfaction, perfect happiness and perfect content. And these three things are – in regard to oneself, the self-respect that will not stoop to that which is low; in regard to our fellowmen, the love which is for ever pure and for ever faithful; in regard to God, the love which issues in true obedience, given not in the fear of God, but in the love of God. If a man's life has these three things, he will covet nothing, for there will be nothing to desire that he does not possess.

Also available in the Fontana Religious Series

What is Real in Christianity?
DAVID L. EDWARDS

The author strips away the legends from Jesus to show the man who is real, relevant and still fascinating. A clear, confident statement of Christian faith taking account of all criticisms.

Parents, Children and God
ANTHONY BULLEN

This book attempts to guide parents in their role as Christian educators. How they may answer their children's questions, how they may meet their children's needs from infancy to adolescence, how they may pray with their children, how they may talk to their children about sex: these and other topics are dealt with.

Ethics in a Permissive Society
WILLIAM BARCLAY

Professor Barclay approaches difficult and vexed questions with his usual humanity and clarity, asking what Christ himself would say or do in our world today.

Dialogue with Youth
AINSLIE MEARES

'This is a first-class general introduction to the world of young adults. . . . (It) is in general terms which convey a wealth of valuable insight . . . a quantity survey which helps to identify and map out a field of personal encounter in which few are competent, many are hesitant, all are involved.'

Church Times

Also available in the Fontana Religious Series

Children with Special Needs in the Infants' School
LESLEY WEBB

'Throughout the book the observations and reports show a deep understanding of, and regard and sympathy for, the children.'
Teaching and Training

Prayers for Young People
WILLIAM BARCLAY

The book includes morning and evening prayers for every week of the year, designed to help young people to pray, and also a fine introductory chapter, 'You and Your Prayers.'

The Plain Man Looks at the Bible
WILLIAM BARCLAY

This book is meant for the plain man who would like to know what to think about the Bible today. The first part deals with what the Bible is and what it is not. The second part shows that the Bible is also a record of certain things that happened.

The Bible Story
WILLIAM NEIL

'Like all his work it is hardly to be faulted, and I have never read so splendid a conspectus of the whole Bible. It will help a great many people to get their ideas sorted out. William Neil writes with such authority and lucidity that it can hardy fail.'
J. B. Phillips